Cultural Hermeneutics

For Paul V.
With gratitude for our friendship,
for our conversations, for our walks in the park
and the reimagining of an idea that has borne fruit.

Cultural Hermeneutics

The World Through the Lens of Theology

Roger Standing

scm press

© Roger Standing 2023

Published in 2023 by SCM Press
Editorial office
3rd Floor, Invicta House,
108–114 Golden Lane,
London EC1Y 0TG, UK

www.scmpress.co.uk

SCM Press is an imprint of Hymns Ancient & Modern Ltd
(a registered charity)

Hymns Ancient & Modern® is a registered trademark of
Hymns Ancient & Modern Ltd
13A Hellesdon Park Road, Norwich,
Norfolk NR6 5DR, UK

All rights reserved. No part of this publication may be reproduced,
stored in a retrieval system, or transmitted,
in any form or by any means, electronic, mechanical,
photocopying or otherwise, without the prior permission of
the publisher, SCM Press.

Roger Standing has asserted his right under the Copyright, Designs
and Patents Act 1988 to be identified as the Author of this Work

Scripture quotations, unless otherwise indicated, are from the New
Revised Standard Version: Anglicized edition, copyright © 1989, 1995
National Council of the Churches of Christ in the United States of
America. Used by permission. All rights reserved worldwide.

British Library Cataloguing in Publication data
A catalogue record for this book is available
from the British Library

ISBN 978-0-334-06081-9

Typeset by Regent Typesetting
Printed and bound by
CPI Group (UK) Ltd

Contents

Acknowledgements	vii
Introduction: Liberty from Slavish Conformity and Seductive Allure	ix
1 Culture: The Inescapable Reality	1
2 Culture and Theology: Exploring the Relationship	22
3 Towards a Theo-cultural Understanding of the World	53
4 Interrogating Culture: Reading and Interpreting the World Around Us	89
5 Cultural Hermeneutics: Reading and Interpreting the World Through the Lens of Theology	120
Conclusion: Evangelizing our Culture	174
Appendix 1: Representative Reflections on Defining the Concept of Culture	182
Appendix 2: Frameworks for Interrogating Culture	191
Appendix 3: Interrogative Questions	196
Bibliography	201
Index of Biblical References	217
Index of Names and Subjects	220

Acknowledgements

My fascination with culture goes back into the mists of time when I was a teenager studying sociology and becoming enthralled with contemporary music, film, politics and life in general. The origins of this book are more recent. Having begun to teach at Spurgeon's College in London, the then Principal Dr Nigel Wright encouraged me to develop modules that matched my passions. Duly approved, the module in Cultural Hermeneutics was a favourite for me. It led to hours of fun and mutual discovery with successive groups of students as we jumped between dense cultural theory and *The Simpsons*, the work of Zygmunt Bauman and *Star Trek*, discovering along the way revealing insights into 'the meaning of life, the universe and everything' accompanied by H. Richard Niebuhr, Neil Postman and Lady Gaga.

My then 10-year-old son Nathan picked up what 'hermeneutics' meant and many happy hours were spent during car journeys together exploring what he was watching on TV while listening to Kermode and Mayo's Film Review on BBC Radio 5 Live with its particular brand of 'wittertainment'. As he became an adult he evolved into something of a film buff himself with the knowledge to read a movie and an ability to deconstruct it that leaves me far behind!

It was my friend Paul Valler who encouraged me to think of writing this book and, on many walks together, gracefully listened to the thoughts that were germinating inside my head. The support and patience of my editor at SCM, David Shervington, kept me on track as deadlines were missed in the wake of Covid-19 lockdown and affirmed the evolving pattern of a project that ultimately looked quite different from what we had started with. I also want to register my thanks to Dave Benson at the London Institute for Contemporary Christianity and Graham Watts for our conversations together bouncing ideas around and their work reviewing the early drafts of what I was writing. Then, last but certainly not least, is my wife Marion. She has proofed everything with her meticulous eye, chuckled as something she was reading tickled her imagination, and got really excited with James Davison Hunter's idea of 'faithful presence'. She has since been telling everyone about it in her work as a Church of England schools' advisor. What follows is all the better for the contributions of each of these friends and colleagues and many others along the way. Without them it would not have seen the light of day.

Roger Standing
St Valentine's Day, 2023

Introduction:
Liberty from Slavish Conformity and Seductive Allure

With a room full of 40 people the small portable record player could hardly be said to have been loud, but the beat was infectious. Feet were tapping.

> God gave rock and roll to you.
> Gave rock and roll to you.
> Put it in the soul of everyone.

As a teenager growing up in the 1970s all the different aspects of my life bled into each other. I was brought up in a church-attending, labour-voting home on a small rural council estate in Norfolk ... and I loved pop music. Having been captivated by Argent's 1972 hit and 'feminist anthem' 'Hold Your Head Up' (Weinstein, 2005, p. 11), I went out and bought their album *In Deep* and discovered the track 'God Gave Rock and Roll To You'. It seemed quite natural, when invited as a 14-year-old to present 'A Young Person's View' to our church's monthly Tuesday Fellowship group, to take along my record player and play them some songs. They listened politely as I demonstrated the gulf that existed between the music of my generation and the old-fashioned hymns we sang on Sundays. Yet I maintained there was still a concern for faith and justice in the rising generation. Young people needed to be understood and respected on their own terms if the church was going to be relevant to them. When I finished speaking their warm appreciation and kindly patience were very encouraging. We concluded with tea and biscuits.

While I had no way of knowing it at the time, it was at this point that the seeds of my future fascination with the relationship between faith and culture were sown. How does my inherited Christian faith understand its cultural context? Does it recognize and own the fact that its present lived reality is a direct product of interaction with its received cultural context? Then, looking in from the other side, how is this faith understood within its wider social setting? How is it incorporated, for good or ill, into the prevailing cultural narratives of how things are?

In a very real sense, the relationship between Christian faith and its surrounding culture has raised critically important issues since the earliest days of the church's life. Key among the first of these to surface, for example, was whether it was possible to be a Christian without being a Jew. Did confessing 'Jesus is Lord' and accepting him as the Messiah require conversion to Judaism? This profoundly theological question was driven by a deeply felt cultural taboo, the 'mutilation of the flesh'. In Greco-Roman culture the naked male body was considered an expression of aesthetic beauty, especially when represented in idealized form as sculpture. Circumcision, by contrast, was a contemptible disfiguring of the body. As long as any converts to 'the Way' of Jesus of Nazareth originated from within Judaism this was not an issue. However, as the apostle Paul took this message beyond the confines of the Jewish synagogue communities dotted around the Mediterranean it did become a problem. Put simply, did non-Jewish males who decided to follow Jesus the Messiah need a further conversion to Judaism and circumcision as believing adults?

With strongly held views on both sides of the question, the matter climaxes at the Council of Jerusalem (Acts 15). At stake in the debate is the place of Mosaic law in the embryonic Christian communities, and whether Christianity would prove itself to be a reforming sect within Judaism or an independent and altogether different movement. While frequently viewed through this pre-eminent theological lens, a second and almost equally important question is addressed in the Council's response: the relationship between Christian faith and issues of culture. By formally dissociating themselves from those pressing for circumcision the Council creates a precedent that will determine the future direction of the Jesus movement. There is no minimizing the significance of this moment, what hangs upon it and how differently the narrative would have developed if other choices had been made.

The outcomes of the Council's deliberations are clear and are unanimously adopted by those present. They determine not to burden the Gentile converts with anything beyond a minimalist four-clause statement of 'essentials' with, by implication, the omission of a requirement for circumcision affirming that Christian faith can be culturally Gentile as well as culturally Jewish. Christian discipleship is therefore transplantable into different contexts and is able to find new ways of expressing its fundamental allegiance to the message and person of Jesus.

With Paul already committed to reaching Gentiles through his expanding missionary enterprise, it is hardly surprising to find him going on to further push at boundaries as he explores and develops his understanding. This is perhaps most clearly on view following his invitation to speak before the Areopagus in Athens after marketplace debates with Epicurean and Stoic philosophers (Acts 17). Using his discovery of an altar dedicated 'to an unknown god' as a point of contact, he frames his presentation with Stoic and Platonic ideas, illustrating the thrust of his argument with quotations from the poetry of Epimenides and Aratus and the writings of the philosopher Cleanthes. While this could be viewed merely as window-dressing, an example of evangelistic opportunism to gain a hearing, Paul's trajectory in the Gentile mission points rather in the direction of a genuine attempt at cultural engagement. Writing to the Christian community in Corinth he was later to articulate the thinking behind his approach with passionate clarity:

> I have made myself a slave to all, so that I might win more of them ... I have become all things to all people, that I might by all means save some. I do it all for the sake of the gospel, so that I may share in its blessings. (1 Cor. 9.22–23)

Indeed, the Christian appropriation and continued use of the quote from Aratus, 'In him we live and move and have our being' (Acts 17.28), demonstrates how effective this endeavour was. Christianity crossed between cultures and found a new landscape of language, ideas and ways of living to inhabit.

Having become established in the Gentile world of the Roman Empire, the conversion to Christianity of the emperor Constantine in the early fourth century marks the beginning of the period that became known in Western culture as Christendom. Christianity was adopted as the state religion and society was identified as being shaped and animated by Christian faith, values and virtues. Such a faith no longer needed to be cross-cultural as it had been before. It was now foundational for the social order and itself provided the framework for comprehending why and how life should be lived and understood. Any debate or difference of conviction about this common order was internal to Christendom culture and did not require the cross-cultural insights and disciplines that lay within the story and experience of the New Testament church.

It was with the birth of the modern overseas missions movement that these cross-cultural issues began to resurface. For example, the Baptist William Carey (1761–1834), on his arrival in India in 1793, quickly appreciated the need for indigenous evangelists and the translation of the Scriptures into language that was native both to the preacher's tongue and to the listener's ear (Stanley, 1992, pp. 47–51). Or again, Henry Venn (1796–1873), Secretary of the Church Missionary Society from 1841, had a vision for the planting of national churches that would be 'self-supporting, self-governing and self-propagating', exhibiting to their perfection and glory 'marked national characteristics' (Walls, 2009, p. 27; Warren, 1971, p. 26; Bosch, 2003, p. 307). Reflecting on what he calls the 'radical indigenization' involved in the missionary translation of the Bible into the vernaculars of Africa, Gambian theologian Lamin Sanneh observed that the relative ease with which Christianity encountered living cultures was remarkable and gave pluralism a concrete indigenous expression while also affirming that culture's merit was not primary but penultimate and relative (Sanneh, 2009, pp. 3, 56).

INTRODUCTION

Sanneh is illustrative of the mature insights into the relationship between Christian faith and its host culture that emerged during the twentieth century. A significant reference point within this developing rediscovery was the American theologian H. Richard Niebuhr, who published his seminal work on the subject, *Christ and Culture*, in 1951. In it he proposed a five-point typological analysis of how different theological convictions led to a range of understandings of, and relationships with, their surrounding culture. While many have found Niebuhr's 'types' to be significantly lacking at several points, the fact that he remains frequently referenced is indicative of the abiding helpfulness of his schema. However, perhaps the most influential thinking on the subject arose out of missiological thinking and practice in the ideas of inculturation and contextualization. Frequently seen as interchangeable, the term inculturation was popularized by Jesuit writers in the mid-1970s (Luzbetak, 1988, p. 69) and the concept of contextualization was widely adopted among Protestants at the same time, becoming particularly influential among evangelicals through the Lausanne Movement (Stott and Coote, 1981; Standing, 2013, pp. 268–78). However, initially articulated in the report *Ministry in Context* of the Theological Education Fund of the World Council of Churches in 1972, the concept of contextualization in theological education was not solely focused on mission studies. Rather, it proposed that theological education itself was contextualized on four levels: missiological, structural, theological and pedagogical (Lienemann-Perrin, 1981, pp. 174–6).

There can be no doubting that great advances have been made over the last half century in both the content and delivery of theological education. Significant investment has been made to develop programmes of study that are fit for purpose for the twenty-first century. In the UK, for example, theology in Higher Education is subject to the same intellectual rigour and inspection as any other discipline through the scrutiny of the regulatory bodies. Then, within the confessional setting of seminaries, theological and Bible colleges and denominational lay-training programmes, this has been supplemented by the growth of practical theology, missiology and contextually rooted, skills-based formation in ministry.

For all these welcome developments, and the laudable objective of theological education at all levels to be relevant and engaged with our contemporary context, too little attention has been given to equipping learners to read, interpret and theologically evaluate that cultural context. Save for a dalliance with sociology while it was a trendy subject in the 1970s, and a penchant for engaging with film studies for which there was a flurry of publications in the early twenty-first century, little has been done. This leaves the Christian community open to two equal and opposite errors. On one side is the pull towards a conservative preservation of received tradition that fails to differentiate between Christian faith and the cultural forms through which it has been transmitted. On the other is an open-armed embrace of contemporary social norms in the name of the gospel, an embrace that neglects to acknowledge our preference for what we intuitively know and in which we have been thoroughly socialized.

Developing a culturally astute theological self-awareness is no easy task. It could be described as a dynamic, three-dimensional puzzle that extends beyond the manageable confines of a convenient table-top to the expanse of the whole of the space-time continuum. It will never be fully known, and even if we were momentarily to achieve such comprehension, even as we appreciated the accomplishment it would begin to slip away from us as that particular moment passed. Is the task, therefore, a futile one? By no means. It is about seeking truth and understanding. It is about grasping the significance of our captivity to established patterns of thinking, whether from our received religious tradition or our culturally conditioned context, and enabling the truth to set us free: free to permit our understanding to be scrutinized by the principles of the Kingdom of God and brought under the Lordship of Christ. Perhaps, in another age, this is what is alluded to in the Letter to the Colossians:

> As you therefore have received Christ Jesus the Lord, continue to live your lives in him, rooted and built up in him

and established in the faith, just as you were taught, ... See to it that no one takes you captive through philosophy and empty deceit, according to human tradition, according to the elemental spirits of the universe, and not according to Christ. (Col. 2.6–9)

To that end, the text of this book is the fruit of my own journey and it is therefore no coincidence that its point of view, the perspective from which it emerges, is British, Christian and post-pandemic, having been written in 2021–23. My own understanding grew out of teaching the subject to undergraduate and postgraduate students in theology, many of whom were preparing and equipping themselves for different forms of Christian ministry. They will certainly recognize the fruit of our conversations in class in the ideas I seek to grapple with and the thoughts I express.

In the five chapters that follow I begin with a 360-degree exploration of our experience of culture, how we are shaped and formed by it and how we might understand and define it. Chapter 2 looks at some classic engagements that theology has made with culture, with particular reference to the work of the theologians H. Richard Niebuhr and Paul Tillich along with the insights of inculturation and contextualization from the study of mission. Chapter 3 takes a step further back and looks to begin to develop a theological understanding of the place of culture and its significance for Christian discipleship. In Chapter 4, among other sources the insights of anthropology, sociology and cultural studies are explored to draw down insights into how culture is read and interpreted. Building on these foundations the final chapter then seeks to develop a cultural hermeneutic 'in the Spirit' by reading and interpreting culture through the lens of theology. The objective is for an inculturated discipleship that embodies a 'faithful presence' of the Kingdom of God in the cultural context in which it is lived out.

Cultural hermeneutics through the lens of theology is about disciples of Jesus knowing the truth, and the truth setting them free. It is about properly understanding the world around us and being liberated both from slavish conformity to inherited culture and from the seductive allure of the 'cultural now'. It is about discovering spiritual agency to live the best life that aligns with the life and the message of the one we call 'Lord', Jesus from Nazareth.

I

Culture: The Inescapable Reality

Experiencing culture

Have you ever just sat and listened to what's going on around you? Normally our lives are so full of tasks to get done, people to see, social media to interact with, books to read, movies to watch, dinner to make, that we rarely take the time. We are therefore very good at filtering out the ambient noise, the things that could distract us, the stuff that is just there in the background, the soundscape of the world immediately around us. But when we do listen it's amazing what we can hear, especially if it's a Spring day and the windows are open. There's birdsong, a dog barking down the road, the rumble of a plane overhead, someone shouting, the sound of builders somewhere, a radio playing, children laughing in the distance and, of course, the ubiquitous and ongoing murmur of traffic. It was there all the time and we just didn't notice it. We accepted it. It was part of the unnoticed ambient hum in the background that is the accompaniment to our lives every day. It is not that we don't hear it or know that it's there, it is just that it's so familiar we don't notice it.

Our experience of culture is very similar. Our cultural home is what we know. It's located in what we experience as normal. It is contained in what seems right to us, whether that has been arrived at through the careful evolution of our thinking and values or, by contrast, is just what we instinctively know to be true. At one level our cultural home seems to be determined by our location against big-ticket items like nationality, gender, class, race, religion, history and tradition. However, that is not the full story. On another level it is altogether more personal.

Our cultural identity is shaped by our day-to-day experience. The TV programmes we consume, the groups we belong to and the organizations we identify with, our families, our social networks, the books we read and the movies we watch all help to establish the cultural postcode that locates us. And therefore, as has been observed, 'Everybody looks at the world from behind the windows of a cultural home' (Hofstede and Hofstede, 2005 p. 363).

Our consciousness is always framed by, and can never be independent of, the social reality in which it is embedded (Hunter, 2010a, p. 210). The intimacy of this reality, the familiarity of our daily experience and the monotony of the mundane all combine to leave us mostly unconscious of the cultural forces and influences that play so large a part in determining our lives. Take language, for example. The words in our vocabulary enable us to think and to order our thoughts, to understand the world around us, to construct ideas, to be creative and to communicate. Yet far from being independent of culture, language itself is a cultural construction that not only carries the 'fingerprints' of its own social and historical location, but rather is a rich repository of cultural DNA. Growing up I had a cuddly black toy that resembled the mascot/trademark on jars of Robertson's marmalade and fruit preserves. I loved it a great deal, but now could not bring myself to even type its name!

Whatever our personal history and the elements that have contributed to the construction of our 'cultural home', it provides the default lens through which we see the world. Some elements of this home we will have freely chosen and are the fruit of our own agency. Other aspects are provided for us through the inherited patterns and structures of life, available opportunities and ways of thinking that constitute the culture in which we live. Both, however, are experienced subjectively. Our cultural home leaves us predisposed and partial in our experience, our understanding and our judgement. Their embedding within our experience predetermines a form of 'truth effect' in our perceptions that makes cultural self-awareness a challenging endeavour to pursue.

Such insight is, of course, far from being a novel revelation.

CULTURE: THE INESCAPABLE REALITY

Herodotus, the Greek historian from the fifth century BCE, observed that given the choice of adopting the best customs from among the nations, after careful examination each nation would select its own. To illustrate his point he recounts a story told of the Persian King Darius the Great. The king first asked the Greeks who were with him, who practised the cremation of their dead, at what price they would eat the deceased bodies of their fathers. Their response was that there was no price. Then he summoned Callatiae Indians, who did eat their dead parents as part of their funerary rites, and asked what would make them willing to burn their dead. They cried out in horror that such an act could even be spoken of. Herodotus concluded, quoting the poet Pindar, 'custom is Lord of all' (Herodotus, *Histories*, III.38).

The role that culture plays is a powerful one, conveying both meaning and identity to individuals and to society as a whole. However, it is much more involved than that. Culture is not static, but rather is an ever-evolving reality in which meaning is generated, embedded, argued over and revised or replaced (Brown, Davaney and Tanner, 2001, p. 5). Sometimes this process evolves over generations; at other times new realities seemingly appear almost overnight. Yet, viewed from within the bubble provided by meaning and identity, the world is, by default, experienced as a place of enduring stability even during times of uncertainty and social volatility. Indeed, at such times, the received traditions of identity and meaning are clung to even more tightly. Change is mostly only recognized as such in hindsight (Hunter, 2010a, p. 78). The *Oxford English Dictionary*'s word of the year for 2021 was 'Vax'. Not a new word, its first recorded use was in 1799 where its definition was from the Latin word *vacca*, which means cow and carries the memory of Edward Jenner's research into smallpox vaccination using bovine cowpox. Its modern usage until 2021 was very rare, but as medical science responded to the Covid-19 pandemic its relevance was undeniable. Added to which, its utility in spawning other words was exceptional, with vaxxie, vax-a-thon, vaxinista and the progressive double-vaxxed or triple-vaxxed mirroring developing vaccination practice.

Culture is inescapable. It determines what matters to us, thus defining the world in which we live and our place within it. It provides the language by which we articulate our understanding along with the social and reasoning tools by which we interrogate it and can seek to change it. Indeed, the creative arts are particularly powerful expressions of our relationship with culture as it is affirmed or challenged. As James Davison Hunter insightfully reflects:

> Culture is far more profound at the level of *imagination* than at the level of argument. Deep structures of culture are found in the frameworks of our imagination, frameworks of meaning and moral order that are embedded in the very words we use. (Hunter, 2010b)

Culture is at one and the same time both liberator and captor. Our ability to understand and think, to create and explore, to communicate and come together as individuals in a shared social environment are all made possible by our common culture. Yet cultural forces shape and limit our thinking according to the time and place within which we live. At the beginning of his *The Order of Things*, Michel Foucault recounts how he burst out in laughter on reading of a Chinese encyclopaedia in which the taxonomy of animals divided them into

> (a) belonging to the emperor, (b) embalmed, (c) tame, (d) suckling pigs to (m) having just broken a water pitcher, (n) that from a long way off look like flies. (Foucault, 1970, p. xv)

It is easy to see the constraints of an alien culture when portrayed in such high relief. Yet Foucault's poignant illustration points to our own potential blindness in examining more deeply our own cultural situatedness. In recognizing that our experience is always context-bound and subjective, we must factor into our reflections who we are and where we come from if we are to have a chance of pursuing greater understanding (Baldwin et al., 1999, p. 14).

Our subjective experience of culture is, of course, multi-layered. For myself, I experience life as someone born into mid-twentieth-century British society. Yet for all the debates about what constitutes Britishness, what is shared is differentiated by endless nuanced and not so nuanced variations. Cultural markers are not only geographically bestowed according to national or ethnic identity. Class, race, gender, religion, education, occupation, politics and the like all contribute to our experience. Indeed, there are almost endless further variations within any category we choose to name. Then, to complicate matters to another level, the evolving nature of culture needs to be acknowledged and understood. Culture is not merely the sum of the unfolding identities that are inherited by each rising generation; rather, it is the fruit of the interplay of all the various component parts that make up the whole. As such culture is continually made and remade. The sociologist Peter Berger identified this perpetual motion within culture as the result of a constant interaction or interplay, a 'dialectic', with itself (Wuthnow et al., 1984, pp. 37–8).

The inherent fluidity of culture means that the subject is, at its very heart, a messy one that appears both complex and haphazard. If this has always been so throughout history, recent decades have further added to the challenge. It was in 1991 that the Canadian novelist Douglas Coupland published his acclaimed *Generation X: tales for an accelerated culture* (Coupland, 1991). In it he sought to illustrate the impact of rapid cultural change on the lives of a group of young twenty-something characters based in southern California. A decade later Zygmunt Bauman interrogated this highly significant late-twentieth-century cultural shift through a succession of books. Rejecting the widely accepted designation of this shift as postmodernism, he argued that it should be more accurately defined and described as 'liquid modernity' (Bauman, 2000; Yakimova, 2002).

> Liquid modern' is a society in which the conditions under which members act change faster than it takes the ways of acting to consolidate into habits and routines ... Liquid life ... cannot keep its shape or stay on course for long ... In short:

liquid life is a precarious life, lived under conditions of constant uncertainty. (Bauman, 2005, pp. 1–2)

Within this cultural shift Bauman goes on to identify the key role played by contemporary consumerism. With culture inherently inclined to evolve, this is heightened and intensified by a consumerist mindset and its perpetual offers of choice put before the individual. The necessary outcome of this is the entrenching of innovation and change as primary cultural values, which then seep into every aspect of life (Bauman, 2011, p.12–13).

Beginning to comprehend the complexity of culture with its vast array of interconnected parts is daunting. From the wide-angled big picture to the zoomed-in and detailed focus on a single object, the prospect of contemplating the substance of culture threatens to be overwhelming. Indeed, any success in describing and probing it only promises what would be a snapshot of one particular moment in time. No sooner is the task of description accomplished than it begins to retreat away from us and be consigned to the repository of our historical understanding.

Culture is, assuredly, a perplexing phenomenon – ubiquitous in presence, complex in detail, and as such overwhelming and incomprehensible in its totality and in its intricacy. Any attempts to grasp it all in analysis will, therefore, be frustrated from beginning to end. (Wuthnow et al., 1984, p. 71)

However, that does not mean that no attempt can be made to grasp some understanding. That would merely leave us as uncomprehending and passive subjects. We would merely be the unwitting victims of our circumstances as we are acted upon and subject to the uncomprehended influence of surrounding cultural forces. What it does mean is that the manner of any enquiry needs, first, to be undertaken with considerable humility. The 'unknown unknowns' will always vastly outweigh what we think we see and our comprehension of it.

Second, any insight we glean, and any understanding that derives from it, are necessarily provisional. They have to be provisional because of what remains unknown. When such knowledge has been properly acquired, appreciated and integrated into our thinking we must still be ready to adapt our understanding. This provisionality also rests on the passage of time. Tomorrow comes, things change and the world moves on. We do indeed 'see through a glass darkly'.

Third, we must beware the temptation to over-simplify. Culture is, by its very nature, a dynamic, interconnected and multi-dimensional living reality. Simon During even suggests that the diffuse and fluid nature of culture makes a methodological approach to understanding it problematic. However, he does acknowledge the pull of the traditional hermeneutic disciplines in seeking to map and understand our cultural experience (During, 2005, p. 8).

Formed by culture

Before we attempt to push on towards a more adequate understanding of culture, we need to acknowledge a further important consideration. If culture does provide the dynamic, interconnected and multi-dimensional reality in which we live, there is an unavoidable implication to this in the deeply embedded structures of human life. It is crucial to both recognize and own the fact that culture is not only something we experience and consume. It is not only the means by which we understand the world around us, it also provides us with the tools to articulate that understanding. However, this is not the end of it, because culture goes deeper still. Indeed, we are not only shaped by our interactions with the world as we know it, we are also formed by it; in absolute truth we are each the product of our cultural location.

Babies do not come pre-loaded with an innate cultural awareness. It has to be learned. Individuals imbibe the norms and values of those around them from the very beginning. The early years of life are an especially intense period in this regard. Berger observed how humans were particularly underdeveloped at birth when compared with other animals, including higher mammals. He concluded that this required a biological and instinctual development outside of the womb that results in a distinct 'world openness' and 'plasticity' in young humans (Wuthnow et al., 1984, pp. 23–4). However, this process does not cease in infancy, puberty or adulthood. Rather, the learning continues throughout the whole of life, though mostly in a more nuanced and sophisticated way in maturity, enabling individuals to develop and adjust as they live as self-aware and skilled social participants. While earlier sociological theories related to the process of socialization have long been frowned upon because of their functionalist conception, there is a more recent recognition of an abiding insight and worth in the concept. This rehabilitation has gained ground as socialization is reconceived within a framework that builds on contemporary insights from cognitive science, pragmatism and the study of language (Guhin, Calarco and Miller-Idriss, 2021, p. 109).

Cultural identity is formed in an individual as they are immersed in the life of the world around them. Through a kind of social osmosis, the experience of everyday life and how things are done, when they are done, why they are done and why they matter is absorbed into them. Thus the values and traditions, customs and beliefs are passed on from one generation to the next and enshrined in the stories we tell. I remember the first Jamaican funeral I went to. The extended singing of gospel songs at the graveside while family and friends backfilled the grave was incredibly moving. I only later learned that these were a part of an extensive pattern of community traditions of common memory – practices that reach back through time into colonial history and slavery in the Caribbean and beyond there to Africa.

Experientially, however the family unit is conceived, it is the primary and foundational source of cultural transmission. Yet, both implicitly and explicitly, wider society also tasks other institutions as the gatekeepers of cultural formation. Education and the arts are obvious contributors, but so are the entertainment industry, the market, the news media, social media, publishing and advertising, not to mention local and national government and the charitable sector (Hunter, 2010a, p. 46). As 'gatekeepers' these institutions contribute to cultural formation in both the transmission of culture itself and its re-formation. The role of the high arts has long been acknowledged but in recent decades the role of popular culture has also been increasingly appreciated. In many ways the history of the twentieth century was one of the increasing influence of popular culture through TV, the movies and contemporary music and their power as storytelling media, providing convincing narratives that enable people to make sense of their lives. This was a new phenomenon, especially as it located a strategic culture-forming influence within the realm of commercial enterprise. In the process, popular culture significantly encroached into territory that was traditionally the domain of the family and a society's shared social institutions and faith communities. Recent decades have seen the entertainment industry consolidate into an ever-decreasing number of media conglomerates that wield immense power and influence. This culture-forming function has become so pervasive that Cobb observes, 'whole generations in the West have had their basic conceptions of the world formed by popular culture' (Cobb, 2005, p. 7).

Speaking of our embeddedness in our historical context, H. Richard Niebuhr memorably pointed out that, 'We are in history as the fish is in water and what we mean ... can be indicated only as we point through the medium in which we live' (Niebuhr, 1941, p. 48). The metaphor holds true for how we are immersed in our cultural context too. We can only be formed by the culture of where we are. But if a fish swims in water, what is the nature of the culture in which we live, move and have our being? Is it merely a 'culture of ideas' that expresses itself in the way we live, in our knowledge, beliefs and values, or is it more than that? This, of course, could be broadened out to embrace the fruit of the expression of these ideas: the creative arts that provide our cultural heritage and cultural inheritance. Through cultural artefacts we express, transmit and preserve the DNA of our culture. However, this would be an inadequate view, because it neglects what is going on beneath the surface of a culture and the role played by the elites, networks and institutions of a society. These groups have access to the levers of privilege, reward and punishment and thereby contribute a disproportionate influence to culture building. It is vitally important to acknowledge these institutional dynamics of culture because their use of power and influence provides the framework and infrastructure that enables a culture to cohere both in time and over time. In this way they help to define and maintain a cultural narrative. Some commentators use computer operating systems to illustrate the point, with social institutions as the computer hardware and culture as the software or programming (Vanhoozer et al., 2007, p. 23; Hofstede and Hofstede, 2005, pp. 2–3). Helpful as the image is, it is also especially necessary to identify the institutions themselves as integral parts of the culture rather than somehow sitting outside or beyond it. Further, Hunter suggests a structuring of these institutions that locates them either at the cultural centre of a society, or in varying degrees towards the cultural periphery (Hunter, 2010b). For example, with a student enrolment of 32,000 the University of Central Lancashire in Preston is a substantial and well-regarded institution of Higher Education that traces its roots back to 1828. Culturally, however, it is on the periphery in comparison to the smaller University of Oxford which, with its 25,000-student body, is actually an international cultural epicentre.

Culture is, therefore, the formative influence of the world we know. In that sense it is something we receive. Yet it is not only the content of what is passed on, it also provides the means to pass it on and the environment within which it is transmitted. Culture is clearly a process and not a thing. It is a constructed reality that is dynamically subject to a life of adaptation, development and reconstruction in real time. As David Morgan sagely observes, 'People built their worlds, and their worlds build them' (Morgan, 2008, p. xiv).

The process of cultural formation shapes our perception of how the world is and how it works. This fashioning and refashioning of accepted worldviews is critically important. At a conscious level it bequeaths the foundational beliefs and ideas which shape how life is lived. It brings coherence and order to lived experience by providing a framework through which life can be understood and interpreted. In a sense it provides the map that orients us to how things are and enables us to articulate this. On a subconscious level a culturally formed worldview acts as an intuitive sense that provides instinctive responses. These are themselves derived from a sensed context that is 'usually sunk to the level of such an unchallenged framework, something we have trouble often thinking ourselves outside of, even as an imaginative exercise' (Taylor, 2007, p. 549). Across a range of disciplines, many refer to this as the 'social imaginary'. With its origins in the work of Jean-Paul Sartre, this carries the idea of a set of values, institutions, laws and symbols that comprise the imaginary 'social whole' within which people live their lives.

Defining culture

All day, every day, we interact with culture at every level of our life and experience. Yet this is not an encounter with a static monolith. There is not just one culture. There are seemingly endless varieties of culture, with overlaps and contradictions. British culture stands within a more generalized Western culture, but for all the similarities, it clearly differs from American, French or Scandinavian culture. For example, while each of these sits historically within the Christian tradition, their experience has been very different. America has a defined separation of church and state, while the British Head of State is the Supreme Governor of the Church of England, France sits within a Roman Catholic tradition and Scandinavia has a Lutheran heritage.

Within Britain cultural differences emerge with clearly defined regional identities in the North, though Scousers, Mancs and Geordies would be very clear about their own distinctiveness. Sub-cultures are everywhere, shaping faith communities, ethnic minorities and activist and interest groups from the whole spectrum of human life. From the macro to the micro levels of society, culture is at work. Indeed, cultural life is a living thing. Cultures grow and develop. They interact with one another and change or morph as a consequence. Sometimes they develop by incorporating elements of another culture, at other times in reaction against them. Historically speaking culture may have been more stable over time than we now experience it to be in the twenty-first century, but cultural difference has always been profuse by time and place.

The innumerable fields and subfields within any culture and their dynamic interaction present what appears to be an overwhelming level of complexity. When taken with their lively proclivity to change, to fragment or retain internal contradictions it is no wonder that there is a great deal of confusion with regard to the term. Added to this is the different way the word culture itself is used, both in general conversation and by academics from differing specialisms. It is no surprise, therefore, that Terry Eagleton begins his exploration of the subject by repeating the observation that culture is 'one of the two or three most complex words in the English language' (Eagleton, 2000, p. 1). However, before looking more closely at what we mean by the word itself, a step backwards may prove helpful. Tracing how the word has come to us and its historic use will set the scene for everything that follows.

Culture in English, *kultur* in German and *colere* in French all have roots that reach back to the Latin *cultura/colere*. This primarily refers to the cultivation of something and is typically used in farming for tilling the soil and the husbandry or care of livestock. In this sense it carries an intriguing balance between what happens naturally and the fruit of human intervention, between spontaneous life and regulated growth, between taking what already is and fashioning it into what it might become. Interestingly, *The Shorter Oxford English Dictionary* identifies seven different meanings for the word that Ben Highmore helpfully distils into three categories: agriculture/horticulture; the cultivation of the mind for the citizen; and culture as 'a way of life' (Highmore, 2016, pp. 3–4).

By the eighteenth century to be a cultured or civilized individual was to be someone who had educated their mind and attended to their manners. This was both a personal and a social trait, made possible by a civilized society that valued learning, refinement and excellence. In this way civilization was seen as

CULTURE: THE INESCAPABLE REALITY

constantly evolving within itself. Then, building on this, because of its progressive nature it was only common sense for a society to view itself as being superior to and in advance of what went before it. More than this, because of a lineal view of its evolution, it also carried an imperialistic implication regarding the 'less developed', 'less civilized' societies of the world in an age of expanding European colonialism (Eagleton, 2000, pp. 9–10).

The idea of culture as 'a way of life' first emerges in the writing of the German philosopher and theologian Johann Gottfried Herder in the late eighteenth century. He is the one who suggests that the process by which people take on the knowledge of the past should be called *kultur*,

> for it is like the cultivation of the soil ... [the] chain of culture ... stretches to the ends of the earth. Even the natives of California and Tierra del Fuego learned to make and use the bow and arrow; they learned their language and concepts, practices and arts, just as we learn ours. (Cobb, 2005, p. 41)

Herder challenged a model of social development that ran on a continuum from primitive to ever more refined levels of civilization.

As Eagleton perceptively observes, Herder pluralizes the term by challenging the notion that culture is 'some grand, unilinear narrative of universal humanity'; rather, he suggests that it is 'a diversity of specific life-forms, each with its own peculiar laws of evolution'. Herder goes on to differentiate between cultures that emerge at the same time and at different times, within distinct social and economic contexts, and indeed within the same nation, and between the nations themselves.

> What one nation holds indispensable to the circle of its thoughts ... 'has never entered into the mind of a second, and by a third has been deemed injurious.' (Eagleton, 2000, pp. 12–14)

If Herder was the first to begin to articulate this kind of understanding, it did not properly begin to take root until the middle of the nineteenth century, and then to become more fully established until the twentieth century. The disciplines of anthropology, sociology and cultural studies have been in the vanguard of developing an understanding of the fundamental nature of culture, although each carries its own conceptual framework and underlying intellectual assumptions. It becomes increasingly obvious that seeking to understand the nature of culture and engage with it is an interdisciplinary task, not only because of the range of the subject itself, but also with regard to the manner in which the task is approached.

By contrast, within the arts *culture* continues to carry the sense of the cultivation of the mind, of refinement and the pursuit of excellence. Works of artistic expression are particularly in view here and are often further identified as 'high culture' over against the work of 'popular culture' that has more mass appeal. Both result in tangible expressions, or artefacts, of culture. Such works of high or popular art can prove to be particularly influential and formative because they are located at the centre, rather than the periphery, of a society's cultural life. As such they should be clearly recognized as key elements of a wider understanding and description of culture.

In looking to define what we are speaking of with this broader concept of culture, two aspects need to be identified and acknowledged as foundational. The first is that culture is a communal phenomenon. It is about shared meaning and activity. A culture, or indeed a subculture, exists because it is 'held in common'. Any network of relationships has the capacity to build a culture that is generated through their shared life. Yet this only happens as they develop common ways of speaking and acting alongside shared narratives of values, objectives and identity. Of course, as Raymond Williams observed, such common culture is 'open-ended' and always in the process of being remade and redefined by those who are a part of it (Eagleton, 2000, p. 119). Consequently, an articulated understanding of a culture always seems to lag behind the innovative edge of its lived experience.

Second, culture is also, by its very nature, clearly cumulative. Our present experience begins with an inheritance that has been passed on to us. Culture is a product of history, 'the past

CULTURE: THE INESCAPABLE REALITY

which survives in the present' as Pierre Bourdieu expresses it, a restatement of the Aristotelian and Thomist understanding of the concept of *habitus* (Hunter, 2010a, pp. 32–3). We never start from scratch, but rather incorporate and build on what has been handed on to us – albeit that the building may also involve displacing, dismantling, replacing and superseding (Crouch, 2008, p. 73). Then, because of the ongoing internal dialogue that occurs within a culture, it also changes over time as new insights and practices establish themselves and historic emphases fade. The result can often make culture seem something of a hodgepodge. As Eagleton observes, 'cultures work exactly because they are porous, fuzzy-edged, indeterminate, intrinsically inconsistent, never quite identical with themselves, their boundaries continually modulating into horizons' (Eagleton, 2000, p. 96). The French may mockingly call the British 'les rosbifs', but the decline in popularity of the Sunday roast means that maybe 'les poulets tikka masala' might be more accurate.

Further to these considerations it is also worth pausing to reflect upon the implications of our own personal inculturation. At its most basic level all our experience is mediated through culture: 'we experience the world *through* culture; through its categories, forms, exemplifications and traditions' (Highmore, 2016, p. 95). Because culture is local to us, it feels intimate and known; we experience it as 'second nature' and common sense, with its source seemingly inside us. The taken-for-grantedness of what is normal for us means that, with our own cultural context, we are most vulnerable to cultural blindness and most in need of cultural self-awareness. This is the idea of 'proximal culture', a phenomenon that gives us a sense of 'what is culturally near and distant, intimate and foreign, common or strange', and it is always a matter of what is local or familiar to us. So, this blindness not only affects how we see ourselves, but it also extends to how we view those different to ourselves. Our own experience is simply that of being human and normal; it is the others who display racial, quirky, or cultural differences. Our views are reasonable while theirs can range from peculiar to extremist (Highmore, 2009, p. x; Eagleton, 2000, pp. 26–7). Of course, this blindness can then inform our intuitive response to cultural difference, a response instinctively driven by the feelings and emotions that are integral to the intimate nature of our own cultural connection. Hence the frequency of conflict in the world that is focused on those identified as the 'cultural other'. Culture is intrinsic to identity. 'Culture ... is what you kill for' (Eagleton, 2000, p. 38). A brutal assessment, yet one that goes a long way to explain the eruption of conflict and the levers of cultural difference that are pulled by those who want to orchestrate it.

Any attempt, therefore, at cultural description and analysis must always be provisional and expressed with humility. T. S. Eliot maintained that, because our sense of our own culture was always more unconscious than conscious, there would always be more to it than we are aware of (Eliot, 1948, pp. 94, 107). Even when such elements are identified and named, our cultural home does not cease to feel any less normal. Cultural self-awareness may make things visible, but it does not necessarily make them feel any less natural (Highmore, 2016, p. 28). Describing our own culture may well give it substance and definition, but it will not necessarily diminish our passionate sense of connection with it.

The final consideration to take into account before turning to more formal definitions of the concept of culture is that of the relationship of culture to power. Already we have seen that an evolutionary idea of culture helped provide an intellectual justification and bulwark during the era of European colonialism. One might even suggest that more recent calls for movements of cultural change and reformation may exhibit similar tendencies towards contemporary forms of cultural imperialism whereby one cultural group seeks to impose its worldview upon everyone else. This might be the 'no platforming/deplatforming' of those whose views are considered unacceptable or offensive by social activists, or reduction of Brexit to a 'zero-sum game'. Or again, with the introduction of the 2009 Anti-Homosexuality Bill in Uganda's Parliament, opposition from NGOs was criticized as 'neo-colonialism' by MP Margaret Muhanga as the West sought to impose its liberal sexual values on the African continent (Muhanga, 2009), while those working among the

NGOs also saw it as 'neo-colonialism', albeit the importation of the homophobic attitudes of conservative Americans through the powerful influence of evangelical churches (Cheney, 2012, pp. 77–95).

Culture is clearly not neutral in relation to power. This power and ability to exert influence is often spoken of as a kind of symbolic 'cultural capital'. While clearly seen in the formal institutions of a given culture, it can be found in individuals as well. The shape and extent of the cultural power of the British monarchy, for example, has risen, fallen and changed over the centuries, most recently with the reign of Queen Elizabeth II. By contrast, the cultural capital possessed by the social influencers of TikTok and Instagram is a far more recent arrival. But for both, cultural capital bestows the credibility to be listened to and taken seriously, with those who are most powerful possessing the ability to define reality itself (Hunter, 2010a, pp. 35–6). This may be easier to see with an absolute monarch or, with the advent of social media, an activist like Greta Thunberg, but potentially it extends down to any workplace or community that possesses its own culture.

As a contemporary concept, our understanding of 'culture' has its roots in the growth and development of anthropology as a discipline from the middle of the nineteenth century. Undertaking to review the evolution of the concept in 1952 and critically trace its gradual emergence and refinement, the American anthropologists Albert Kroeber and Clyde Kluckhohn identified 164 different definitions. As the first professional attempt to create an inventory of definitions of culture, they arranged them in groups or classifications as descriptive, historical, normative, psychological, structural and genetic. Reflecting on the development of the concept, they concluded: 'In explanatory importance and in generality of application it is comparable to such categories as gravity in physics, disease in medicine, evolution in biology' (Kroeber and Kluckhohn, 1952, p. 3). While the use of the concept of culture has been adopted across the humanities, the flourishing of sociology and arrival of Cultural Studies in the latter part of the twentieth century has further added to the cornucopia of definitions and applications.[1]

If the subject matter of culture is 'the complex whole of life', then Highmore is prudent in identifying three intrinsic dangers that perpetually accompany it: superficiality, inflation and exoticism (Highmore, 2016, pp. 8, 20–2). The danger of superficiality is obvious given the breadth of the subject, but it goes deeper too. Merely studying and knowing about something does not mean that the subject is properly known and understood. The cultural study of religion is a case in point; only a participant believer will properly understand what it is like to believe and have faith. Second, inflation is the lax assumption that the cultural perspective is the only one that matters because it encompasses 'the complex whole of life' and therefore nothing is outside its purview. Such a kleptomaniacal tendency is an overreach that seriously diminishes the impact of the material realm, dismisses transcultural or extracultural phenonema and can result in an innate analytical complacency and reductionism. Third, exoticism is the lure away from the common and mundane to those things that are strange and different.

That the anthropological approach to culture is so widely embraced across the different disciplines as they explore it is evidenced by the frequency with which the ideas of the American anthropologist Clifford Geertz are cited by a wide range of writers (e.g. Eagleton, 2000, pp. 33–4; Lynch, 2007, p. 77; Vanhoozer et al., 2007, pp. 24–5; Carson, 2008, p. 2; Morgan, 2008, pp. 4–8; Highmore, 2016, p. 66; Chatraw and Prior, 2019, p. 24). For Geertz, culture is a signifying system where patterns of meaning are embodied in symbols and signs:

> Human beings, says Clifford Geertz ... are animals suspended in webs of significance that they themselves have spun. 'Culture' is the name for these webs. It is what we make of the world, materially, intellectually and spiritually. These dimensions cannot be separated: the Word is necessarily flesh. In constructing the world materially we interpret it, set values on it. To talk of values is to talk of a culture's self-understanding, its account of its priorities. (Gorringe, 2004, p. 3)

CULTURE: THE INESCAPABLE REALITY

Geertz was concerned about how unusably comprehensive the concept of culture could be and sought to limit its meaning to the 'still extensive "webs of significance" humankind spins for itself' (Inglis, 2000, p. 113). John Frow more succinctly offers 'the whole range of practices and representations through which a social group's reality (or realities) is constructed and maintained' (Eagleton, 2000, p. 35).

H. Richard Niebuhr, in his classic treatment of *Christ and Culture* from 1951, defined culture as

> the 'artificial, secondary environment' which man superimposes on the natural. It comprises language, habits, ideas, beliefs, customs, social organization, inherited artifacts, technical processes, and values. This ... the New Testament writers frequently had in mind when they speak of 'the world'. (Niebuhr, 1951, p. 32)

A more contemporary treatment by theologian Kevin Vanhoozer views culture as

> *made up of 'works' and 'worlds' of meaning.* Culture is a *work* because it is the result of what humans do freely, not a result of what they do by nature to produce something significant. Let us call the products of such work *cultural texts* ... Culture is a *world* in the sense that cultural texts create a meaningful environment in which humans dwell both physically and imaginatively. (Vanhoozer et al., 2007, p. 26)

In highlighting that culture is made up of 'works' and 'worlds' in this way, Vanhoozer clearly guards against culture only being seen as works of artistic merit on the one hand, or as a philosophically based worldview on the other, restricting it solely to the sphere of ideas. Identifying the products of cultural activity as 'cultural texts' is a helpful designation too, as it clearly indicates that they are objects, the meaning of which can be 'read' in their own right.

The sociologist Peter Berger captures the internal dynamic of a society's cultural life when he says:

> The fundamental dialectic process of society consists of three moments, or steps. These are externalization, objectivation, and internalization ... Externalization is the ongoing outpouring of human being into the world, both in the physical and the mental activity of men. Objectivation is the attainment by the products of this activity (again both physical and mental) of a reality that confronts its original producers as a facticity external to and other than themselves. Internalization is the reappropriation ... of this same reality, transforming it once again from structures of the objective world into structures of the subjective consciousness. It is through externalization that society is a human product. It is through objectivation that society becomes a reality *sui generis*. It is through internalization that man is a product of society. (Berger, 1990, pp. 3–4)

More simply, in introducing the concept of 'culture' for the discipline of Cultural Studies, Ben Highmore settles on the intriguingly crafted 'culture is the word we give to the plurality and contradiction of meanings, feelings and practices that circulate in the world and, crucially, to their circulation' (Highmore, 2016, p. viii). However, my own preference sits with the definition advanced by literary theorist Terry Eagleton, not least for the positive and affirming trajectory with which he imbues it.

> Culture can be loosely summarized as the complex of values, customs, beliefs and practices which constitute the way of life of a specific group. It is 'that complex whole', as the anthropologist E. B. Tylor famously put it in his *Primitive Culture*, 'which includes knowledge, belief, art, morals, law, custom, and any other capabilities and habits acquired by man as a member of society'.
>
> Culture is not only what we live by. It is also, in great measure, what we live for. Affection, relationship, memory, kinship, place, community, emotional fulfilment, intellectual enjoyment, a sense of ultimate meaning: these are closer to most of us than charters of human rights or trade treaties. (Eagleton, 2000, pp. 34, 131)

The truth is, most of the time we are unaware of the culture that has been bequeathed to us and that we freely and unconsciously embrace. This 'taken-for-grantedness' enables us to live the life we know intuitively and without thinking. It comprises everything that is important to us and significant for us. Without it, like the air we breathe, it would be impossible to live.

As our perceptions about culture begin to sharpen their focus Highmore suggests that there are two questions that should be borne in mind. The first is about what we are doing when we identify something as cultural. The second addresses our objective. What does recognizing something as cultural allow us to do by way of interrogation and analysis (Highmore, 2016, p. vii)? We have already gone some way towards responding to the first question in exploring our experience of culture, the issues that are raised by reflection on that experience and the kind of criteria that have been deployed in a more formal definition of the concept. Chapters 2 and 3 that follow will take these questions further by setting their exploration within a framework of biblical theology. Chapters 4 and 5 will then look at the analytical task and the insights that can be drawn from across disciplinary divides to help facilitate the theological task of cultural hermeneutics, of interpreting the context in which we live as Christian disciples.

Note

1 While these are too many to map or reference, a selected sample of definitions and the discussions around them is included in Appendix 1.

2

Culture and Theology: Exploring the Relationship

Let earth and heaven combine,
Angels and men agree
To praise in songs divine
Th' incarnate Deity,
Our GOD contracted to a span,
Incomprehensibly made man.

So wrote Charles Wesley in one of his *Hymns for the Nativity of Our Lord*, first published in 1745 (Wesley, 1745, pp. 7–8). With an incarnational theology at the heart of explaining the very nature of Jesus Christ, the relationship between Christianity and culture was always going to be a complicated one.

It is no surprise to discover, therefore, that the appreciation of this complex relationship between culture and theology has mirrored the growing fascination with the nature of culture in wider society. The roots of this enthralment lie in the experience of colonialism and the overseas missionary movement. An exposure to societies that were very different to those of post-Enlightenment Europe raised enormous questions yet, at the time, led to very little cultural self-reflection. Rather, the application of Darwin's evolutionary insights into anthropology produced the doctrine of 'social evolutionism' in which all societies were understood to be somewhere in a developmental sequence ranging from 'primitive' to 'civilized'. Evolving trajectories were identified and could be mapped across a range of intellectual forms and social institutions. For example, the development of the religious dimension of life would progress from a belief in primitive magic, through a more codified religious understanding which is then itself superseded by a scientific comprehension of the world (Tanner, 1997, p. 16). Effectively justifying the superiority of the colonialists, 'social evolutionism' resulted in attitudes and behaviours ranging from benevolent paternalism to the worst forms of racist oppression, exploitation and abuse that the age of empire facilitated.

In many ways the missionaries merely embodied the prevailing worldview of their colonial context. Their endeavours were enabled by imperial expansion and, as Joe de Graft's prophetic play *Muntu* highlights (de Graft, 1977), they arrived on the same ships with the traders, settlers and colonial administrators who provided the infrastructure of empire and exploitation. The missionaries' thinking, living and ministering were an expression of that world. Yet they could also be much more than this. Theirs was also a genuine missionary movement animated by a biblical vision to reach the nations with the gospel of Jesus Christ, rather than a vocation to be the religious agents of imperial rule and chaplains to its institutions. It is a lazy analysis that fails to recognize the far more complex cultural encounter that accompanied the missionaries. For example, while they were hugely shaped by their experience of empire, their understanding of the gospel also carried a deep-seated conviction that in Christ there was 'no longer Jew or Greek ... for all of you are one in Christ Jesus' (Gal. 3.28). Such a profound conviction contributed its own unique outcomes to the missionaries' cultural engagement with schools, hospitals and hospitality at the very heart of their work. Or again, the translation of the Bible into the local vernacular was both affirming and empowering for the subjects of empire (Sanneh, 2009, pp. 250–1), as was the commitment to the indigenization of the church. Henry Venn, the Honorary Secretary of the Church Missionary Society between 1841–73, advocated for a 'three-self principle' of missionary endeavour that looked to establish self-governing, self-supporting and self-propagating churches. He held that the outcome of his strategy would be the liberating autonomy of these young churches and 'the euthanasia of the mission' itself (Jenkins, 2011, p. 48).

However, it was not until the mid-twentieth century that more substantial theological reflection emerged that sought to explore the relationship between culture and theology more closely. As T. S. Eliot observed in 1948,

> Just as a doctrine only needs to be defined after the appearance of some heresy, so a word does not need to receive this attention until it has come to be misused. I have observed with growing anxiety the career of this word *culture* during the past six or seven years. (Eliot, 1948, p. 13)

With the idea of 'culture' gaining both intellectual and social traction, a theological response was inevitable. It was two mid-twentieth-century American Protestant theologians who were particularly to rise to the challenge. In his landmark work, *Christ and Culture*, H. Richard Niebuhr (1951) addressed the range of Christian responses to culture by identifying the underlying theological convictions that generated the response. Paul Tillich's approach was very different. Throughout his career his aim was to articulate a *Theology of Culture* (1959), but this involved both the redefinition of the theological task and what was understood to be its substantive content. A third strand of response was to emerge in the 1960s and 70s from those engaged in missiological research and practice. The coming of age of non-Western churches and the experience of cross-cultural mission led to a rapid appreciation and adoption of the insights of inculturation and contextualization theory.

H. Richard Niebuhr's typology

Originally delivered as a series of lectures at the Austin Presbyterian Theological Seminary in 1949 and published two years later, Niebuhr acknowledged that the gestation of his ideas was the result of 'many years of study, reflection and teaching' (Niebuhr, 1951, p. xi). That the book has remained in print since 1951 is testimony to its significance, as are the accolades that it has accrued across the spectrum of theolog-

CULTURE AND THEOLOGY

ical opinion: 'influential' (Tanner, 1997, p. 61), 'famous' and 'immensely influential' (Gorringe, 2004, pp. 12, 16), 'an icon' (Carson, 2008, p. xi), a 'masterwork' (Hunter, 2010a, p. 214), 'the classic study of this' (Graham, 2017, p. 117), 'a headwater of all subsequent discussion of the huge issues he addressed' (Stackhouse, 2008, p. 13) and 'one of the most widely discussed Christian texts about the relation of religion and culture' (Volf, 2011, p. xiv).

Arranged as a descriptive typology, Niebuhr seeks to tease out how Christians respond to 'The Enduring Problem': the competing authorities of culture on the one hand and the Jesus Christ of the New Testament on the other. Having surveyed the history of the church and its accompanying theologies, he proposes five 'ideal types' that account for the different responses he identifies:

- Christ Against Culture (radicals).
- The Christ of Culture (liberals).
- Christ Above Culture (synthesists).
- Christ and Culture in Paradox (dualists).
- Christ the Transformer of Culture (conversionists).

In taking a typological approach he acknowledges his indebtedness to the sociologist Ernst Troeltsch and the *Psychological Types* of Carl Jung. There is no doubt that his work epitomizes the era of post-war reconstruction and the end of colonialism in which it was written (Gorringe, 2004, p. 13). Yet, while it has many identified weaknesses, it has remained a key theological reference point in all serious discussion of the relationship between Christianity and culture ever since. Had a more effective approach than Niebuhr's idealized 'types' emerged, it would have long since been displaced. That they continue to be cited is indicative of the highly effective way in which they simplify the bewildering range of possibilities that would exist without them (Stassen et al., 1996, pp. 9–10).

What Niebuhr conceives in his work is a continuum of typology, the first two providing polar opposites with the remaining three holding nuanced understandings of a middle range.

Christ Against Culture sets being 'in Christ' over against being 'of the world'. For these 'radicals' their faithfulness to Christ requires a separation from contemporary culture, which is seen as being at odds with God's revelation. There is nothing to be gained from it because it is incompatible with Christian discipleship. Of course, the world cannot be so easily escaped and rather than originating outside of culture, faith is mediated through it. Ironically, in so uncompromisingly affirming the sole Lordship of Christ they either take into themselves the culture of the Judaeo-Greek world that formed Jesus and the early Christian community, or some other inherited cultural form from their own antecedents to which they are seemingly blind. Unconscious of this, they also reject reason and miss the Lordship of Christ over the world of culture he created. For Niebuhr, such an approach can be seen in the teaching of Tertullian and the orientation of monasticism and the Mennonites to wider society (Niebuhr, 1951, pp. 45–82).

The ***Christ of Culture*** type stands at the opposite end of the continuum and no conflict is perceived between Christ and culture. Rather, the 'Christ of Culture' view tends to be a chameleon that blends into the prevailing landscape, more comfortable with the social elite and reductionist in its theology. Jesus is little more than a great teacher who gives kindly liberal advice to good people who want to do right. Christian teaching is therefore seen as the expression and fulfilment of all that is good in human life, and Christianity as embodying everything that a culture might aspire to. Niebuhr sees this as characteristic of the dominant form of Protestantism that, in accommodating to culture, has saved Christianity from becoming a withdrawn sect. Theologically liberal, it tends to overvalue reason and underestimate sin and can be seen as underpinned in the writings of Abelard, Kant, Schleiermacher and Ritschl (Niebuhr, 1951, pp. 83–115).

Christ Above Culture is viewed by Niebuhr as the historic position of the church, where Christ is seen as being high above the realm in which people live. This is a middle or synthetic response that seeks to synthesize the insights of the two poles. All that is good in culture points towards Christ and he is the fulfilment and restorer of its life and institutions. Yet there is something in Christ that neither arises out of culture nor contributes to it. Christ cannot be reached solely by building on the goodness of society. Seen in the work of Justin Martyr and Thomas Aquinas, a synthesis is attempted that maintains the distance between Christ and culture and yet affirms his Lordship over it. However, the approach fosters a conservativism towards culture and its institutions that leads it to be overly optimistic and lacking in a sense of the importance of divine judgement (Niebuhr, 1951, pp. 116–48).

Christ and Culture in Paradox is, by nature, dualistic and seeks to do justice to a believer's loyalty to Christ and responsibility for culture. The whole of creation is fallen, including culture, and yet God sustains it. Any attempt to describe this reality leads to statements that seem paradoxical in the embrace of concepts like wrath and mercy, law and grace. Christians are called to be citizens of two worlds that are not only discontinuous but also largely opposed to one another. There is a recognition of the radical nature of sin in human culture, but also of the fact that believers cannot get out of this world. In this sense it is a dynamic, experiential understanding that mirrors the struggles of actual life, yet antinomianism and cultural conservatism easily flow from its pessimism towards cultural improvement. Niebuhr sees this more as a theological motif than a school of thought, but discerns it in Marcion, Luther and Kierkegaard (Niebuhr, 1951, pp. 149–89).

Christ the Transformer of Culture belongs to the great central tradition of the church. It sees a radical distinction between God's work in Christ and human endeavour in culture but is not separatist. History is the story of God's interaction with humanity and humanity's response. Created good, human nature was corrupted by the fall and redeemed through the atonement. Culture does not need to be reformed or replaced, but rather to be reborn. Culture needs conversion through

Christ so that it might be transformed. John's Gospel demonstrates cultural conversion in undertaking to translate the good news into the ideas of its Hellenistic readers and in lifting ideas like Logos and truth to new levels of meaning in Christ. This conversionist approach appears to be Niebuhr's preferred type because he places it last in his account and offers no criticism of it. However, he does observe that its vulnerability to perversion also leads to its openness to transformation, thereby making a weakness into a core strength. In this sense, cultural engagement is always essential, and Augustine, Calvin and F. D. Maurice are deployed as its exemplars (Niebuhr 1951, pp. 190–229).

Niebuhr concludes that there is no definitive Christian answer to the problem of Christ and culture. The five types he outlines are not wholly exclusive of each other and Christian believers have to step beyond theoretical understanding as they move from insight to action. For him, decisions are always relative and existential: relative to incomplete knowledge, partial faith and the individual's historical and social position; existential because Christians are so by faith not by doctrinal purity.

> When one returns from the hypothetical scheme to the rich complexity of individual events, it is evident at once that no person or group ever conforms completely to a type. (Niebuhr, 1951, pp. 43–4)

Herein lies one of the most widespread misunderstandings of Niebuhr's approach, that is, confusing the difference of purpose between a typology and a taxonomy (Stackhouse, 2008, pp. 32–3). When his work is described as the 'most seminal taxonomy of Christian responses to culture' (Chatraw and Prior, 2019, p. 35), too great an expectation is placed upon it. Where a typology offers a hypothetically constructed range of 'Ideal Types', a taxonomy implies a far more precise and scientific approach to the classification of how things actually are. Criticizing the typology for not working as a taxonomy is just unfair.

Beyond Niebuhr's own self-criticism, other observations have also been made that question the usefulness of his typology. At the most fundamental level is the implied assumption that culture is a static and monolithic entity. However, culture defies being used as such a fixed and global category (Gorringe, 2004, p. 15). Life is far more varied and complicated than a rigid two-dimensional model with five alternatives allows. Yoder concludes that an unintended consequence of the typology is that it leads readers to make too much of the 'normative rigidity' presented through the five types (Stassen et al., 1996, p. 47). This also leads to culture being portrayed as too concrete and thus downplays its dynamic and internal diversity. Indeed, Christ and culture as outlined in Niebuhr's thesis are not the discrete and separable entities that they are inferred to be. Rather, they are closely inter-connected and always in some form of inter-relational tension (Stackhouse, 2008, p. 31; Carson, 2008, pp. 62–4; Howell and Paris, 2011, p. 40). Other theologians have analysed Niebuhr's typology at a more granular level, critiquing its biblical, theological and historical assumptions and understanding (for example, Gorringe, 2004, pp. 12–16; Carter, 2006, pp. 64–71; Carson, 2008, pp. 31–43, 59–64).

While it is somewhat disingenuous to criticize Niebuhr merely because the knowledge, insight and sensitivities of the twenty-first century are alien to him, sometimes these underlying presuppositions can be critically important. Craig Carter highlights the significant flaw that Niebuhr's presumption of Christendom brings to his account of the relationship between Christ and culture. An understanding of Christendom is the background assumption for each of the five types and is taken for granted in all the subsequent discussions about them. Here the Constantinian settlement bestows upon the state the guardianship of Christian civilization and legitimizes the use of coercive violence to maintain it. For Carter this does not stand theological scrutiny (Carter, 2006, pp. 14, 114).

Perhaps the most telling critiques of *Christ and Culture* are those that examine 'its unspoken axioms, its tacit biases and lacunae, and the way it directs and diverts attention' (Stassen et al., 1996, p. 32). Many have noted that Niebuhr presents last his favoured type, 'Christ the Transformer of Culture', and offers no list of weaknesses as he did for the other four. This undeclared weighting of his argument is then combined with an apparent objectivity as he appears to dispassionately stand back and describe the five types. This subtly enables him to justify his own position as a pluralistic liberal Protestant whose theology provides a justification for a pluralistic liberal democracy like America (Hauerwas and Willimon, 1989, pp. 39–42; Stackhouse, 2008, pp. 37–8).

Evaluations of the usefulness of Niebuhr's typology range from its qualified embrace to outright rejection. Elaine Graham is typical of the mildly affirmative because she appreciates its usefulness as a heuristic tool but finds it limited insofar as it oversimplifies complex perspectives (Graham, 2007, p. 75). Robert Jenson has more of a questioning indifference: 'it is no accident that while everyone reads it, and most praise the book, no one seems to be much enlightened by it' (Holmes, 2008, p. 48). Hauerwas and Willimon provide a more trenchant assessment that 'few books have been a greater hindrance to an accurate assessment of our situation', not least because they observe that behind Niebuhr's 'seeming innocuous pluralism' lies 'a prime example of repressive tolerance' (Hauerwas and Willimon, 1989, pp. 40–1). A more measured response is provided by Tim Gorringe who, having identified the typologies' many problems, calls for them to be dropped in favour of a more complex mapping of the interrelation of the gospel and culture (Gorringe, 2004, pp. 15–16). However, it is probably John Stackhouse's defence of the 'abiding usefulness' of the basic typology that is the most realistic assessment of this 'groundbreaking' work (Stackhouse, 2008, pp. 13, 41).

With all the shortcomings contained in Niebuhr's *Christ and Culture*, it is interesting to reflect on why these insights are still so often referenced over 70 years after their initial publication. Why has this creaky typology not been superseded by a more nuanced and thoroughly inter-disciplinary approach that is fit for purpose? The answer is threefold. First, and most importantly, Niebuhr's five types each embody a particular theological response to culture that is recognizable and approximates to what is found in the wider church. Second, the task is altogether more difficult to accomplish than it is to state. For all the dangers of over-simplification, Niebuhr accomplishes a schema that provides at once a comprehension of the task at hand alongside a rudimentary map to begin to explore it. With the appropriate qualifications it provides an entry-level access to the task. It remains a staple reference point because no alternative has, to date, done it better. Third, while both its substance and methodology have been justifiably questioned, it also provides a place to begin constructing approaches that might be more adequate for the task. A brief foray into some of the models that have been advanced over recent years is revealing in this regard.

The turn of the twenty-first century saw a rapid growth in interest in combining theology with film studies. From the outset, Niebuhr's typology provided a helpful theological reference point for those practitioners who were developing interrogative frameworks to facilitate their analytical work. Clive Marsh suggested a distillation into three main ways that the relationship between theology and culture could be understood: theology against culture, theology immersed in culture and theology in critical dialogue with culture (Marsh and Ortiz, 1997, pp. 24–8). Robert Johnston, by contrast, developed a graphic matrix with a range of approaches spanning engagement with film and an ethics/aesthetics continuum, namely avoidance, caution, dialogue, appropriation and divine encounter. Having concluded his introduction, he confesses his indebtedness to Niebuhr, whose framework he considers he is applying (Johnston, 2006, pp. 55–79).

Outside of theology and film, popular speaker Tim Keller outlines four ways in which Christians relate to culture: the Transformationist model, the Relevance model, the Counterculturalist model and the Two Kingdoms model (Keller, 2012, pp. 194–217), while Catholic theorist Michael Paul Gallagher, SJ, suggests a three-fold analysis of 'Hostility towards the culture', 'Innocent acceptance of the culture' and 'Discernment of dispositions' (Gallagher, 1997, pp. 117–23).

Each of the above adapts or applies Niebuhr's typology, while Craig Carter provides a more thoroughgoing revision to take account of post-Christendom thinking and the issue of coercive violence (Carter, 2006, pp. 111–96). Niebuhr's insights take a more sociological turn in the writing of Gordon Lynch as he explores theology and popular culture with his applicationist, correlational, revised correlational and praxis models (Lynch, 2005, pp. 101–5). Gorringe makes good on his determination for a richer understanding of the relationship between church and culture by partnering with cultural studies, using insights from ideas of 'ideology' and 'hegemony' to interrogate the notion of power (which he believes Niebuhr ignores) and mission as the inescapable cross-cultural aspect of the church's life (Gorringe, 2004, pp. 21–2). Pete Ward also believes Niebuhr to have been influential in missiological thinking, as evidenced in Stephen Bevans' six models of contextual theology: translation, anthropological, praxis, synthetic, transcendental and countercultural (Ward, 2008, p. 54; Bevans, 2002). By contrast, Australian missiologist Dave Benson uses the Niebuhrian types as a conversation partner in constructing a biblically based narrative journey toward 'shalom' with six modes of cultural engagement (Benson, 2020, pp. 114–23).

For all their flaws, Niebuhr's types have lasted because they have provided a perceptive language and helpful framework with which to interrogate the relationship of Christ and culture. Having located his own thinking in reference to Niebuhr, Miroslav Volf expresses in the simplest of terms a more deeply nuanced, sophisticated and Christological approach that builds upon it:

> there is no single way in which Christian faith relates and ought to relate to culture as a whole ... The relation between faith and culture is too complex for that. Faith stands in opposition to some elements of culture and is detached from others. In some aspects faith is identical with elements of culture, and it seeks to transform in diverse ways yet many more. Moreover, faith's stance toward culture changes over time as culture changes. How, then, is the stance of faith toward culture defined? It is – or it ought to be – defined by the center of the faith itself, by its relation to Christ as the divine Word incarnate and the Lamb of God who takes away the sin of the world. (Volf, 2011, p. xv)

Paul Tillich's *Theology of Culture*

By contrast with Niebuhr, the writing of Paul Tillich is much less well known. His work is surprisingly absent from contemporary philosophical theologies and his contribution to the rapidly expanding theological interest in culture is strangely overlooked. Given his connection to the influential 'Frankfurt School' of thinkers exploring critical social theory during the interwar years, and his influence in creating the discipline of 'theology of culture' that has led a generation of theologians and sociologists of religion to look for religion outside its organized expression, Cobb sees this omission as 'stunning' (Re Manning, 2015, p. 2; Cobb, 2005, pp. 98–9). Yet Alister McGrath agrees that he is the most influential American theologian to have emerged since Jonathan Edwards (McGrath, 1998, p. 234) and Russell Re Manning seeks to address this oversight and re-present Tillich's 'explosive mix of prophetic critical Protestantism, revolutionary religious socialism, ecstatic rational mysticism, and avant-garde cultural progressivism [that] mark him out as a truly radical thinker for today's radical situation' (Re Manning, 2015, p. 2).

Born in 1886 and already possessing a doctorate in philosophy and having been ordained and served as a Lutheran pastor in a working-class district of Berlin, in 1914 he volunteered for military service in the German army within months of the outbreak of the First World War. For four years he served as a chaplain among the trenches of the Western front, ministering amidst the carnage of death and dying that came to epitomize this ugly and brutal chapter of European history. With the maelstrom of the war threatening to overwhelm him, he discovered that he could divert his attention and sustain himself and his faith by looking at reproductions of great paintings in the books and magazines that were available at the front. After the end of the war he determined to view some original works of art in the museums of Berlin. It was while he was viewing Botticelli's *Madonna with Singing Angels* that he experienced what was to be a life-changing revelation. He later recalled:

Gazing up at it, I felt a state approaching ecstasy. In the beauty of the painting there was Beauty itself. It shone through the colors of the paint as the light of day shines through the stained glass windows of a medieval church.

As I stood there, bathed in the beauty its painter had envisioned so long ago, something of the divine source of all things came through to me. I turned away shaken.

That moment has affected my whole life, given me the keys for the interpretation of human existence, brought vital joy and spiritual truth. I compare it with what is usually called revelation in the language of religion. (Cobb, 2005, pp. 90–1)

Within a few months, in the aftermath of the war, having begun to teach at the university to a student body seeking to come to terms with everything that had happened, Tillich was invited to give a lecture to the Kant Society of Berlin. The 1919 lecture, 'On the Idea of a Theology of Culture', was to set the course of his academic career to the extent that, forty years later in the Foreword to *Theology of Culture* he could write, 'It is a source of great satisfaction to me that ... I can take the title for this volume from my first important public speech' (Tillich, 1959, p. v).

Tillich's opposition to Hitler led to his emigration to the United States and successive posts at Union Theological Seminary, New York, Harvard Divinity School and the University of Chicago prior to his death in 1965. His legacy is as 'the preeminent "theologian of culture"' (Marsh and Ortiz, 1997, p. 30), the archetypal mid-twentieth-century theological liberal who was willing to 'transcend theism' (Re Manning, 2015, pp. 1, 7) and whose ideas are to be found 'under-sitting' neo-liberal attempts at articulating a 'secular theology' that are tantalizingly accused of being 'crypto-theology' by their nay-sayers (Grimshaw, 2018, p. 6). If his career was at the height of its influence in the mid-century, it had significantly waned by its close, due in part to a changing theological method and outlook alongside reservations about Tillich's personal ethics (Marsh, 2018, pp. 36–7).

In his 1919 lecture Tillich made it clear that moral theology and theological ethics could no longer be pursued as they had in the past. His sense was that the war had left the 'whole house in ruins'. Struck by the 'intolerable gap' that had opened up between religion and culture, he made the revolutionary proposal to revise the very nature and task of theology. As Re Manning has observed, 'his radical assessment of the true challenge facing the future of theology ... [was] the rise of an excess of faith (in both its religious and cultural guises)' (Re Manning, 2015, p. 3). Rather than repairing the fracture of old certainties, what needed to be addressed was far more fundamental: in short, the very cultural framework of modern life (McKinney, 1976, pp. 274–5).

In addressing this task he differentiates between the 'theology of the church' and the 'theology of culture'. The 'theology of the church' is the familiar work undertaken with those elements that make up the religious sphere of life such as the religious knowledge of myth and dogma, religious aesthetics, cultus and the religious formation of the person. The 'theology of culture' is looking for the religious 'substance' contained in the other spheres of culture such as art, science, morality, politics and the economy. Tillich wrote:

> the theological method ... is the universal application of theological inquiry into every cultural value ... The task of a theology of culture corresponds to this. It carries out a general religious analysis of all cultural creations, it offers a philosophical–historical and typological classification of great cultural creations from the point of view of the religious substance realized in them, and from its own religious standpoint it fashions the ideal design for a culture religiously fulfilled. (Nuovo, 1987, pp. 26–7)

In what he proposes Tillich uses the idea of religion in two different ways. First, it refers in the received sense to that defined sphere of culture of sacred texts, liturgies, symbols, clergy and institutions. Then, second, he goes in a different direction altogether in what will prove to be the basis of his distinctive contribution. Here Tillich uses religion to identify the deep and 'unconditioned' sense of meaning that lies beneath all spheres of culture, giving them worth and value and thereby sustaining them and ensuring ongoing participation within them. Religious substance, or meaning, is therefore embedded in all expressions of culture in which people discern a sense of meaning (Cobb, 2005, p. 92). Tillich will later name this as 'ultimate concern'.

Tillich also goes on to seek to explore more fully the relationship that exists between the 'theology of culture' and the 'theology of the church'. Recognizing that the 'theology of the church' is itself a product of culture, this implies that it should be part of a broader 'theology of culture' rather than a separate entity on its own. Indeed, he recognizes that they are deeply entwined together and never truly separate. For example, he argues that to experience the religious values of a culture and then seek to articulate a 'theology of culture' requires a religious culture to have preceded it and made such an identification possible. However, making them distinct in abstract, he argues, is a psychological necessity to more fully understand and appreciate them, as it is in other areas of knowledge (Nuovo, 1987, p. 35). Yet it is in Ultimate Concern that the deep interconnection between culture and religion is most clearly seen. Writing his more mature reflections towards the end of his career, Tillich observes:

> Religion as ultimate concern is the meaning-giving substance of culture, and culture is the totality of forms in which the basic concern of religion expresses itself. In abbreviation: religion is the substance of culture, culture is the form of religion. Such a consideration definitely prevents the establishment of a dualism of religion and culture. (Tillich, 1959, p. 42)

In this way Tillich opens up every sphere of culture as an appropriate subject of theological consideration and establishes the legitimacy of a robust use of theological resources and insights in its analytic task.

> Judging means seeing both sides. The Church judges culture, including the Church's own forms of life. For its forms are created by culture, as its religious substance makes culture possible. The Church and culture are within, not alongside,

each other. And the Kingdom of God includes both while transcending both. (Tillich, 1959, p. 51)

Religion and culture are so much a part of each other that to separate thinking about either is to fail to properly engage with both (Grimshaw, 2018, p. 5). Thus Tillich sets up a dialogue in his 'theology of culture'. As the Ultimate Concerns of culture are expressed, especially through modern philosophy and the creative arts, theology formulates answers to the questions and thereby correlates the gospel with contemporary culture. There is mutuality in this conversation in that it leaves both open to correction and enrichment; but, at the very beginning, to engage in the dialogue theology must both hear and understand the expressed concerns of culture. This identification of Ultimate Concern is the fruit of practising a form of cultural hermeneutics: how do we interpret the world around us? For Tillich, the theology of culture is no less than being faithful to the received theological tradition while also properly engaging with the contemporary situation as the opposite pole of theology (McKinney, 1976, p. 273). It is

> the attempt to analyze the theology behind all cultural expressions, to discover the ultimate concern in the ground of a philosophy, a political system, an artistic style, a set of ethical or social principles. (Cobb, 2005, p. 99)

The whole of Tillich's *Theology of Culture* is guided by this conception of Ultimate Concern and, according to Re Manning, in this bold, assertive and radical move he relocates theology from religion to culture (Re Manning, 2015, pp. 3–4).

In some ways this might be viewed as a form of apologetic theology. Tillich was clear that 'The Christian message is the message of a new Reality in which we can participate', and yet that participation takes upon itself the anxieties and despairs revealed by the expressed Ultimate Concern (Tillich, 1959, p. 208). This is not an apologetic that seeks to convert the secular world by translating biblical religion into the language, thoughts and feelings of its host culture. Rather, it offers something wholly different, 'a faithless theology of doubt' (Re Manning, 2015, p. 8). For Tillich, following Kant, 'God' cannot be the object of theology, as if God were amenable to investigation. He prefers, therefore, to talk of God in non-personal terms, such as 'being-itself' or 'the ground of meaning and being' and of Jesus Christ as the 'bearer of new being'. So theology has nothing to do with an object called 'God' or with a particular body of revelation (McKinney, 1976, p. 275). As a consequence, a new locus for theology must be found. While Schleiermacher has his 'subjective turn' that moves towards faith, piety and the believer's experience being the subject of theology, for Re Manning Tillich is far more radical than this. A 'supra-natural' God merely reduces him to the 'supra-finite'. Rather than follow Bultmann's call to 'demythologize', Tillich aims at a 'deliteralization' where religious language is always symbolic. Then, as theology has no real subject of its own, everything can properly become its subject (Re Manning, 2015, pp. 11–12, 3; Nuovo, 1987, p. 20; Grimshaw, 2018, p. 6).

The theological idea that ties together everything that Tillich seeks to accomplish is the methodology of 'correlation'. Once the Ultimate Concerns of anxiety, despair, estrangement and their like have been exposed, the task of religion is to provide answers by correlating its symbols, narratives and practices to these expressed Ultimate Concerns. Tillich's objective was to make Christianity meaningful to a generation in which it seemed to be losing its public credibility (Wade, 2020, p. 4; McGrath, 1998, pp. 234, 335–6).

Brief summaries of Tillich's contribution frequently fall back on his abbreviated strapline 'religion is the substance of culture, culture is the form of religion' (Tillich, 1959, p. 42). Ultimate Concern is the substance of culture and is discerned by theology through its analysis of culture. This is the very depth of culture, what matters most to it and therefore provides the centre of its religious or spiritual dimension. The expression of this Ultimate Concern in culture is then the form that religion takes in its social organization and cultural expression (Re Manning, 2015, p. 8; Grimshaw, 2018, p. 6). In all of this, therefore, John Heywood Thomas suggests that a theology of culture is primarily concerned with the substance of culture, rather than its form (McKinney, 1976, p. 287).

In passing, it is also worth noting Tillich's understanding of religious symbols. As with all symbols, he sees them as vehicles for revealing a level of reality that would otherwise be hidden. Because of the nature of religious symbols, the 'depth dimension' they connect with is that of ultimate reality, the fundamental level, the level of being itself. Such religious symbols therefore become a means of opening up 'the experience of this dimension in the depth of the human soul'. This dimension of ultimate reality is the dimension of the holy, yet, while religious symbols participate in the experience of the holiness of the Holy, they are not Holy themselves (Tillich, 1959, pp. 58–9). This is an important distinction because it means that religious symbols are provisional and if they cease in their function they die. He also sees a similar provisionality in language, which is itself the result of 'innumerable acts of cultural creativity' (Tillich, 1959, p. 47). This gives Tillich significant freedom in his use of symbol and language. As Harvey Cox observed in his introduction to the third edition of Tillich's *The Courage to Be*.

> There is a quality of daring in Tillich's thinking. He took risks, ... One of the risks he took was to abandon any fetishism of particular words. He knew, both from his keen observation of modern culture and through his own spiritual struggles, that the words 'grace' and 'faith' and even 'God' had not only lost much of their original power, but had also been so distorted that they had often been evacuated of meaning. So he boldly experimented with new vocabulary. If the word 'God' no longer speaks to you, he once wrote, say 'depth.' Instead of 'sin,' say 'separation.' Instead of 'forgiveness,' say 'acceptance.' (Tillich, 2014, p. xxiv)

The fact that Tillich is much less well known is probably accounted for by the fact that he was very much a child of his times. Much that was ground-breaking and vital in his work in the first half of the twentieth century has not aged so well. With the Frankfurt School he showed an exclusive preference for the products of high culture where the artists, poets and philosophers of the avant-garde, 'the great works of the visual arts, of music, of poetry, of literature, of architecture, of dance, of philosophy', were the true expressions of culture (Tillich, 1959, p. 46). This was little more than a kind of liberal accommodationism for the intelligentsia, an expression of social privilege and social superiority. In this reading of culture, Marx and Freud, for example, were awarded a prophetic status. By contrast, their attitude towards the kitsch of mass or popular culture ranged from disdain to aversion. Having seen how Hitler marshalled such populism in the 1930s, and the American culture industry similarly used mass media to further capitalism after the Second World War, the influences at work in his thinking are clear to see (Cobb, 2005, pp. 97–8). However, as Marsh poignantly observes, such an approach is too constraining as 'even poor art might be revelatory' (Marsh, 2018, p. 40).

Theologically Tillich has had his critics too. For example, McGrath considers his treatment of Jesus as Christologically reductionist. Jesus becomes merely the symbol of universal human possibility. This represents a 'degree Christology' that is not interested in the historical figure of Jesus of Nazareth, but rather treats him as a symbol of our perception of God (McGrath, 2001, pp. 369–70). Or again, Thomas believes that the significant influence of Hegel on Tillich's 'Theology of Culture' leaves him open to a pantheistic doctrine of God as he draws upon the mediation of the Infinite through the finite in a thoroughly reciprocal relation (McKinney, 1976, pp. 279–80). Over more recent decades it is the shortcomings in the economic and socio-political implications of Tillich's work that are highlighted (Marsh, 2018, pp. 43–4), though Re Manning suggests that the 'retrieval of the *politically* radical Tillich' is a realistic objective (Re Manning, 2015, pp. 5, 14).

For all Tillich's lack of visibility in contemporary theology, there can be no doubting his contribution in laying the foundations for a theological engagement with culture. He demonstrated that it was possible to theologically read the world around us and skilfully synthesized the German tradition of attempting to generate an all-encompassing vision of the world with American pragmatism and experimentalism (Wade, 2020, p. 7). In focusing on the present cultural situation John Clayton memorably observed that Tillich had given his theology 'a planned obsolescence' that precluded its future relevance (Re Manning, 2015, p. 13). Indeed, Clive Marsh sagely concludes that Tillich's approach brings theology much closer to journalism than it might care to admit. Further, as he explores theology's engagement with film, Marsh calls for this encounter not to be about establishing relevance but rather about an interdisciplinary quest for truth (Marsh and Ortiz, 1997, pp.33-4). For Marsh, though, any theologian who follows in the footsteps of Tillich needs to be aware of Trevor Hart's warning of fitting the gospel to the '*Zeitgeist* [spirit of the age] rather than the *heilige Geist* [Holy Spirit]' (Marsh, 2018, p. 34).

Missiology's concepts of Inculturation and Contextualization

In 1986 the missiologist Lesslie Newbigin made a rather telling observation that there was now nothing new in discussing the relationship between gospel and culture; yet he wryly remarked, as he referenced Niebuhr's 'classic study' and Tillich's 'massive work', that it 'has mainly been done ... by theologians who had not had the experience of the cultural frontier' (Newbigin, 1986, p. 1). The frontier that interested him was, of course, that provided by the missionary movement. The preceding twenty years had witnessed a particularly fruitful period of theological creativity in which Roman Catholicism, the World Council of Churches and the evangelicalism of the Lausanne Movement all developed parallel and complementary understandings of the relationship between the gospel and culture. Though there are significant differences of vocabulary, Catholic insights into inculturation and the Protestant understanding of contextualization are largely shared and the two overarching terms are often regarded as being synonymous (Archbishops' Council, 2004, p. 90).

While both terms are relatively recent, the ideas that underpin them have long roots that track back through church history. Indeed, Raymond Brown observes that even in early Judaeo-Christianity different forms of practice emerged as Christian faith grappled with the competing cultural implications of the movement's Jewish origin and the ensuing Gentile mission. Its foundations in Judaism made the Torah an issue along with ritual purity, circumcision, religious conversion, the Temple and the place of sacrifice. These quickly became matters of concern and conflict, with different emphases spinning off and influencing the assorted communities and strands of the movement. Some insisted on circumcision, like those from Jerusalem who found support in Galatia and Philippi. Others, who aligned themselves with James and Peter, were not so much concerned with circumcision as a deeper commitment to maintaining Jewish purity laws. Then there were the gentile churches that followed the lead of Paul, and among whom a tendency towards a greater tolerance and diversity developed (Brown, 1985, pp. 133–4). In what was a historically unique development, Christianity as a religious expression parted company with both the faith community and the language into which it had been born (Sanneh, 1993, pp. 118–19).

Inculturation

The term 'inculturation' itself was first used in 1962 by Fr Joseph Masson, SJ of the Gregorian University in Rome. It quickly spread and supplanted the terms 'accommodation' and 'adaption' that had been most popular up to this point. These were viewed as implying a superiority to the existing Eurocentric form of Catholicism, along with a more static understanding of the expression of faith. The adoption of inculturation also moved away from the more romantic and exotic notions conjured up by 'indigenization', which was also considered to be rather conservative and backward-looking. Inculturation, by contrast, pointed towards a more creative and dynamic relationship between the Christian message and the cultures it encountered and inhabited (Shorter, 2006, pp. 10–11).

While still Cardinal Ratzinger and Prefect of the Congregation for the Doctrine of the Faith, the future Pope Benedict XVI declared, 'faith itself is culture'. Here there is no 'pre-cultural' or 'de-cultured' faith; faith must become culture to be received and lived (Gallagher, 1997, p. 103). This has to do with both the communication of the faith and its lived reality. Inculturation, then, is not merely a transcultural encounter or even a fruitful dialogue. It is only when it has moved beyond these stages to a symbiosis that is neither syncretistic on one side, nor culturally imperialistic on the other, that inculturation can be understood to have occurred.

> The possibility of Christian inculturation is proved by actual experience. The normal consequence of successful evangelization is that Christianity becomes 'at home' in the evangelized culture. It becomes 'customary' – part of a people's custom. (Shorter, 2006, p. 62)

Evangelization therefore addresses the shape and form of culture and not just the individual with a view to their conversion. It also suggests a 'double movement' that involves not only the inculturation of Christianity in a way that does not compromise the message as it is reinterpreted and reformulated, but also the Christianization of the host culture itself. Yet a significant flaw in this concept is the implied sense of it being accomplished when the faith is fruitfully implanted in its receptor culture – thus potentially undermining its advance on the older idea of indigenization. Because culture is not a static entity and no culture can perfectly inculturate the gospel, Christianity must always resist being domesticated by its context and must therefore maintain a critical and discerning orientation to the world around it. For all the importance of the principle of inculturation, there remains a dimension of its relationship with a host culture in which Christianity must remain 'out of step', on the margins and 'foreign' (Bosch, 2003, pp. 454–6).

Recognizing the attractive power of the Christian life well lived, inculturation can be understood as embedding the 'essence of the gospel' in the lived witness of human beings. These authentic and readily identifiable qualities – such as love, self-sacrifice, forgiveness, abnegation, spiritual poverty – are therefore of critical importance (Shorter, 2006, pp. 60–1). The evangelization of a culture cannot therefore be artificially induced or self-consciously constructed. As the Sri Lankan Jesuit theologian Aloysius Pieris perceptively pointed out, it happens naturally and is the 'by-product' of people living and interacting together. In this sense it is truly formational and consciously seeks to accomplish this by hastening a process of mimetic learning. By contrast, the 'questions that are foremost in the minds of inculturationists are, therefore, totally irrelevant' (Gorringe, 2004, pp. 199–200).

The concept of inculturation gained currency among the Jesuits and also received advocacy from the African bishops and theologians who saw it as an ally in ensuring a genuinely African expression of Christianity in their newly independent and post-colonial context. Pope Paul VI and then Pope John Paul II both firmly espoused it, effectively neutralizing the resistance of Western church leaders to embracing it (Shorter, 2006, p. xi; Bosch, 2003, p. 452; Gorringe, 2004, p. 199). In more recent times inculturation has found new prominence, having been adopted as the term of choice in the Church of England's influential *Mission-shaped Church* report. Following its publication in 2004 the report provided the initial impetus and foundational thinking that gave rise to the Fresh Expressions of church and pioneer ministry movements that quickly became a ubiquitous feature within international Anglicanism and more widely in other Protestant denominations (Archbishops' Council, 2004, pp. 90–3; Moynagh, 2018, pp. 2–3).

Contextualization

Within the Protestant world it was the work of the World Council of Churches' (WCC) Theological Education Fund (TEF) that gave the word 'contextualization' its theological birth in its 1972 report, *Ministry in Context*. Under the direction of Shoki Coe the Fund was committed to raising the academic standards of theological education in the global south, along with enabling students to competently engage with the gospel in full consideration of their own culture, ways of thinking and human situation (Chang, 2012, pp. 122–3). Coe knew these issues within himself. A family background in Taoism and shaped by the post-war situation in South East Asia, he had studied in Japan and Cambridge, marrying Winifred while giving instruction in Japanese at the School of Oriental and African Studies in London (Wheeler, 2002, pp. 77–80). Their mandate from the WCC directed them to help the churches reform training for Christian ministry in the light of the 'widespread crisis of faith', 'issues of social justice and human development' and 'the dialectic between local cultural and religious situations and a universal technological civilization' (Theological Education Fund, 1972, p. 17). In the light of this task, they defined their key concept of contextualization as

> all that is implied in the familiar term 'indigenization' and yet seeks to press beyond. Contextualization has to do with how we assess the peculiarity of Third World contexts. Indigenization tends to be used in the sense of responding to the gospel in terms of a traditional culture. Contextualization, while not ignoring this, takes into account the process of secularity, technology, and the struggle for human justice, which characterize the historical moment of nations in the Third World. (Theological Education Fund, 1972, p. 20)

Trying to catch something of the flavour of the move from indigenization to contextualization, Al Krass, writing in the magazine *The Other Side* in 1978, observed that where indigenization was a subject covered in *National Geographic*, contextualization was more the kind of thing you read in *Time* magazine (Nicholls, 2003, p. 22).

The report proposed that if contextualization was the chief characteristic of theological reflection, then applications for support would be judged according to evidence discerned at four levels: Missiological, Structural, Theological and Pedagogical (Theological Education Fund, 1972, p. 20; Lienemann-Perrin,

1981, pp. 174–6; Hesselgrave and Rommen, 1989, pp. 31–2). Theological reflection was to be intentionally focused on the local and situational context, yet it was held that this could only be accomplished if a wider interdependence was maintained. Chronologically there was an inseparable link with the history and future of a specific context, and internationally there was a required 'solidarity with all people in subordination to a common Lord'. In this process false contextualization always succumbed to uncritical accommodation to its setting, whereas authentic contextualization was prophetic because its rootedness in God's Word and its contemporary context led to a challenge to change.

> Contextuality, it is claimed, is the capacity to respond meaningfully to the gospel within the framework of one's own situation. Contextualization is not simply a fad or a catchword but a theological necessity. (Theological Education Fund, 1972, pp. 20–1)

The term became popular very quickly and was soon being incorporated into the evolving socio-economic theologies (political theology and theology of development) and the revolutionary approaches of liberation, black and feminist theology (Bosch, 2003, pp. 420–1). So ubiquitous did this understanding of the contextual nature of theology become that Stephen Bevans opens his substantive treatment of the subject with the statement, 'There is no such thing as "theology"; there is only *contextual* theology' (Bevans, 2002, p. 3).

Given that the idea of contextualization emerged from the World Council of Churches and was quickly adopted by more liberal approaches to theology, it is something of a surprise to see it also taken up by those who were more theologically conservative. Though many had reservations, it was at the 1974 Lausanne Congress on World Evangelization that serious questions were raised in this regard. The *'Gospel and Culture'* consultation subsequently took place in 1978 at Willowbank, Bermuda, with 'contextualization' at the heart of the discussions and clearly under the spotlight. The conference concluded that God's self-disclosure in the Bible was always given in terms of the hearers' own culture and that there was no hope of communicating the gospel if the culture factor was ignored (Stott and Coote, 1981, pp. 313, 319).

The endorsement of the Lausanne Movement paved the way for contextualization as an idea to move into the mainstream of evangelical thinking. The influence of theologian practitioners like Lesslie Newbigin furthered the cause by bringing intellectual rigour, the experience of cross-cultural ministry and missiological insights to bear on contemporary theological reflection. Having spent most of his life as a missionary in India, Newbigin returned to the UK and realized that what Western culture needed was a 'missionary encounter' with the gospel. At the heart of this encounter he wanted to place what the missionary movement had learned about the importance of contextualization.

> The value of the word *contextualization* is that it suggests the placing of the gospel in the total context of a culture at a particular moment, a moment that is shaped by the past and looks to the future. (Newbigin, 1986, p. 2)

Newbigin wanted to think through what was involved in communicating the gospel. What were the dynamics of this missionary encounter? He saw it as requiring a triangular model involving the three cultures he discerned as being at work in any such encounter – the culture of Christ and the Bible, the missionaries' own culture and the target or receptor culture (Hunsberger, 1998, pp. 237–8). This encounter required a coming together of personal self-awareness, biblical knowledge and cultural insight. To begin with, the communicator needed to understand how they had already recontextualized the biblical world into their own and how they inhabited it. Much of this is an unconscious process that builds on past experience, inherited understanding and the instinctive reaction that tries to make sense of things. Stripping the process of contextualization of these cultural accretions and assumptions, the objective is to then recontextualize the gospel message into the cultural space of the hearers. Now the message is to be constructed in terms of the experience and understanding of the receptors. According to Charles Kraft the goal is to produce a 'dynamic equivalence' of effect in the language and conceptual framework of the hearers that was experienced in the original biblical context (Kraft, 2005, pp. 216–27).

Historically this translation model of contextualization has been seen as moving along a continuum, where any authentic and legitimate attempt at contextualizing sits somewhere between the poles of cultural isolation and irrelevance at one end and cultural syncretism and assimilation at the other. Herein lies a dilemma: 'In the attempt to be relevant one may fall into syncretism, and in the effort to avoid syncretism one may become irrelevant' (Newbigin, 1986, p. 7). These alternatives are stark: compromise or obscurantism, a comfortable and familiar message or one that is veiled and hidden and makes no sense – the dangers of over-contextualizing or failing to contextualize.

The decades since the TEF report and the Lausanne consultation have witnessed the growing influence of missiology in theological education and ministerial formation and of contextualization as its key foundational principle. Mission studies are now part of core curricula, if not the shaping principle around which the whole curriculum itself is formed (Banks, 1999). John Corrie summarizes these developments as embracing three distinguishable levels: first, language and the need to communicate in the forms of speech and understanding of an intended audience; second, the identification of the concerns and those things that are important within a given culture such as foundational traditions, shared values, perceived needs or owned priorities that may be in harmony with the gospel and to be embraced, at odds with the gospel and to be rejected, or indifferent to the gospel and may be accepted purely on the basis of their cultural significance; and third, the transformational level that is the product of interactive dialogue operating at the level of meaning where, on one side, new dimensions of gospel significance are revealed and, on the other, individuals and communities are transformed by Kingdom values and meaning (Corrie, 2002, p. 3).

Contextualization is the process by which a local Christian community integrates the gospel message (the 'text') with the real-life context, blending text and context into that single, God-intended reality called 'Christian living'. (Luzbetak, 1988, p. 133)

While there is a range of understanding within Protestant circles of the scope of contextualization, Scott Moreau's 'holistic approach' is demonstrative of the progress of fifty years of reflection on the ideas initially tabled by TEF. Having discovered Ninian Smart's dimensional approach to religion, Moreau transposes this seven-dimensional framework into his own treatment of contextualization as social, mythic, ethical, artistic/technological, ritualistic, experiential and doctrinal, where his expanded social dimension includes separate chapters on association and kinship, economics, education and politics (Moreau, 2018).

In short

Broadly speaking, as theology has sought to understand its relationship with culture the three approaches identified above have been most influential. Niebuhr takes a sociological path and wants to understand how different theological traditions can relate to culture so differently. In contrast, Tillich has a more iconoclastic methodology as he takes the cherished orthodox categories of theology and reuses them by redefining and developing them with the objective of seeking a deeper insight and understanding of wider human life.

> To say that Niebuhr and Tillich influence nearly every theologian who correlates theology and culture will only be a slight exaggeration. The importance of their work cannot be underestimated. (Long, 2008, p. 62)

The missiological and apologetic readings of culture, or at least elements of them, then provide the third major strand of theology's response to culture, looking to provide bridges of engagement, understanding and evangelization with the world. This, however, is not the full story.

As the twentieth century progressed it is hardly surprising that the wider fascination with culture also fed back further into theology itself. The emergence of contextual, intercultural and postmodern theology is testimony to this. Contextual theology explores how a cultural context shapes theological thinking. Stephen Bevans, for example, identifies six models of contextual theology that he names as translation, anthropological, praxis, synthetic, transcendental and countercultural (Bevans, 2002). Intercultural theology then takes this further by bringing systematic theology into conversation with cultural studies to provide a theological interpretation of the issues at stake (Gruber, 2018, p. 12). Postmodern theologies are all rather more difficult to pin down, but largely map a theological response to writers like Derrida, Foucault, Lyotard and Baudrillard and the theological/philosophical debate that has subsequently ensued (Ward, 2005, p. xxiv; Smith, 2006, pp. 18–20; Caputo, 2007, pp. 134–8).[1] Some theologians have pushed back at what they have seen as an over-dependence on the fruit of social science. Most notably, John Milbank has contended that theologians have allowed their work to be 'policed' by the intrinsic logic of the social sciences. He proposed a different logic of 'radical orthodoxy' that was primarily founded on the doctrine of the incarnation, along with a robust ecclesiology. Believing that the church was an idealized community that, by virtue of its institution, was already a 'reading' of other human societies, he argued:

> For theology to surrender this claim, to allow that other discourses – 'the social sciences' for example – carry out yet more fundamental readings, would therefore amount to a denial of theological truth. (Milbank, 2006, p. 390)

This is a critically important issue to consider. That theology is a part of culture (Tanner, 1997, p. 63). George Lindbeck's 'cultural-linguistic' activity (Long, 2008, p. 94) – is undeniable.

Yet in itself theology believes it is much more than this. There is a 'receivedness' about its truth that transcends the mere transmission of historic insight. Its truth has a divine source that is given as a revelation. However, missiology aside, much of the theological response to its heightened awareness of the role of culture has been 'inward' looking and carried on at a rarefied level.

A more fundamental question needs to be asked if a more outward orientation is to be achieved along with a more grounded understanding that facilitates Christian discipleship. It requires taking a step further back. It is the question that addresses the why of it all. If culture is an inescapable reality, how do we understand this 'givenness' in the creative purposes of God? Herein will lie the actual substance of a theology of culture, rather than a theological explanation of a sociological observation, an appropriation of theological concepts as a vehicle to aid philosophical explanation or an instrumental engagement with culture to facilitate a missiological end.

Note

1 *On contextual theology:* Bevans sees its innovation as moving beyond theology as 'a kind of objective science of faith' based on Scripture and tradition and somehow beyond historical and cultural conditioning. Admitting human experience into the equation provides a new locus of theological attention that incorporates culture, history and contemporary thought-forms. While acknowledging that this is a radically new way of understanding theology, he also maintains that it is thoroughly in continuity with what has gone before. Indeed, he begins his account by stating 'There is no such thing as 'theology'; there is only *contextual* theology' (Bevans, 2002, pp. 3–4).

On intercultural theology: Understood as evolving out of missiology, intercultural theology seeks to understand the variations in theological understanding that different cultural contexts produce. While still a nascent discipline around which there are a variety of perspectives, definitions, constituencies, allegiances and objectives (Cartledge and Cheetham, 2011, p. 1), its focus is an important one. Such as: given the plural, fragmented and evolving nature of theological understanding that differing contexts give rise to, how are the universal claims of

Christianity held within a variety of particular contextual theologies? Or: who gets to decide what is Christian, and on what basis (Wrogemann, 2016, p. xiii)? As Gruber highlights,

> The epistemological changes brought about by the Cultural Turn put the universal claim of Christianity's message into a precarious tension with its particular local formulations. A theological accounting of faith thus demands that we relate the normative unity of faith to its plural testimonies and consider the normativity of formulations of Christian identity in relation to their historical and cultural contingency. Theology after the Cultural Turn requires a model of universality that is based on epistemological particularity: How can we maintain the universality of the Christian message without erasing the disparate particularities of Christian identity? (Gruber, 2018, p. 11)

For a fuller account see Cartledge and Cheetham (2011), Gruber (2018), and Hennig Wrogemann's *Intercultural Theology* trilogy (2016, 2018 and 2019).

On postmodern theology: Kevin Vanhoozer takes an optimistic view that Christianity has always grown through its encounter with 'the other'. He therefore deploys a seven-fold typology to bring some semblance of an overview to developments within the realm of postmodern theology. He suggests that these are:

1 A theology of communal practice.
2 Postliberal theology.
3 Postmetaphysical theology.
4 Deconstructive theology.
5 Reconstructive theology.
6 Feminist theology.
7 Radical orthodoxy.

He then goes on to map what is, for him, a central theme in reading culture:

> Theology returns, not as a modern science, but as a Theo-drama that situates the human within the narrative of God's creative and redemptive activity. The suggestion, therefore, is to situate modernity and post-modernity alike within the story of what relates both what God is doing in the world through Jesus Christ and the Holy Spirit and what the world is doing in response. Postmodernity here appears as a properly *theological* condition. (Vanhoozer, 2003, pp. 19–21)

3

Towards a Theo-cultural Understanding of the World

The response of theology to the twentieth century's increasing appreciation of culture through the development and popularity of the disciplines of anthropology, sociology and cultural studies has varied. Niebuhr is best viewed as the father of it all as he seeks to provide a theological account of why Christian communities varied so greatly in their sociological orientation to the culture around them. By contrast, Tillich's 'theology of culture' is a wholesale reconception of the theological task and the philosophy of religion. The missiologists, as would be expected, are far more confessional and practical in their engagement with issues of culture. For evangelistic, apologetic or pastoral purposes, theology is deployed to interrogate and 'read' subjects such as film (Goodwin, 2022), contemporary music (Scharen, 2011), sport (Parker, Watson and White, 2016) or for a more general engagement with popular culture (Gould, 2019). Other more substantive volumes cover similar ground, but with a more serious and intellectually rigorous intent (Loughlin, 2004; Till, 2010; Harvey, 2014; Clark and Clanton, 2012).

One further approach is worth noting and involves using an existing theological system or specifically identified theological categories as templates by which to construct an understanding of a cultural context. Calvinism particularly lends itself to such an endeavour, as is demonstrated in the work of Henry Van Til. Here the template is provided by a four-stage biblical plot of creation, fall, the redemptive plan that begins with Israel and is fulfilled in Christ, and then the new creation that is the fruit of the Second Coming of Christ. Van Til then goes on to deploy Augustine, Calvin and Dutch Reformed 'neo-Calvinists' like Abraham Kuyper to illustrate how these profound insights of biblical plot are best drawn out for understanding culture (Van Til, 2001). William Romanowski uses a similar approach but takes a different tack, suggesting four fundamental faith beliefs to reveal 'a biblical vision into the cultural landscape'. These are the core contours of Christian experience which are deployed to represent what it is to live within this landscape:

- God is at work in the world, and an invisible spiritual world exists.
- Believing people inhabit this landscape, and faith is integral to all of life.
- Human sin is real, and evil exists.
- God offers forgiveness and the possibility of redemption. (Romanowski, 2007, pp. 144–58)

For all this thinking, writing and engagement with culture, what is most often missing is one step further back. It has to do with a theological understanding of the nature of culture. Prior to religious explanations, theological reinterpretations, missiological readings and doctrinal analysis something more basic is needed. What do our theological insights have to reveal to us about the givenness of culture in our experience? Culture is a universal and inescapable reality, an experiential certainty for every human being that not only shapes our experience but also provides us with the tools to articulate that experience, to reflect upon it and respond to it. What might the existence of culture suggest about the nature of God? What role does culture play in the redemptive purposes of God narrated in Scripture? What fresh light does our cultural insight throw onto the exercise of Christian discipleship and how we fundamentally conceive it?

While culture has been an ever-present given in human experience throughout the ages, that presence has been largely stable and familiar. By contrast, in the twenty-first century other forces are at work, with profound cultural impact. Globalization, the culture industry and social media, for example, highlight the very strange new world in which we now find ourselves. Understanding how these forces are at work is vitally important and the growth of the cultural sciences in the academy is evidence of a recognition of this. Having a theology of culture that is fit for purpose is also essential for the Christian community, not least because understanding the dynamics of what is going on should inform the most important question of all: 'What then shall we do?' Stephen Holmes draws an analogy of this 'pressing need' with the rise of the natural sciences in the seventeenth century. Those who did not engage with this new world were 'regarded as old-fashioned, wilfully obscure or simply irrelevant' (Holmes, 2008, pp. xiv–1).

Before exploring what a theology of culture might look like, there are several things that need to be held in mind. They are important qualifications of the task that is to be undertaken. First, as has already been acknowledged, language is at the very heart of culture. It is the expression of a specific context and the means of expressing the context from within. Any expression of theology therefore has a particular cultural location and will bear the marks of its origin in the use and meaning of words, metaphors and idioms. The architecture of a given language will simultaneously enable, limit and shape the theology that is articulated through it. The words in our vocabulary open the door for our theological reflection, but they also establish boundaries because it is difficult to express that for which we lack words, or for which we have words that do not quite fit. For good or ill, the way our language works and the associations it creates also have a shaping effect in what we attempt to say, with tenses, the grammatical genders of masculine and feminine and so forth all playing their part (Gümüşay, 2022, pp. 1–15). In many ways our use of language will reflect the social concerns and preoccupations of its wider environment. Just as Jesus' teaching reflects the economy of the rural poor in Galilee under Imperial rule, as José Pagola has extensively demonstrated (Pagola, 2012), so Paul too regularly deploys military images drawn from his experience of daily life in the Empire (Eph. 6.10–17; 2 Tim 2.3–4).

Language is also, of course, a dynamic expression and words can change their meaning over time. This fluidity in meaning is clear with the children's nursery rhyme *Monday's Child* that was first recorded in A. E. Bray's *Traditions of Devonshire* in 1838. Progressing through the days of the week it declares in its hebdomadal climax,

> And the child born on the Sabbath day
> Is bonny and blithe, good and gay.

For most of the twentieth century this conveyed a carefree light-heartedness that is now mostly lost on a contemporary audience.

The cultural rootedness of language highlights the need to have clear understanding of the nature of revelation and its relationship to the theology that expresses it. In essence, revelation is non-propositional, it is beyond words and cannot be contained by them. Our expressed theological language is an attempt to articulate what we perceive of the revelation. The words are not the revelation but are rather windows through which we can see what is described or alluded to. A different formulation of words provides a further window that allows the subject to be considered from a different angle or point of view. The result may or may not be clearer, but it helps to form a three-dimensional perspective of the subject under consideration.

Second, our cultural locatedness has a further, profound impact. It leaves us completely subjective as we theologically ruminate upon the meaning of life, the universe and everything. For Colin Gunton this is about recognizing the principle of 'indwelling'. A godlike 'objectivism' is not possible as we view reality from the inside (Montefiore, 1992, p. 85). Or, as Karl Barth wryly observed, 'we can no more speak outside of culture than we can jump out of our own skin' (Gorringe, 2004, p. 43). We all speak from somewhere. If our experience, our language and our imagination are all shaped by our cultural starting point, that conditioning is an integral part of our theological journey (Tanner, 1997, p. 168). This, then, clearly begs a question of Christian theology of whether there can be any real or substantive connection between a first-century Roman-occupied Galilee and a globalized twenty-first century with all its culture wars, cultural challenges and cultural memes. If Vincent of Lérins' test of orthodoxy was that which had been believed everywhere, always and by everyone, does anything now pass that test? The Roman Catholic theologian Nicholas Lash frames it like this: if the good news contained within the life, death and resurrection of Jesus of Nazareth is God's Word to humanity, this must remain consistent over time. He concludes that while nothing is immune from the processes of history, what remains is the historicity of the life, death and resurrection of Jesus and the intention of the Christian community in its shared life to assemble and respond to the Word of God under the guidance of the Holy Spirit in different cultural contexts (Lash, 1973, pp. 67–9).

This, then, leads to a third consideration of how to conceive the interplay between theology and culture. Is it about following the lead of the anthropologists in exploring the role of theology in culture, or rather talking about the role of culture in theology? Lash would clearly land the discussion with the latter. A more Calvinistic reading of the issues would do the same, albeit grounding such an understanding in a theology of the sovereignty of God. If God is sovereign over everything as part of a divine prerogative, this has to include the cultural processes at work in collective human activity. These then, in turn, must be central to God's purposes in creating humanity (Van Til, 2001, p. ix). In this way there is no dualism between 'the gospel' and culture, though it would be easy to conceive of how such a separation and opposition of ideas might occur.

Fourth is a more general observation about the nature of the theological task itself in the light of all this. At the most basic level the widely embraced epithet that theology is 'faith seeking understanding' sums it up very well. As Gerard Loughlin sagaciously points out, the faith component is essential, for without it there is no real object of learning. The task might as well be an aspect of the history of ideas or a form of religious studies. Properly construed, theology has to be undertaken in faith by those who understand themselves to stand in relation to God and want to explore the implications of that relationship (Loughlin, 2005, pp. 3–4).

Properly understood, theology has both inward- and outward-facing dimensions. Inwardly, its growing understanding adds to the richness and depth of reflection and self-awareness of the believing community. As such it is the beating heart of the church's teaching ministry. Externally, theology informs the apologetic explanation and prophetic challenge to the communities' cultural context while also shaping the practical day-to-day discipleship of believers and the community of which they are a part.

The vital necessity of having some form of cultural hermeneutics in the range of theological resources available to the church is therefore obvious. Inwardly, it provides a reflective function to help analyse the influence of received culture through the faith tradition. Outwardly, it enables a comprehension of the impact on the community of faith of the cultural forces present in its own context. With both it enables an analysis and evaluation to take place that seeks to ensure the authenticity of its faith commitment and its continuing theological fidelity and integrity. Outwardly speaking it is of the highest importance for apologetics to have the fullest possible understanding of what is going on around it, why it is going on and the theological issues that it raises. Without such understanding the apologetic voice makes little or no connection and fails in its task. Similarly, if the prophetic challenge does not comprehend that of which it speaks and how to effectively communicate with its audience, it is easily dismissed as simply irrelevant. Arguably, however, it is in shaping day-to-day discipleship that the theological task of cultural hermeneutics has its most important function. Here it equips believers to understand the world in which they live and to live authentically as faithful witnesses to the spiritual truth they have embraced and the faith commitment they have undertaken. Of course, none of this is new.

Finally, it is worth stating the obvious: that there are no biblically equivalent concepts or ideas that match our contemporary understanding of culture. While what we know to be culture has been an ever-present reality, bringing unity and difference between people, it would be anachronistic to read a contemporary understanding behind any of these elements, however they are observed and commented upon. When the biblical text refers to 'the world' or 'the nations', for example, the lazy temptation to read back twenty-first century concepts into the ancient narrative needs to be strongly resisted. As is always the case, the intent of the biblical author in using the language available to them is the key to understanding what they are trying to say.

A Theo-cultural creation

The relatively recent arrival of culture as a concept into the lexicon of human understanding should not deter placing it under theological scrutiny. While some might demur and argue that Christian thought appears to have managed quite successfully without it, yet having named it as inescapable, its ubiquity is unmissable. Our predecessors may not have had either the linguistic or conceptual tools that we have now, but they still lived under the sway of their own culture. Of course, those living under the sway of a Christendom worldview had their vision and perception radically shaped and influenced by the privileged position that Christianity enjoyed.

Rather than being merely a contemporary muse that distracts attention into the fripperies of present-day living, culture is an essential part of human life and experience. As John Stott simply observes, 'Every human being who has ever lived has been a creature of culture' (Stott, 1992, p. 189). At the most fundamental level this raises a question of origin that has profound theological implications. Is culture just an accident of life, an unanticipated consequence of the human condition, or is it rather an intentional and integral component of God's creation? In the divine will, is culture of little importance and merits only passing consideration, or is it so important as to actually be revealing of God's nature and creation intent? It will come as no surprise in this volume that the latter is my strong conviction. It is my contention that the reality that we know and experience is best understood as a Theo-cultural creation. That is, the phenomenon that we have come to identify and describe as culture has been hardwired into the creation by God. Yet this is not merely a mechanical law of the universe that leads to our 'cultural imprisonment' (Stott, 1992, p. 189) or a 'secondary environment' (Van Til, 2001, pp. xvii, 26–7, 32–3) that is imposed on nature by humanity in the exercise of the 'creation mandate' as some kind of a God-like 'dominion' over the earth. Rather, culture is better understood as part of God's original 'blessing' of the creative endeavour that is fundamentally reflective of the nature of the creator and is declared in essence as 'good' (Gen. 1.26–28). As such, the creative fecundity of culture is immense. From the wide-ranging and commonly held cultural forms of ethnic groups to the infinite variety of micro cultures found in family groups, workplaces and social networks, the diversity is both rich and seemingly never-ending in its variety. Not only is it integral to the multiple levels of human relationship, but it is also a dynamic phenomenon that is constantly changing, developing and adapting. It is a complex and shifting reality that, while attempts might be made to curate, shape or engineer it, is ultimately uncontainable. Its natural spontaneity, seemingly inexhaustible creativity and its ability to facilitate human connection and the production of artefacts of incredible beauty, amazing technical utility and profound insight into the nature of things are staggering in their range and richness.

Seeing the parallels between the natural and cultural worlds, the Dutch theologian–politician Abraham Kuyper was enthralled by this principle of fecundity and insisted 'that God has programmed the creation to display a marvellously complex diversity, including a complex array of spheres of human interaction' and that multiformity was intrinsic to creation because God loves 'many-ness' (Mouw, 2012, pp. 23–4). Crouch concludes that culture is both God's original plan for humanity and God's original gift (Crouch, 2008, p. 175).

At the end of the creation narrative God viewed everything that had been made and concluded that it was 'very good' (Gen. 1.31). That may be, but this is only part of the story. Human culture also has a darker side. Because of human agency it not only reflects the original blessing, it also embodies the consequences of original sin. The fallenness of humanity also leads to cultures that are prejudiced, oppressive, exploitative and discriminatory; the inspiration towards creative beauty is supplanted by a controlling impetus toward domination and repression; healthy relationships dissolve into fractiousness and conflict; community cohesion and cooperation is replaced by mistrust and suspicion, while constructive creativity succumbs to violence and destruction. In our cultural experience, at one and the same time we have the possibility of great goodness while also staring into the face of our potential for selfishness and depravity. How we theologically comprehend this reality can depend upon our dogmatic predisposition. In the alternatives that Richard Mouw wryly offers, do we say 'Fallen, but *created*' or, 'Created, but *fallen*' (Mouw, 2012, p. 20)? Are we realistic about sin while being optimistic regarding the potential goodness in God's creation of culture or, while recognizing the goodness of what God intended, are we pessimistic because of the unavoidable corruption of all human nature that taints everything?

If the freedom to be culture creators is part of the fabric of creation and thereby reflects the image of the creator, then it is clearly a gift of common grace. Such grace is given to everyone irrespective of belief in God or standing in holiness and is part of the deep fabric of reality. Nothing will change humanity's status as image-bearers of God, and insofar as that image expresses itself in the formation and expression of culture, whether conscious of it or not, this is something that has already been declared 'very good'. There is a robustness to the goodness of God in the created realm and an abiding strength in the reflection of the creator that cannot be lost, however much it is overlaid, misshapen and warped by the consequences of the fall. Evidence of the goodness of God is littered throughout every iteration of culture for those who have eyes to see. While it may be a naive approach that fails to recognize and acknowledge the 'sinfulness of sin' and the depravity to which humanity has frequently stooped, yet to over-estimate it seriously compromises an understanding of God's sovereign goodness in creating and sustaining life in Christ, for in him all things in heaven and on earth were created, things visible and invisible, whether thrones or dominions or rulers or powers – all things have been created through him and for him. He himself is before all things, and in him all things hold together. (Col. 1.16–18)

Given that we now acknowledge the significance of language as an integral part and carrier of culture, it is fascinating to note that establishing Christ's role in creation, as Paul does here, is mirrored in John's Gospel with Christ depicted as the pre-existing 'Logos/Word' (John 1.1–3).

God spoke the world into being in Gen 1, and John's contemporaries continued to celebrate this ... [one] title for God was 'the One who spoke and summoned the universe into being'. (Keener, 2003, p. 379)

As the Eden story progresses towards its climax God speaks again, but this time to issue what has been called the 'Creation Mandate'. Adam and Eve are instructed, 'Be fruitful and multiply, and fill the earth and subdue it; and have dominion' (Gen. 1.28). In more recent years this has also come to be identified as the 'Cultural Mandate', especially among the neo-Calvinists, and in the process it has acquired an expanded life. For Kuyper, 'God invested the original creation with complex cultural potential, which human beings were expected to actualize' (Mouw, 2012, p. 41). Fulfilling this task to subdue the earth and have dominion is therefore core to the identity and purpose of humanity in God's creation intent, and thus to bring God glory. Even following the fall, sin did not destroy the 'cultural urge' to rule because humanity was still God's image-bearer, albeit that the image was marred and open to misuse and abuse (Van Til, 2001, pp. 34–5). Such a view of a 'cultural mandate', however, inclines towards a far more pre-programmed perspective. The task is to discern and enact God's predetermined will as obedient servants. This does not properly match a creation that is complex, diverse and in a dynamic state of perpetual motion like some endlessly turning cultural kaleidoscope. As Steven Bryan highlights, the divine purpose in creation is played out as humanity fills the earth and, as a result, it is 'teeming' with cultural diversity (Bryan, 2022, pp. 35–43).

One further element to note with regard to the Theo-cultural nature of creation is the place of narrative and storytelling as the vehicles for establishing identity, passing on culture and conveying theological truths. We have already seen how language is intimately integrated into the fabric of culture and, of course, without the facility of language the art of storytelling does not exist. In this sense narrative is the younger sibling of linguistic skills. Brian Wicker is deeply evocative of our human experience as he maps the thorough-going manner in which narrative has taken control of our consciousness:

> For we dream in narrative, daydream in narrative, remember, anticipate, hope, despair, believe, doubt, plan, revise, criticise, construct, gossip, learn, hate, and love by narrative. (Wicker, 1975, p. 47)

Human experience tells us that we bring unity to our lives and make sense of the constant flow of human consciousness by developing a memory of what has happened alongside imagining the future and anticipating what is to come. At the most rudimentary of levels a narrative is therefore born that is unique to each one of us. No-one has lived our life before. As Gerard Loughlin notes, 'narrative is basic in human life, beyond culture and rooted in nature' and that human experience is narratively structured (Loughlin, 1996, pp. 64, 66). It truly does seem that God has created us to live in a universe where narrative and stories define who we are. Indeed, even the Bible itself comes to us as largely a collection of narratives, woven between a beginning and the garden of Eden and the climax of history in the heavenly city of the book of Revelation. In the words of the old Sunday School song, 'God has given us a book full of stories'. By the most conservative estimates somewhere in excess of two-thirds of the Bible is written in some form of narrative. Indeed, the narratives of the Bible are literary creations, they are representations of how things are. God does seem to have created us to live within a narratively defined experience of history.

The correspondence between the narrative form and the biblical writer's basic perception of reality may also tell us why there is no biblical term for 'story'. In the Bible, narrative is not a device; it is an expression of the way things are. (Long, 1989, p. 69)

It is hardly surprising, therefore, that through the ages preachers have been schooled in enabling their listeners to connect their personal stories with the trove of narratives contained within the Scriptures, and thereby to establish a kind of mimetic dialogue. It is through the biblical stories that Christian disciples conceive of the world and how they themselves are to live in the world. Following Hans Frei and Karl Barth, Loughlin suggests that the task of theology is to fit the world into the story of God, rather than God into the story of the world (Loughlin, 1996, pp. 19, 34, 37). Thus, in Christian theology it is the story of the life, death and resurrection of Jesus of Nazareth, the Christ, that becomes the organizing heart of a theological reading of culture.

A Christo-cultural incarnation

If Jesus Christ is the central organizing heart of Christian theology, it is essential to explore his own relationship with culture. A great deal flows from this, defining how the Christian tradition will understand and interact with contemporary culture. Is the cultural moment to be passively accepted as a fait accompli, forcefully rejected as sinfully compromised, or energetically transformed through redemptive social action? Or is it none of these and something wholly different?

We know that Jesus was a historical figure. He lived a real life, in a particular place, at a specific point in history. His was a world that was profoundly influenced by Judaism, along with the Hellenism of Alexander the Great and imperial Rome. Jesus' natural tongue would have been Aramaic though he was also able to read the Jewish scriptures in Hebrew and, having ministered in the Decapolis (Mark 7.31), it is highly likely that he spoke Greek. In addition, there is the probability he also understood the administrative language of the Empire, Latin, thus making him a potential quadra-linguist. He understood the cosmopolitan life of Galilee and the nature of living in a state that had lost its autonomy to an occupying military power. These facts would have been in sharp relief for him having established Capernaum as the centre for his early ministry (Matt. 4.13). The city was located on a provincial border and had its own custom post and resident Roman garrison on the Via Maris trade route. His ministry was not confined to one particular group within society; rather, he moved easily among the rural poor and urban religious elite, with imperial collaborators and nationalist freedom fighters, with respectable women and those who made up the shady under-belly of Palestinian society.

This historical locatedness is fundamental to the Christian story of the man Jesus. However, the Christian tradition goes much further and insists that in a unique way Jesus is God's anointed or chosen one. He is a one-of-a-kind who is both wholly human and wholly divine. He is God incarnate, or 'en-fleshed'. If this is not so, then any worship of Jesus is pure idolatry. If it is so, then it begs many questions of the nature of this incarnation and the implications of an act by which God enters and participates within the created order and its cultural embodiment. Indeed, it begs questions of God's purpose and objective in doing so.

Incarnation

If the life of Jesus is the climax of God's self-disclosure, then the manner of his coming is highly significant. John 1.1, 14 is central in this regard:

> In the beginning was the Word, and the Word was with God, and the Word was God ... And the Word became flesh and lived among us, and we have seen his glory, the glory as of a father's only son, full of grace and truth.

C. K. Barrett makes the assertion that John wants the whole of his Gospel read in the light of verse 1. The deeds and words of Jesus are the deeds and words of God (Barrett, 1979, p. 156). Certainly, the beginning of the Gospel would have caught the attention of Jewish listeners because 'In the beginning' has strong echoes of Genesis 1.1. This is particularly significant when it is remembered that the Jews of this period referred to the books of the Bible by their opening words, so 'In the beginning' was the de facto name for Genesis. In addition, the entire first phrase points beyond merely the original beginning of things. Merrill Tenney suggests a literal translation as 'When the beginning began, the Word was already there'. With the introduction already having suggested divinity, Tenney further demonstrates that this is underlined by the following phrase, that the logos was 'with' God, a phrase that can be rendered 'face to face' or 'in fellowship with', which establishes his equality of identity and yet distinctiveness in relation to God. Finally, 'the Word was God' clearly affirms the deity of the logos (Tenney, 1995, pp. 28–9).

The choice and use of the word *logos* is a masterful stroke by John. A word of common usage that implied the meaning or thought carried by words, yet in Greek philosophy, through Heraclitus, was also used for the supreme wisdom by which all things are steered (Beasley-Murray, 1987, p. 6). In this context the concept would have been comprehensible to Jews too, tying it in with God's spoken word of creation. The Word of God was the expression of the divine personality. God spoke and it happened. John's association of the person of Jesus with the divine Word makes it clear that in his life and action the will, person and personality of God are revealed and accomplished.

In verse 14 John summarizes his thesis: 'And the Word became flesh and lived among us, and we have seen his glory.' He was God but he 'became' a man, involving a change of state and a new dimension of existence, becoming something that he was not before (Beasley-Murray, 1987, pp. 13–14). John then continues that he 'lived among us', with the Greek literally meaning 'to pitch a tent, to dwell temporarily' or to be 'tabernacled'. While this may only point to the incarnate life not being permanent, Tasker sees an allusion to the presence of God, previously located in the tabernacle and later in the temple, but now fully present in Jesus, the Word made flesh (Tasker, 1997, p. 48). Also significant in this context is that the incarnation brings the presence of God into the world of personal observation. Those who met Jesus had 'seen' him:

> It is precisely because the gospel emerged in history that we have to understand it as also incarnated in a culture. It did not fall from the skies with the swiftness of a meteor, nor was it received from space like a radio signal ... we will look in vain for a 'pure gospel', if by that we mean an original message as if wafted to earth from Gabriel's horn ... it is also a cultural product – brought to life by the person and deeds of Jesus – and forged in the crucible of cross-cultural developments. Strictly speaking, it is not even a Jewish product, because the gospel comes to us from Israel under Roman tutelage, and in the language of the Greeks. (Walker, 1996, pp. 18–19)

In the incarnation, therefore, Jesus' own cultural education was as a first-century Jew. His cultural identity also deeply immersed him into what we would now identify as intercultural processes through encounters with the minority Samaritan subculture and the culturally dominant presence of Imperial Rome. A fascinating implication of all this is that, through the incarnation of Jesus, something new entered into the knowledge and being of God that had not been there before. At its core is the first-hand knowledge of being immersed in, subject to and contained by human culture. Some consider that one of the most theologically creative contributions of the Second Vatican Council was to locate the starting point of understanding the process of inculturation in the incarnation (Shorter, 2006, pp. 79–81).

Kenosis

Looking to tease out the implications of the incarnation, Paul reflects in his letter to the church at Philippi on the manner of Christ's coming in the incarnation and what it involved for him:

> who, though he was in the form of God, did not regard equality with God as something to be exploited, but emptied himself, taking the form of a slave, being born in human likeness. And being found in human form, he humbled himself and became obedient to the point of death – even death on a cross. (Phil. 2.6–8)

This action on the part of Christ has been called kenosis after the verb '*kenoo*' in v. 7, 'but emptied himself'. The term has been a controversial one due in part to its usage by some German and English scholars at the turn of the twentieth century. However, the poetic and rhythmic nature of the verses was recognized as long ago as 1899 by Johannes Weiss and is now widely recognized to be the content of an early Christian hymn rather than a systematic theology (Hawthorne, 1983, p. 76). In context, Paul's purpose in quoting it had little to do with Christology and everything to do with the ethics of everyday Christian living. The telling application that the apostle is making is that what Christ sacrifices has to do with giving himself in the service of others. He empties himself of the privileges, honour, role and status of his pre-incarnate being by taking on the role of a servant, one who had no rights or privileges except to serve his master. In doing so he both obeys God and serves humankind. Paradoxically, in his kenosis he becomes what he was not before and rather than subtracting from himself, adds to himself the humanity of the incarnation.

The identification of a double action of kenosis in the mind of Christ, in the idea that he 'emptied himself' and 'humbled himself', is particularly helpful. The first relates to sacrifice (what he renounced) and the second to service (how he identified himself with humanity and put himself at its disposal). In renunciation Christ surrenders the status he enjoyed as the Son of God in glory, the independence of his omnipotence, and his immunity from temptation, limitation, need and pain. Regarding his humble service of identification with humanity, it is manifested through the identification of his 'flesh and blood' experiences of life, ministry and crucifixion (Stott and Coote, 1981, pp. 323–34).

Further to this, while not framing it in terms of a theology of kenosis, James Davison Hunter explores how Jesus uses power. He sees him clearly eschewing the path of worldly power that tends towards manipulation, domination and control, with a predisposition to exploitation and self-aggrandizement and an inclination towards abuse. By contrast, according to Hunter, Jesus exercises a completely different kind of 'social power' to accomplish his objectives. He identifies four characteristics that demonstrate what the incarnation of this alternative pattern of power looks like. First, it is derived from the intimacy of his relationship with the Father and his desire to do the Father's will. This is particularly to the fore in John's Gospel and is articulated most profoundly as Jesus prays on the night of his betrayal. He is conscious both of completing the task the Father had given him to do, and that his disciples might share this intimacy of relationship that he has experienced with the Father (John 17.4–5, 20–23). Second is his rejection of status, power and privilege that the Philippian hymn alludes to. Not only did the incarnation imply the humility of becoming a man, but as a man he took on the form of an obedient slave on the pathway to death. Third is the animating principle of love. As Hunter says, 'Compassion defines the power of his kingdom more than anything else. It was the source, the means and the end of his power.' Finally there was the non-coercive way in which he dealt with people. His kingdom was available to all: rich and poor alike, Jews and pagans, the powerful and the powerless are all free to receive his teaching or walk away. Enemies are to be loved, persecutors are to be prayed for, other cheeks are to be turned and calling down fire from heaven is not to be resorted to as a form of punitive action (Hunter, 2010a, pp. 188–93).

The command to make disciples

Jesus' final command to his immediate group of friends, as recorded in Matthew's Gospel, has proven to be very influential over the years. Indeed, many would agree with David Bosch's affirmation of the 'pivotal' nature of these verses (Bosch, 2003, p. 57). In his final resurrection appearance Jesus issues his 'Great Commission' by making the statement:

> 'All authority in heaven and on earth has been given to me. Go therefore and make disciples of all nations, baptizing them in the name of the Father and of the Son and of the Holy Spirit, and teaching them to obey everything that I have commanded you. And remember, I am with you always, to the end of the age.' (Matt. 28.18–20)

With the resurrection providing the divine vindication of Jesus' ministry and teaching, it is with authority that he issues this charge to his disciples, a charge that has echoes of the Lord's promise to Abram (Gen. 12.3). This linkage had already been established at the beginning of the Gospel with Jesus' genealogy explicitly identifying him as 'the Son of Abraham' (Matt. 1.1). Indeed, the LXX uses exactly the same Greek phrase in relation to the promise to Abraham (Gen. 18.18; 22.18) that Matthew here ascribes to Jesus, *'panta ta ethne*/of all nations'. The word *'ethne'* is perhaps best translated in contemporary terms as 'ethnic, tribe, people or culture group' rather than the geopolitical nation states of the modern world. Indeed, in a rather sophisticated way the phrase refers to the world as a whole while also acknowledging its particular, diverse and segmented parts (Datema, 2022, p. 146). In context, Jesus' command is then sustained by the statements that frame it on either side, namely the all-encompassing authority and promised presence of Jesus.

Here is the crucial transition point in the Jesus movement that sees it quickly moving away from its Jewish roots and successively penetrating different cultural milieus. This is no small historic matter to consider. The cultural shifts that follow are of immense proportion. Very quickly the mother-tongue of the founder is abandoned in favour of the common-denominator language of the empire. Then, as Christianity breaks out of the expatriate, diaspora Jewish communities to which it had spread into the wider pagan society, the question is swiftly raised as to whether the movement's adherents needed to convert to Judaism. A gathering of leaders in Jerusalem, recorded in Acts 15, concluded that they did not. Christianity was not to be distinguished by its cultural traits, or to be culturally distinctive. It could be incarnated, in the name of Christ, into any cultural context. Its identity was to be preserved by obeying the teaching of its founder and inhabiting those principles of the Kingdom of God summed up in the love commands (Matt. 22.34–40). It is worth noting too that the disciple-making is defined by the discipleship of obedience to Jesus rather than in purely evangelistic terms of seeking the conversion of allegiance to Christ.

This sets up a particular cultural dynamic for those who wish to follow Jesus. On the one hand the good news of the gospel is that individuals are accepted for who they are, with an existing cultural conditioning and all that implies. We are cultural beings and our identity is enmeshed in the broad themes, the intricate minutiae and the complex set of predispositions and relationships that are part and parcel of everyday life. The missiologist Andrew Walls calls this the 'indigenizing principle'. Following Christ does not require a migration to another culture, but there are times when devotion to Christ puts us out of kilter with our culture, if not at odds with it. This 'pilgrim principle' establishes a critical distance between the Christian disciple and their cultural home. They remain fully part of it, but also carry an allegiance that has a higher call on their loyalty. In passing, Walls also notes that whatever an individual's cultural experience, on joining the faith family of Christianity they automatically acquire an adoptive cultural history stretching back over thousands of years. Not only does this embrace the tradition of the church, but it also covers the history of Israel. Together they provide 'a whole set of ideas, concepts, and assumptions that do not necessarily square with the rest of their [own] cultural inheritance' (Walls, 2009, pp. 7–9).

The fallenness of the world can make the level of 'out-of-stepness' starkly obvious, yet it does not require withdrawal into a sanctified cultural community, hermetically sealed off from the rest of the world to avoid contamination. Rather, it begs the question, what does cultural obedience to Christ – or inculturated discipleship – look like here?' Abraham Kuyper, giving the inaugural address at the Vrije Universiteit in Amsterdam that he had co-founded, declared: 'There is not a square inch in the whole domain of our human existence over which Christ, who is sovereign over all, does not cry: "Mine!"' (Mouw, 2012, p. 20).

A Pneuma-cultural discipleship

John's account: 'Receive the Holy Spirit'

> When it was evening on that day, the first day of the week, and the doors of the house where the disciples had met were locked for fear of the Jews, Jesus came and stood among them and said, 'Peace be with you.' After he said this, he showed them his hands and his side. Then the disciples rejoiced when they saw the Lord. Jesus said to them again, 'Peace be with you. As the Father has sent me, so I send you.' When he had said this, he breathed on them and said to them, 'Receive the Holy Spirit ...' (John 20:19–21)

This first appearance of the resurrected Jesus to his assembled disciples provides 'the pneumatological climax to the gospel' (Keener, 2003, p. 1196). Within the narrative it serves to establish the purpose of discipleship as carrying on the mission of Jesus under the direction, enabling and empowering of the Holy Spirit. Jesus' own ministry was not dissimilar. According to John the Baptist, the Holy Spirit had authenticated Jesus' divine mandate as the Son of God and indicated to him that he was also to be the baptizer/immerser of others in the Holy Spirit (John 1.32–34).

Later, speaking with the inquiring Pharisee Nicodemus, Jesus plays with the linguistic resonances between the words for Spirit and breath to demonstrate how the Spirit brings life. Then, further developing the play on words with the metaphor wind, he observes how it blows freely and mysteriously wherever it chooses. Those who are 'born from above' know and experience a similar freedom and liberty of life in the Spirit (John 3.1–8).

This underpinning of the life in the Spirit then comes into full focus in Jesus' 'farewell discourse' with those who were closest to him (John 14–16). He maintains that it is better for them that he departs because then, with the Father, he can send another Advocate, the Spirit of Truth, who will be both 'with' them and 'in' them (John 14.14–16, 26; 15.26; 16.7). The Greek word for Advocate, *paracletos*, in its widest sense identifies one who comes alongside to help. More specifically it also carries a legal allusion referring to the one who pleads your cause in a court of law or before another party. Jesus then goes on to identify a further instructional role for this intimate accompanist, a role that is critically important in understanding the central part the Holy Spirit will play in what is to come. Indeed, the Holy Spirit will be Jesus' de facto replacement. He 'will teach you everything, and remind you of all that I have said to you' (14.26–27). 'When the Spirit of truth comes, he will guide you into all the truth; for he will … take what is mine and declare it to you' (16.13–14).

If this inward-facing work of the Holy Spirit enables Jesus' disciples in his absence to understand and articulate and live by the message of the Kingdom, it is also counterbalanced by an outward-focused activity in the wider world:

> And when he comes, he will prove the world (*kosmos*) wrong about sin and righteousness and judgment: about sin, because they do not believe in me; about righteousness, because I am going to the Father and you will see me no longer; about judgment, because the ruler of this world has been condemned. (John 16.8–11)

The Johannine account is clear. The Holy Spirit is indispensable for any ongoing discipleship to Jesus. Acting as a surrogate for Jesus, the Spirit both accompanies and indwells the disciple, acting as a guide, a teacher and a memory prompt in making connections between the lived life and Jesus' message of the Kingdom. However, this same Spirit is also at work outside in the wider world through prevenient grace revealing fundamental spiritual realities to a world disconnected from the divine.

Luke's account: 'and to the ends of the earth'

As Luke navigates the transition from the life and ministry of Jesus to the birth of the early church, once again the Holy Spirit takes a central place. As his Gospel draws to a close, Jesus identifies the proclamation of repentance and forgiveness of sins 'to all nations' (*panta ta ethne*) as the future trajectory of his mission. Alongside this he instructs his disciples to wait in Jerusalem until they are 'clothed with power from on high' as he sends upon them what the Father has promised (Luke 24.46–49). The beginning of the Acts of the Apostles takes up these themes as Jesus directs the disciples, following their receipt of divine power when the Holy Spirit has come upon them, to be his witnesses 'in Jerusalem, in all Judea and Samaria, and to the ends of the earth' (Acts 1.8).

The inauguration of this outward push from its Jewish point of origin then begins at the pilgrimage festival of Pentecost as the fledgling Christian movement is immersed in the enabling and empowering presence of the Holy Spirit. With the population of Jerusalem swollen by pilgrims to up to three times its normal size of 30,000 (Bruce, 1984, p. 643), the city was transformed into a cosmopolitan melting pot drawn from the surrounding regions of the Roman empire. As Jesus' disciples worshipped at the Temple[1] the Spirit came upon them and they 'began to speak in other languages, as the Spirit gave the ability' (Acts 2.4). What was surprising was that the gift of speech was not in the common languages of Aramaic or Greek that the others in the Temple would have readily understood, but in their own languages of home (Acts 2.5–12). From Parthians to Egyptians and Romans to Arabs, Luke records that 'All were amazed and perplexed, saying to one another, "What does this mean?"'

From the outset the Spirit draws the disciples into a multi-lingual, multiracial and multicultural expression of the nature of the Kingdom of Christ (Stott, 1990b, p. 68). The question of meaning is, however, a significant one. As Craig Keener observes, in the Acts 2 list of 15 distinct and representative places of origin for the crowd, 'The biblically literate ... might perceive a model in the foundational biblical list of nations in Gen 10' (Keener, 2020, p. 130) and, of course, the story that immediately follows in the Genesis narrative is that of the Tower of Babel. Indeed, many scholars therefore go on to see the events of Pentecost as 'a reversal of Babel'. This is important, not least because Genesis 10–11 have been considered the most significant narratives in understanding God's intention regarding cultural plurality in the world (Hunsberger, 1998, pp. 243–4).

In summary, Genesis 10 gives the account of the dispersion and cultural development of the offspring of Noah following the great flood, with the so-called 'Table of Nations' listing some seventy different ethnic identities. Genesis 11 follows with the retelling of the incident at Babel in which the building of the infamous tower incurs God's swift judgement.

> Therefore it was called Babel, because there the Lord confused the language of all the earth; and from there the Lord scattered them abroad over the face of all the earth. (Gen. 11.9)

In Acts 2 the list of points of origin for the visiting pilgrims establishes the connection to Genesis 10. Then their hearing of the apostles speaking in their own language indicates the reversal of the confusion of language brought by God's judgement in Genesis 11. Babel is reversed. At Babel the tower was the means by which the people sought to make a name for themselves, but God's judgement brought linguistic confusion and scattered the nations throughout the world. By contrast, in the Pentecost event God receives the glory as the language barrier is removed and new believers are united in the Spirit as they are dispersed back throughout the empire.

For Lesslie Newbigin, reflecting on Genesis 10, the initial variety of nations in the story is part of God's 'primal covenant of blessing'. God's goal has always been for a unified diversity rather than some monolithic and uniform ideal of unity or the presumed restoration of a lost former expression of unity. As illustrative of this he notes that when the curse of Babel is reversed at Pentecost, the variety of languages remains, the Holy Spirit provides 'the baptism of languages, not their extinction' (Hunsberger, 1998, pp. 252–4).

God's intention to bless the nations is then picked up in the story that follows Babel in Genesis 12, where even in the act of calling Abram and the promise to make his descendants into a great nation, God declares that 'in you all the families of the earth shall be blessed' (Gen. 12.3).

In Luke's theological presentation of the Day of Pentecost in Acts 2 there is a clear affirmation of cultural difference and diversity. What has been explored above in the Theo-cultural nature of creation and Christo-cultural basis of the incarnation is now demonstrated as foundational to life in the Spirit and thus provides a Pneuma-cultural basis for Christian discipleship.

At Pentecost the seeds are sown that will quickly lead to the Christian movement's centre of gravity leaving its cultural home and spreading throughout the eastern half of the Roman empire, and ultimately to Rome and beyond. Pentecost was an endorsement of a pluralism in which no culture was to be the exclusive bearer of the norms of truth (Gorringe, 2004, p. 197). Along the way there were to be many cultural barriers to overcome as the message of Jesus encountered different worldviews with which to wrestle, different contexts to inhabit and different languages in which to express itself. The first of these was to be expressed in the pivotal question, 'Do you have to be a Jew to be a Christian?'

In many ways early Christianity was a radical and revolutionary movement. The levels of social and cultural mixing, along with the accompanying boundary-breaking, were without precedent. The missiologist David Bosch is clear that it was without analogy and, in its cultural context, a 'sociological impossibility' (Bosch, 2003, p. 48). Consequently, it was inevitable that points of friction would be generated that had the potential to completely derail the new movement. The question about how Jewish the first Christian communities needed to be sat behind the presenting issue of male circumcision and it was at Antioch that it reached the critical point of needing to be addressed.

It was at Antioch that disciples of Jesus were first called 'Christians', having developed a cultural distinctiveness that meant they were no longer mistaken for a Jewish sect. This is hardly surprising given what is known about the cultural mix of the community's leadership. Barnabas was a Greek-speaking Cypriot, Manaen was a 'foster brother' to Herod Antipas, Lucius was from North Africa, Simeon was also called 'Niger' – probably because he was a black African –, and Paul a highly trained rabbi from the Jewish diaspora (Acts 13.1). This 'Antiochan experiment', as Dean Gilliland calls it, included a withdrawal of the requirement of male circumcision, the ministry of the laity and an openness to the Holy Spirit in worship (Gilliland, 1989, pp. 53–5). It was perhaps predictable that it was a church like this that would be the catalyst to force the growing Christian movement to squarely face up to the growing tension. If Christianity was to be a genuinely transcultural movement then there were implications to be addressed as a consequence of what was driving their progress around the eastern Mediterranean.

When some men arrived at Antioch from Judea teaching that salvation was impossible without circumcision according to Mosaic custom, a sharp dispute broke out. Paul and Barnabas were delegated to take the matter back to the mother church in Jerusalem. There the issues were rehearsed with the believers who belonged to the party of the Pharisees pushing for the adoption of their more conservative and traditional beliefs. I. Howard Marshall points out that it is easy to underestimate the colossal step involved in converted Pharisees adopting a new way of thinking. Added to which, he maintains that with growing nationalist pressure in Judea, Christians had to tread carefully lest they be seen as disloyal to their Jewish identity (Marshall, 1998, p. 249).

If circumcision was the presenting issue, two matters of concern lay behind it. The first was that Jewish Christians found it difficult to understand how Gentiles could be saved without becoming members of the people of God with obligations to the Jewish law. Secondly, how could Jewish Christians who remained faithful to the law have table fellowship with those who were not faithful to the law and were therefore ritually unclean? The crux of the issue that the church had to wrestle with was how far the gospel was to be allowed to be contextualized in a Gentile setting (Marshall, 1998, pp. 242–3). At this vital moment in the development of Christianity were Gentile converts to Christianity to be required to convert to Judaism and take on board Jewish culture, or was the Christian message truly transcultural?

In James' moderation of the gathering in Jerusalem a way forward is discerned (Acts 15). In his summing up he acknowledges that God had made from among the Gentiles a 'people' for himself, and that therefore nothing should be done to make it difficult for the Gentiles who were turning to God. Any thought of circumcision being required was put to one side because three of the four prohibitions they were to go on to agree (food polluted by idols, meat of strangled animals, and blood) were all concerned with maintaining table fellowship between Gentile converts and Jewish Christians who continued to observe the dietary laws. The fourth prohibition addressed sexual immorality. As James said in his letter to the church at Antioch, these matters relating to the contextualization of the gospel in the Gentile world 'seemed good to the Holy Spirit and to us' (Acts 15.28). In this way the transcultural future of Christianity was embedded in the life of the developing Christian network. This was liberating news for the growing number of Gentile believers as it made clear that they did not have to surrender their ethnic identity to be faithful to Christ.

Paul's account: 'I have become all things to all people'

'The importance of the Holy Spirit for Paul can hardly be exaggerated, not least when it comes to understanding his ethics' (Wenham, 1995, p. 230). Indeed, the centrality of the gift of the Spirit is foundational for Paul's understanding of Christian discipleship (Dunn, 2003, p. 419). In both the evidence of his ministry record in the Acts of the Apostles and in his preserved correspondence, he is frequently wrestling with what a Spirit-led, culture-crossing discipleship looks like.

For Paul, the qualities of Christian character and experience are demonstrated by the 'fruit' of the Spirit's activity in love, joy, peace, patience, kindness and so forth (Gal. 5.22–23), while the ministering charisms of the Spirit are 'gifts of grace' as diverse as those of an apostle and an administrator, gifts of healing and speaking in tongues, with diligent leadership and the cheerfully compassionate service of others (Rom. 12.4–8; 1 Cor. 12.27–30; Eph. 4.11–13). Paul's letters are, in fact, peppered with such observations, insights and exhortations to faithful Christian discipleship. However, it is as he ministers that he is confronted by the cultural friction points that emerge between Christianity's Judaic place of origin and its increasing penetration into the non-Jewish, gentile world. Paul is particularly well-equipped to navigate this transitional moment as he was a man of both worlds. While he was born in the Hellenistic city of Tarsus in Cilicia and was a Roman citizen, he was also reared in a strict Jewish home, lived as a Pharisee and was proud of his faith heritage (Ladd, 1982, p. 360). Yet through all his ministry it was the call to be 'in the Spirit' and to 'walk ... according to the Spirit' (Rom. 8.9, 4), to be 'taught by the Spirit' (1 Cor. 2.13) and to be 'guided by the Spirit' (Gal. 5.25) that directed his path. This too was the source of his creative innovation when confronted with the inevitable challenges that were to present themselves.

The Spirit was not only the enabler of authentic discipleship but was also the mediator of access into the divine presence. Rather than only being reliant upon received tradition and its reapplication into the present world, in the Spirit the believing community had immediate access to God. This informed the statement of the Jerusalem elders that it 'seemed good to the Holy Spirit and to us' as they responded to the letter from Antioch. Paul explores this further in 2 Corinthians 3 as he celebrates the freedom of those who are in the Spirit to have their lives transformed by their encounter with the glory of the Lord as they see and understand. By contrast, when the old covenant law received by Moses is read, a veil lies over the minds of the hearers that is only removed in Christ. 'Now the Lord is the Spirit, and where the Spirit of the Lord is, there is freedom' (v. 17). In this way the Spirit facilitates communion with the living God, and the progressive experience of discipleship whereby believers are transformed into conformity with Christ 'from one degree of glory to another, for this comes from the Lord, the Spirit' (v. 18) (Martin, 1986, pp. 73–4).

In the letter to the Galatians this creative theological freedom in the Spirit is expressed at the very pinch point of cultural conflict. When the apostle Peter withdrew from table fellowship with the gentile members of the community for fear of those advocating the circumcision of Christian men, Paul recalls, 'I opposed him to his face, because he stood self-condemned' (Gal. 2.11–12). He then goes on, in one of his most profound theological statements, to articulate the radical inclusivity of the Christian message:

> There is no longer Jew or Greek, there is no longer slave or free, there is no longer male and female; for all of you are one in Christ Jesus. (Gal. 3.28)

And the theme continues throughout the letter. 'For freedom Christ has set us free. Stand firm, therefore' (5.1); and again, 'For you were called to freedom, brothers and sisters, only do not use your freedom as an opportunity for self-indulgence, but through love become slaves to one another' (5.13). 'Live by the Spirit, I say, and do not gratify the desires of the flesh ... By contrast the fruit of the Spirit is love...' (5.16, 22).

In his own ministry Paul sought to embody this Spirit-led transcultural understanding of discipleship. Defending himself

TOWARDS A THEO-CULTURAL UNDERSTANDING

to the church at Corinth against accusations of being a flatterer and only telling people what they want to hear, Paul powerfully expresses what he is doing, and why:

> For though I am free with respect to all, I have made myself a slave to all, so that I might win more of them. To the Jews I became as a Jew, in order to win Jews. To those under the law I became as one under the law (though I myself am not under the law) so that I might win those under the law. To those outside the law I became as one outside the law (though I am not free from God's law but am under Christ's law) so that I might win those outside the law. To the weak I became weak, so that I might win the weak. I have become all things to all people, that I might by all means save some. I do it all for the sake of the gospel, so that I may share in its blessings. (1 Cor. 9.19–23)

Paul's response is clear: he is not a flatterer, rather he is making himself a slave to everyone because of his obligation to the gospel. Having undertaken such a spiritual obligation, Paul will do whatever it takes to communicate the gospel in whatever context he finds himself. When he is with Jews he will gladly follow the dictates of Jewish law as occasion demands. His taking of a Nazirite vow in Acts 21.23–26 is consistent with this, even though Paul will also argue strongly for his own freedom from the law of Moses. While there is some evidence of Jewish missionary practice that sought to make the law no more burdensome and offensive than was necessary for potential converts (Barrett, 1979, p. 211), Paul goes much further than this. He is prepared to abandon Judaism altogether. He could only write 'To the Jews I became as a Jew' (1 Cor. 9.20) if, having been a Jew, he had ceased to be one and become something else.

This radical change in Paul's self-perception involved separation from his inherited cultural and religious traditions when the gospel was advanced by his conformity with the social and religious environment in which he was ministering. Communicating the message of the gospel had priority, 'that I might by all means save some. I do it all for the sake of the gospel, so that I may share in its blessings' (vv. 22–23). This is not, however, a capitulation to an alternate set of cultural norms through pragmatic adjustment or intentional assimilation because Paul remains under 'Christ's law' (v. 21). This is his theological lodestone; anything else is negotiable. While some may see this as inconsistency on Paul's part, F. F. Bruce observes that appeals for consistency are the preserve of 'little minds'. Rather, Paul's 'inconsistency, as some thought it (cf. 2 Cor. 1.17ff.), was subject to a higher consistency – the more effective discharge of his apostolic commission' and was evidence of his adaptability and versatility (Bruce, 1980, pp. 88–9).

Paul's approach meant neither the Hellenization of the Jews or the Judaization of the Greeks and, by implication, means that 'It is not necessary for Christians from different backgrounds to become carbon copies of one another (Bosch, 2003, p. 136). Spirit-led discipleship is specific to the cultural location of each believer. The gospel is not bound to any particular cultural expression and Paul is prepared to waive his personal freedoms in Christ to share more fully the life of those among whom he is ministering in the hope of removing unnecessary obstacles in the path of the gospel message. His opportunity to debate with Epicurean and Stoic philosophers at the Areopagus in Athens highlights this approach at work.

While Athens at this point was not the place it had been and was only home to around ten thousand people, its illustrious past had ensured its status as a 'free city' in the empire and it remained a cultural and philosophical centre of considerable importance.

Having preached regularly in the marketplace Paul was courteously invited to address a meeting of the Areopagus on Mars Hill (Acts 17.16–34). This was a group of thirty men who comprised the most exclusive court in the city. They tried murder cases as well as overseeing public debate. Paul was not on trial but rather giving an account of his 'new' teaching that had piqued local interest. He addresses his audience in the style and with the modesty with which they were familiar. He avoids a direct confrontational attitude of challenge and denunciation, choosing instead to come alongside his hearers with ideas and language that they knew. He commends them for being 'very religious' and uses an altar dedicated to 'an unknown god' that he had discovered in the city to establish a bridge between their respective spiritual worldviews. Then, using the rhetorical technique of 'insinuatio', which would also have been familiar to them, Paul attempts to arouse their curiosity rather than launching into a full explanation of the fundamentals of his teaching (Baasland, 1997, p. 19). Yet underpinning his whole address is the same vision that sits beneath the reversal of Babel in Acts 2.

> From one ancestor he made all nations to inhabit the whole earth, and he allotted the times of their existence and the boundaries of the places where they would live, so that they would search for God and perhaps grope for him and find him. (Acts 17.26–27a)

Paul is convinced that the message of Jesus contains the fulfilment of their yearnings and so he uses their philosophy to affirm their insights and provide the opportunity for the gospel to interact with them. Following the statement above he angles his application to the pantheism of the Stoics, 'he is not far from each one of us' (v. 27b), then adding a quote from the poet Aratus, 'For we too are his offspring' (v. 28b). He quotes the Old Testament in a way that those familiar with Plato would understand, adapting Exodus 20.11 and Isaiah 42.5 in v. 24 by including the Greek *kosmos* for 'world', to which there is no corresponding term in Hebrew (Marshall, 1998, p. 287), but which carries the sense of not only everything that is, but also what we mean by 'my world' and 'our world' (Watkin, 2022, p. 11). He then utilizes his knowledge of Greek philosophy by quoting from Epimenides, 'For "in him we live and move and have our being"' (v. 28), demonstrating that he is quite prepared to use pagan thought when it reflects the truth, and in the process applies what was said of Zeus to the Judaeo-Christian God (Marshall, 1981, pp. 25–6).

Having spoken clearly of the resurrection of Christ and the

need for repentance (vv. 30–31), Paul's reception is mixed. Some sneered (probably the Epicureans as they did not believe in resurrection of the dead), some expressed a desire to hear him again, and a few, like Dionysius and Damaris, became believers (v. 34).

Paul's foray into the Athenian bastion of intellectual society is viewed in very different ways. For Ernst Baasland it is 'a masterpiece of contextualization' (Baasland, 1997, p. 19), and John Stott saw it as a model for present-day Christians in the academy, the arts and the media who can engage

> with contemporary non-Christian philosophies and ideologies in a way which resonates with thoughtful, modern men and women, and so at least gain a hearing for the gospel by the reasonableness of its presentation. (Stott, 1990b, p. 281)

By contrast, a few believe this incident tells another story completely and consider the Mars Hill debate to be a great mistake. Rather than being a model to follow, as only a few people believed, it clearly demonstrates the failure of Paul's culturally accommodationist strategy. Two pieces of evidence are cited for this argument. The first is that the full gospel was clearly not preached in Athens and that Paul is mocked as 'a babbler' – in Greek the word *spermologos* literally implies a bird, especially a crow, that flies around picking up scraps from different places. Second is the fact that no church appears to have been formed in Athens, with Corinth proving to be the first fruitful location for Paul (1 Cor. 16.15). 1 Corinthians 1.17–2.5 is then interpreted as a commentary on what Paul learned from the experience: 'For Christ did not send me ... with eloquent wisdom, so that the cross of Christ might not be emptied of its power' (1 Cor. 1.17). However, there is common agreement among New Testament scholars that there is no evidence to suggest that Paul thought his preaching at Athens was a failure at all, let alone one that caused him to reassess his approach (Bruce, 1980, p. 37; Larkin, 1995, pp. 260–1; Barrett, 1979, pp. 62–3). Indeed, the African theologian Lamin Sanneh views Paul's preaching in Athens as being of great significance and the 'symbol of the crossroads of God's providential design and the particularity of cultural self-understanding (Sanneh, 2009, p. 192).

As the early Christian movement embodies its discipleship to Jesus and explores the extent of the mission that he bequeathed to them, two underlying convictions have a determinative role to play in what that discipleship will look like. First, it must be 'in the Spirit', 'you are in the Spirit, since the Spirit of God dwells in you. Anyone who does not have the Spirit of Christ does not belong to him' (Rom. 8.9–10). Second, its trajectory is to 'the ends of the earth' and therefore of necessity has to grapple with the issues raised by its transcultural migration. As they act upon Jesus' commission to make disciples of all nations no cultural barriers must impede its progress (Gal. 3.28; Col. 3.10).

> The scripture says, 'No one who believes in him will be put to shame.' For there is no distinction between Jew and Greek; the same Lord is Lord of all and is generous to all who call on him. For, 'Everyone who calls on the name of the Lord shall be saved.' (Rom. 10.11–13)

Towards a Theo-cultural understanding of the world

From the early days of the twentieth century, theology has increasingly risen to the challenge of engaging with culture. Niebuhr recognized that the theology of a believing community was formative of how it viewed culture and interacted with it. Tillich had an altogether grander project in mind, how to thoroughly reinvent the discipline of theology by using its insights and categories as a way of understanding the ubiquity of culture. Cross-cultural missionary workers were confronted by cultures very different to their own and, from the early days, were not merely the lackeys of their imperial compatriots. Indigenization, inculturation and contextualization are the mature fruit of seeking to communicate and inhabit the message of Jesus in culturally authentic ways while retaining fidelity to Christ. In the more analytical approaches that theology has taken more recently, with subjects such as popular culture and film studies playing the role of conversation partners, the result can be quite profound insights into the human condition.

Yet for all the theological reflection on culture, a step further back is needed. What is our theological understanding of culture? What does it tell us about the nature of God and his redemptive purpose? In tentatively seeking to answer this question and beginning to move towards articulating what I have called a 'Theo-cultural' understanding of the world, I have been gently surprised that what has emerged has the semblance of a trinitarian form. Given the inescapable reality of culture in human experience, it is patently clear that culture is part of the fundamental nature of things and clearly an intentional component of God's good creation.

Given that culture matches the wider created order with a dynamic and interrelated complexity that is ever shifting suggests that this is something that God has placed at the heart of all he has created. Indeed, to provide for the creation to have this potential for creativity signals a divine delight in difference and diversity and the creative a 'new thing' that is coming. It is truly a 'Theo-cultural creation'.

That being so, the Christ event and our understanding of the incarnation is also intimately and inextricably a cultural event. Jesus lived at a particular place, at a particular time and understood the world as it was at a particular cultural moment. His language, accent and experience were culturally determined. As Craig Keener observes, 'If we had not guessed otherwise, the incarnation would show us that history and historical particularity matter' (Keener, 2016, p. 99). This brought something new into the experience of the Godhead, yet this cultural moment was not frozen in time as the only vehicle to transport Jesus' message and preserve its spiritual wisdom and power. Very quickly the movement that issued from Jesus' ministry leaves his home country, religion and language. This is the nature of the 'Christo-cultural incarnation'. This movement then follows Jesus' direction and, animated by the Holy Spirit, becomes a movement of discipleship to the nations. Facilitated by the Pax Romana, the followers of 'the Way' spread out around the known world bringing the life-changing message of the Kingdom of God. Jesus' instruction to 'make disciples of all nations' epitomizes the fact that his mission is one of 'Pneuma-cultural discipleship'.

What is the point of all this? What is the objective of understanding the world through the lens of theology? It is about understanding the God-given nature of our cultural experience and recognizing our cultural home as the context in which to practise a discipleship that is obedient to the teaching of Jesus. Thankfully we do this together as a community of disciples and together with the Spirit of God who is the one who 'comes alongside to help'. He is the one who leads us into all truth, who instructs us in matters of 'sin, righteousness and judgement' as we work out what they mean in our context. We 'walk in the Spirit' and are empowered to live lives that demonstrate the fruit of such a spiritual liaison.

Fascinatingly, in the Revelation of John, as the heavenly city comes into view, the epithet based on 'every tribe and language and people and nation, is repeated seven times (Rev. 5.9; 7.9; 10.11; 11.9; 13.7; 14.6; 17.15). And as John sees a vision of the City of God, the New Jerusalem, it is one that

> has no need of sun or moon to shine on it, for the glory of God is its light, and its lamp is the Lamb. The nations will walk by its light, and the kings of the earth will bring their glory into it. Its gates will never be shut by day – and there will be no night there. People will bring into it the glory and the honour of the nations. (Rev. 21.23–26)

This could be a fourth element of our Theo-cultural account of things, an 'Eschato-cultural vision'. As such, it confirms how the message of Jesus is affirming of cultural difference and, indeed, of its abiding value and worth. The idea of the 'glory and honour of the nations' being brought into the heavenly city by the 'people' is an intriguing one (Standing, 2016, pp. 16–27; Watkin, 2022, pp. 581–3). However, for the moment, it is beyond the scope of this exploration.

Note

1 A close reading of Acts 2 suggests that rather than hiding away in the upper room the disciples were at the Temple. See, for example, (1) on the day of a pilgrimage festival they were 'all together in one place', v. 1; (2) the sound of the violent wind 'filled the entire house where they were sitting', v2, and 'the House' was the colloquial name for 'the House of the Lord', Acts 7.47; (3) there is no account given of leaving 'the house' and getting to a public place where the public could witness what was happening and form a puzzled crowd, v. 6; (4) the size of the crowd was such that three thousand responded and were baptized. Only Temple Mount in the ancient city was large enough to accommodate so many. Indeed, the pilgrims would have been there already, participating in the worship, v. 41; (5) water to baptize so many would have been in short supply; however, archaeological excavations on Temple Mount in the 1960s discovered sufficient ritual Mikva (immersion pools) to enable the large number of worshippers to ritually cleanse themselves before entering the Temple precincts. For a fuller account see Standing, 2004, pp. 100–6 (especially pp. 103–4), 161–8.

4

Interrogating Culture: Reading and Interpreting the World Around Us

> Throughout the world, culture has been doggedly pushing its way onto the center stage of debates not only in sociological theory and research but also throughout the human sciences. (Alexander, 2003, p. 11)

From history to psychology and literary studies to political science, the twentieth century witnessed a growing appreciation of the significance of culture. Once historians themselves recognized that they were the product of a cultural context as much as those they studied, history became cultural and culture became historical (Tanner, 1997, p. 39). In psychology, Freud published *Totem and Taboo* in 1913. Some have claimed this to be the first attempt in modern times to formulate a comprehensive theory of culture. Built on a Darwinian notion, his ideas of cultural evolution were inherently colonial and racist. Surprisingly, they had no basis in scientific research or observation but were rather rooted in the imposition of his own presuppositions on certain contemporary anthropological ideas (Groh, 2020, pp. 12–13, 24–5). Yet the relationship between psychology and culture is immense and undeniable, as further reflection has clearly demonstrated.

Given the all-encompassing reach of the idea of culture, it is hardly surprising that each branch of the humanities and social sciences has gradually engaged with it. Each has done so from their own perspective and with their own intellectual agenda. Pioneering this trend was anthropology, which is, broadly speaking, the study of the development of human societies and their cultures. Hence the classic picture of the anthropologist undertaking immersive ethnological research in remotely located and exotic societies. Developing in the wake of anthropology, sociology also focuses on human societies but has historically been more concerned with the study of social relationships within societies and their institutions as experienced in everyday life. From the outset its focus has been more contemporary in outlook and has tended to be on its own cultural context as its subject of inquiry.

By contrast, the cultural scrutiny of artistic and intellectual activity has progressed through the academic disciplines of the humanities and especially in philosophy, history, literary studies and, latterly, film studies. Building on all the above, the more recent arrival of cultural studies as a distinct subject in its own right has provided what Ben Highmore has described as a 'permission slip' for cross-disciplinary or interdisciplinary exploration to be understood as the only way to properly analyse culture (Highmore, 2009, pp. ix, 115). Having its roots in British Marxism, cultural studies uses a range of analytic approaches and explanatory paradigms that include feminism, postcolonialism, LGBTQ+ and multiculturalism for a more politically engaged approach that deals with fundamental issues of domination and the exercise of power. As almost anything can be conceived of as cultural, nothing is really out of bounds in the quest to make sense of how life is experienced, organized and governed within society.

This increasing penetration of the idea of culture across the academy grew much stronger from the 1970s through to the close of the century and beyond. With this period now widely acknowledged as incorporating the 'cultural turn', several texts proved to be instrumental in laying the foundation of its progress.[1] Hayden White's *Metahistory* (1973), Clifford Geertz's *The Interpretation of Cultures* (1973), Michel Foucault's *Discipline and Punish* (1977) and Pierre Bourdieu's *Outline of a Theory of Practice* (1977) all fulfilled this function.

Beyond the more obvious subjects that might have been swept up in this turn to culture, the approach found a home in disciplines as diverse as geography (Cook et al., 2000), translation studies (Bassnett, 2014, p. 85), international development (Labadi, 2019) and health care (Pescosolido and Olafsdottir, 2010). In healthcare, for example, cultural analysis was seen as helpful in investigating glaring discrepancies such as why mental healthcare for children can be seen as highly appropriate in a population and yet the take-up remain disproportionately low (Pescosolido and Olafsdottir, 2010, pp. 655–76). Or again, in the work of international aid, where a worker on her first assignment with UNESCO used cultural considerations as a tool of reflection and came to the realization that,

> to my own dismay, I might have involuntarily become one of those 'colonial missionaries' ... in my attempt to convert the targeted beneficiaries to a new life aligned with Western aspirations and values. (Labadi, 2019, p. 10)

It would be foolish to underestimate the significance of this 'turn' to culture that has been identified as 'a pivotal moment in social theory' (Alexander, 2003, p. 12) or as 'one of the most influential trends in the humanities and social sciences in the last generation' (Jacobs and Spillman, 2005, p. 1).

With the groundwork for a renewed theological engagement with culture already in place through the work of Niebuhr, Tillich and those engaged with the overseas missionary movement, it is no surprise to see the 'cultural turn' also having a theological dimension. The rapid development of missiological ideas around inculturation and contextualization, in particular, caught the wind of this intellectual zeitgeist, as did an increasing fascination with the interplay between theology and popular culture, film studies and theories of leadership and management. Clive Marsh stated the obvious: '[if] religion is part of human culture ... then cultural studies must grant a place within its brief to religious studies and theological enquiry' (Marsh, 2004, pp.129–30). Yet some theologians, like Gordon Lynch, had already recognized the inclusive nature of this interdisciplinary wave and jumped on board (Lynch, 2007, p. 109). Indeed, where theology is frequently criticized because of the partiality of its approach, the increasing awareness that no analysis can be free of the cultural influences and convictions of its interpreters removes such a reproach at its source. Reflecting on this a quarter of a century after the publication of his work *Metahistory*, the American scholar Hayden White wrote:

> I do not believe for a moment that it is possible to produce a science of society that is not contaminated with ideological preconceptions ... I believe this is a good thing, that any science of society should be launched in the service of some conception ... of what a good society might be. (White, 1999, p. 316)

On such a premise the place of theology as a lens through which to view the life we live is both legitimized and affirmed.

The 'cultural turn' in our understanding of the world around us has certainly placed a premium on those academic disciplines that can provide insight and a frame of reference that enables our cultural context and experience to be interrogated. The key subjects are anthropology, sociology and, latterly, cultural studies. One of the helpful outcomes of the 'cultural turn' has been the emergence of a new lingua franca as the fruit of common epistemological and methodological concerns and the ensuing dialogue (Bonnell and Hunt, 1999, p. 25). Therefore, before exploring how we might utilize theology in enabling culture to be read and interpreted, an overview of these three core cultural specialisms, along with additional insight from postmodern philosophy via the American neo-pragmatist Richard Rorty, will provide a helpful point of entry.

Anthropology

Coming from a combination of the Greek words *anthropos* (human) and *logos* (what is spoken, thought or known), the development of the latter into the common English suffix -ology gives the subject a seemingly grandiose definition that could be taken as the 'study of everything human'. This breadth of scope is evidenced in the development of the range of specialized fields that have emerged since anthropology began to gain a self-conscious awareness of itself as a discipline in the later part of the nineteenth century. Necessarily at the intersection of the natural sciences and the humanities, these differing branches of knowledge span out in vastly differing directions. This is clearly demonstrated in the American approach that identifies four major branches of anthropology which, while sharing the same anthropological outlook, have developed their own separate methodologies and theories:

- *Physical anthropology* focuses on biology and human evolution.
- *Archaeological anthropology* is the study of material artefacts of the past, from prehistory to more recent times, to understand their cultural or societal setting.[2]
- *Linguistic anthropology* explores how human language has developed, shaped and encoded culture and social life across the 6000 languages identified as spoken throughout the world in the twentieth century.
- *Cultural anthropology,* also sometimes identified as *social or sociocultural anthropology*,[3] uses finely detailed studies of everyday life to understand how and why societies function as they do.

A vast array of subfields of study do justice to the all-encompassing purview of anthropological interest. For example, psychological, educational, religious and urban anthropology have each, along with ethnomusicology, developed considerable bodies of research and insight. Some have argued that applied anthropology is a fifth major branch of the subject, but in truth most of the fields of anthropological study have an applied dimension that serves practical community or organizational needs. Essentially, because culture characterizes a group of people, when an anthropologist identifies a culture they do so by viewing it from above as a single, if complex, whole. Internalized by those who live within it, culture is an ordering principle for social behaviour because it includes the norms, values, beliefs, attitudes, dispositions and sentiments that give meaning and shape to their community (Tanner, 1997, pp. 29–32).

The first generation of anthropologists relied heavily on the second-hand reports, information and artefacts gathered by sundry colonialists, missionaries and a committed cohort of travelling gentleman scholars. Later, the emergence of the characteristic approach of immersive fieldwork, that was in many ways to become the hallmark of anthropological research, only properly developed from its roots in the early decades of the twentieth century. Bronislaw Malinowski and Margaret Mead helped to establish this methodological foundation in both the discipline and the wider popular understanding of the subject. Bronislaw Malinowski's monographs on the Trobriand Islands (1922–35) were the fruit of having spent two years living among the islanders in 1915–18 (Young, 1979, p. 1), and Margaret Mead's *Coming of Age in Samoa* (1928) followed a nine-month immersion in village life on the island of Ta'u. While the posthumous publication of Malinowski's diary in 1967 led Clifford Geertz to characterize him during his time in the Trobriands as a 'crabbed, self-preoccupied, hypochondriacal narcissist, whose fellow-feeling for the people he lived with was limited in the extreme' (Young, 1979, p. 12), his influence on this emerging field of study was immense. For all his faults and the inherent racism that lurked behind the commonly embraced evolutionary views of culture of the time, Malinowski helped to establish that the anthropologist's ethnographic task was summed up in the attempt 'to grasp the native's point of view, his relation to life, to realize his vision of his world' (Malinowski, 1922, p. 25).

A more social or cultural dimension to anthropology began to emerge from the 1920s and throughout the century developed into one of the major branches of research and cultural analysis. Aiming to explain the many dimensions of culture, it is built upon the foundation of ethnographic field research and the collection of primary data that can then be analysed and either explained or interpreted. An early emphasis on studying contemporary hunter-gatherer or pastoralist communities from the so-called 'developing' world was based upon the assumption that societies were culturally self-contained and integrated systems (Hiebert, 1985, p. 20). While anthropological research has long since broadened out into working within any contemporary cultural context, there remains a commitment to evolutionary analysis as a key element in understanding cultural change. This, however, is no longer rooted in the 'Social Darwinism' of Herbert Spencer and his notion of the 'survival of the fittest', and the accompanying 'unilineal theory of cultural evolution' first proposed by E. B. Tylor. Often deployed as an intellectual justification for colonialism, this view held that all cultures had to progress through the same stages of development. This conscription of a 'pseudo-evolutionary theory' to legitimize imperial ambitions was in decline after World War 1 and almost universally discredited after World War 2. In anthropology the rejection of these more generalized theories by Franz Boas and those who followed him led to the adoption of a more 'particularized' view. Here each culture was acknowledged as a unique expression and representation of its own history and context (Howell and Paris, 2011, pp. 232–5).

Because of the hybrid and multidisciplinary breadth of anthropology, it straddles the quest to develop general scientific laws on one side and a process of interpretation and developing cultural understanding on the other. While the various branches of anthropology each seek to benefit from a strict adherence to the scientific method, it is cultural anthropology for which this is least helpful because it more properly requires the skill set provided by hermeneutics. From the 1970s this became most evident in the influential work of Clifford Geertz who maintained that because anthropology was the study of people it could not be reduced to purely scientific observation (Hiebert, 2009, p. 112). In *The Interpretation of Cultures* (1973) Geertz advocates that anthropology should take a different path.

> The concept of culture I espouse ... is essentially a semiotic one. Believing, with Max Weber, that man is an animal suspended in webs of significance he himself has spun, I take culture to be those webs, and the analysis of it to be therefore not an experimental science in search of law but an

interpretive one in search of meaning. It is explication I am after. (Geertz, 1973, p. 5)

Geertz advocated anthropology moving away from attempts to explain and predict human behaviour and towards a methodology of description and interpretation. Semiology was an integral part of this reading of culture, focusing on the signs – or meanings – that are attached to the life of the world people inhabit. He did not, however, see semiotics as merely a means of communication or signs to be decoded. Rather, it was understanding them as modes of thought and idioms to be interpreted. Culture is symbolic and public in visible and audible ways and the question to ask is 'What is getting said?' Because culture is shared it has to be public, like the common meaning it carries in its signified behaviours and things it produces (Inglis, 2000, pp. 1, 113). Indeed, Geertz was later to coin the term 'dramaturgical' to highlight how human life could be seen as a drama in which individuals take on roles and play their part on the cultural 'stage' (Howell and Paris, 2011, p. 238).

Central to Geertz's interpretive approach is the process of description or, as he describes it, 'an elaborate venture in, to borrow a notion from Gilbert Ryle, "thick description".' Geertz then uses the British philosopher's own illustration to demonstrate what he is getting at. Ryle had pointed out the essential similarities between straightforward descriptions of a boy with a twitch in his eye, a boy winking badly, and another boy mimicking the poor attempt at a wink. However, such a thin description would not differentiate between a physical affliction, a conspiratorial communication and parody (Geertz, 1973, pp. 6–7). By contrast, 'thick' descriptions needed to aim at being comprehensive and distinguishing between these nuances, yet also recognizing that they are always partial and incomplete. Indeed, says Geertz, 'Cultural analysis is (or should be) guessing at meanings, assessing the guesses, and drawing explanatory conclusions from the better guesses' (Geertz, 1973, p. 20). In this sense Geertz sees a dual action in hermeneutics. As the interpreter explains what is going on in their own words and 'makes up' their own interpretation ('making up' to 'make out'), they produce their own object which itself can become a subject for interpretation. In this sense the fingerprints of the analyst are always all over the work they have produced. While early anthropologists believed themselves to be following the scientific method and approached their observation with objectivity, such naivety is not sustainable. Geertz is the epitome of a more self-aware approach. 'It has been both the tenor and vehicle of Geertz's work to indicate in advance of postmodernism, how refracted and unabsolute truths are, how partial impartiality, how subjective objectivity' (Inglis, 2000, p. 172). Fascinatingly, cultural anthropologists do appear to have been early adopters of postmodern insights and have since benefitted from the insights of the place of power, social structure and gender and the importance of standpoint theory in their work (Howell and Paris, 2011, pp. 239–42).

For Geertz, the anthropologist tells stories, but is more than just a storyteller. Behind the discipline is a systematic process and rigour of a social science to interpret what is described in the narrative (Inglis, 2000, pp. 113–17).

Cultural sociology

In the most general of terms, if anthropology is the study of humans, sociology is the study of society. While there is a clear overlap between the disciplines and, over the years, a significant cross-fertilization of ideas and insights, still their perspectives differ. Where anthropology focuses down to Geertz's 'thick description' of specific contexts, sociology has tended to take a wide-angled approach to social structure, institutions and phenomena. Historically, themes such as social stratification, social mobility, the family, secularization, race, gender and deviance have been the subject of sociological scrutiny and analysis. A variety of theoretical approaches such as positivism, functionalism, phenomenology and social action theory are used within the subject alongside analytical frameworks drawn from Marxism, feminism and critical theory analysis.

Given that society is run through with culture, however it

is understood and defined, it is surprising that sociology has only relatively recently been fully engaged with the idea of it as a critically important area of study. In part this may be down to 'a generally accepted division of labor between sociologists and anthropologists, whereby the former have focussed their attention on society and the social, and the latter ... culture and cultural practices' (Bryant and Peck, 2007, p. 131). This had not always been the case. Classical works in the early twentieth century, like Max Weber's *The Protestant Ethic and the Spirit of Capitalism* and Emile Durkheim's *The Elementary Forms of the Religious Life*, effectively seeded the study of culture within sociology for the future. However, it was not until sociology's own 'cultural turn' that those seeds would properly germinate. It was the American scholar Jeffrey Alexander who would build on Durkheim's work and give birth to what he named and defined as 'cultural sociology'.

Picking up on a famous metaphor used by the French anthropologist Claude Lévi-Strauss, that the study of culture should be like the study of geology – where surface features are accounted for by underlying conditions – Alexander proposed engaging in a seismographic enterprise that would reveal a 'fault line' running straight through such a conception (Alexander, 2003, pp. 11–12). While sociology had always acknowledged the importance of culture, it had viewed it as the fruit or product of social structures and institutions. Marx, for example, saw culture as the embodiment of the ideas and values of the ruling class. Culture is therefore a derived and secondary phenomenon and is determined by the way society is organized. This approach Alexander identified as a 'sociology of culture'. By contrast, 'cultural sociology' looks for culture to be the expression of meaning. Here he draws on Durkheim's work on religion and the nature of the sacred and profane, aligning culture with the idea of the sacred. Like the sacred that identifies the ideas, icons and representations of the divine, culture is about meaning and the values, symbols and stories that shape and are shaped by those who embrace them (Tomley et al., 2015, p. 207).

To believe in the possibility of a cultural sociology is to subscribe to the idea that every action, no matter how instrumental, reflexive, or coerced vis-à-vis its external environments ... is embedded to some extent in a horizon of affect and meaning ... Similarly, a belief in the possibility of a cultural sociology implies that institutions, no matter how impersonal or technocratic, have an ideal foundation that fundamentally shapes their organization and goals and provides the structured context for debates over their legitimation. (Alexander, 2003, p. 12)

Viewed from a distance the 'sociology of culture' and 'cultural sociology' look very similar. They are dealing with the same landscape and a common vocabulary of values, codes and discourses. However, they are profoundly different perspectives. One views culture as derived from, and explained by, social structures; the other 'argues for a sharp analytical uncoupling of culture from social structure' and embracing of Geertzian hermeneutic of 'thick description' that explores the realm of meaning. Such a 'thick description' is no mere academic journalism that simply describes what meanings are present. Rather, it is also analysing the interactions of social structures, institutional dynamics and their interplay with other actors. Such a hermeneutic should not be ambiguous or shy in specifying how and why culture makes a difference (Alexander, 2003, pp. 13–14, 22; Lynch, 2012, p. 50).

This is the task of a cultural sociology. It is to bring the unconscious cultural structures that regulate society into the light of the mind. Understanding may change but not dissipate them, for without such structures society cannot survive. We need myths if we are to transcend the banality of material life. We need narratives if we are to make progress and experience tragedy. We need to divide the sacred from profane if we are to pursue the good and protect ourselves from evil ... Cultural sociology is a kind of social psychoanalysis. Its goal is to bring the social unconscious up for view. To reveal to men and women the myths that think them so that they can make new myths in turn. (Alexander, 2003, pp. 3–4)

To properly understand culture, or to understand it better, it has to be understood from the inside. This can only be attempted through engaging with the values, meanings and symbols that people use in their attempts to make sense of the world and their experience. This, for Alexander, is vitally important, because a person's internal life is the secret of their 'compulsive power'. Values, meanings and symbols press into deeply held convictions, issues of personal and communal identity and consciously/unconsciously generated responses, and that can be highly emotional and even visceral in nature. In the process the sociologist has no alternative than to adopt a richly hermeneutical or interpretive approach.

How people interpret an event can never be completely anticipated and is only truly accessible to the sociologist in hindsight. Alexander illustrates this meaning and myth-making process in a 2001 essay, 'On the Social Construction of Moral Universals: The "Holocaust" from War Crime to Trauma Drama' (Alexander, 2003, pp. 27–84). In it he highlights how, in the aftermath of the Second World War, the Holocaust was not viewed with the same fierce denunciation as the epitome of evil as it has been by more recent generations. European antisemitism and the ethnic distinctiveness of Jewish communities had precluded a more empathetic response. Alexander observes that it was only as they became more thoroughly integrated into their host cultures that the Holocaust could be re-narrated and recoded as an act of evil. A notable part of this was the powerful narrative of suffering portrayed through the publication and dramatization of Anne Frank's diaries (Lynch, 2012, p. 43).

Also contributing to the development of cultural sociology have been two other strands of sociological thinking. From the sociology of organizations and the sociology of knowledge emphasis has been put on how different organizations, institutions and networks generate and influence emerging patterns of meaning. Or again, from pragmatism and practice theory scholars have explored how social interaction and social practice become meaning-making processes, and how individuals and groups bestow meaning on particular actions (Spillman, 2007, pp. 924–5).

Within sociology the concept of culture has been the principal source of theoretical innovation since the 'cultural turn' of the 1980s. Cultural sociology itself has been the most heavily involved stream of sociology to be engaged in interdisciplinary approaches, even adopting neuroscience as a conversation partner in exploring the substance of meaning (Strand and Spillman, 2020, p. 43). Within the subject itself, exploring the question of meaning has contributed to easing the classic sociological tensions between interpretation and explanation, social structure and human agency, consensus/solidarity and conflict/resistance, along with linking everyday social interaction (micro settings) with large-scale (macro) social processes. The introduction of meaning as a focus to pursue in the 'identity' subjects of class, gender, race, sexuality and other axes of distinctiveness, the role of meaning-making of social and political movements and in sustaining engagement in them, not to mention its significance in religion, politics, the arts and civil society, has significantly deepened sociological discourse and insight. It has also brought the spotlight onto recently emerging issues such as how new communications technologies influence social identity and the place of meaning-making in a transnational and global context of migration. Helpfully, it has assisted in guarding the subject against the ever-present temptation of over-generalization about cultural processes (Spillman, 2007, p. 926).

Cultural studies

In many ways cultural studies is a very different and distinctive subject to anything else. Positioned at the intersection of the social sciences, and especially sociology, with the wider humanities and literary studies, it has no well-defined methodology or clearly established fields of study of its own (During, 1993, p. 1).

In Britain the subject emerged after the Second World War, drawing on the influence of writers like Raymond Williams, Richard Hoggart and E. P. Thompson. It then took a more substantive form under Hoggart with the formation of the Centre for Contemporary Cultural Studies (CCCS) at the University of Birmingham in 1964, funded by the owner of Penguin Books in appreciation of Hoggart's help in their defence during the *Lady Chatterley's Lover* court case (During, 2005, p. 20; Cobb, 2005, p. 53).[4] Within Cultural Studies all of its pioneers were 'men of the left' who challenged received tradition and emphasized a wider and more inclusive understanding of culture.

Hoggart's *The Uses of Literacy* (1957), Raymond Williams' *Culture and Society* (1958) and E. P. Thompson's *The Making of the English Working Class* (1963) laid the foundation for the critical analysis of what they preferred to call 'lived experience', or the lost sense of culture as 'ordinary'. However, they wanted to take it further. Such an analysis had to account for how social institutions, history and the exercise of power and privilege provided the broader context with its formative potency and influence (Long, 2007, pp. 913–14; During, 2005, pp. 20–1). Thus the study of culture is analysing not only the effect of human activity, but also how that activity itself constructs social reality. This analysis is then exercised with the aim of offering a critical perspective that examines the political implications of mass culture. Indeed, Stuart Hall, who was Director of CCCS between 1969 and 1976, had as one of his chief concerns how those with power used mass culture, and especially how they used what was represented through it, to exercise control. For Hall, a case in point was 1960s-era TV 'Westerns':

> with a clear-cut, good/bad Manichaean moral universe, its clear social and moral designation of villain and hero, the clarity of its narrative line and development, its iconographical features, its clearly registered climax in the violent shoot-out, chase, personal show-down, street or bar-room duel, etc. For long, on both British and American TV, this form constituted the predominant drama-entertainment ... [the] Western was so clear-cut, its action so conventionalized, stylized, most children ... soon learned to recognize and 'read' it like a 'game': a 'Cowboys-and-Injuns' game. (Hall, 1973, p. 5)

In this way the real historical West was selectively transformed into a 'symbolic or mythical' West. A view of the 'West' that was to evolve into '*the* archetypal American story' (Hall, 1973, p. 6). Half a century after Hall's paper was first delivered, the portrayal of firearms, summary justice and the indigenous community of native Americans in 1960s TV Westerns is as formative of a contemporary American mythology and as problematic as it ever was.

In many ways, because cultural studies is a relatively recent arrival its foundation myths are still in a state of flux. One has the CCCS as 'heroic, dissident British academics ... battling for democratization against elitism and hegemony in the sixties and seventies', while another views the subject as the fruit of the international movement of the 'new left' of the 1960s–70s encountering the powerfully influential emergence of popular culture at the same time (During, 2005, p. 14).

The international perspective is an important one because around the world the subject takes a variety of forms with differing approaches and emphases. In the United States, for example, it has evolved to major on issues of multiculturalism and the analysis of race and power. It does have a wider scope, but identity and power tend to be centre stage. In Australia, by contrast, the subject has more fully developed along the line of cultural policy studies, looking to understand how a culture is organized to influence governance and the future shaping of culture (During, 2005, pp. 19–26, 73).

In Germany the Frankfurt School has been heavily influenced from the beginning by a Marxian reading of society. Having firmly established itself in the 1930s, this group of academics was one of the first to take popular culture seriously. They viewed it as a product of capitalism that provided an illusion of happiness for the masses. This new 'opiate of the people' that arose through the evolution of Western consumer economies and the production of mass entertainment now underpinned the power structures of capitalism. Their analysis, provided by the development of 'critical theory', endeavoured to unmask what was really going on and thereby set society free from its bondage to commodification (Vanhoozer et al., 2007, p. 38).

Over recent decades Jürgen Habermas has been the preeminent voice out of the Frankfurt tradition. Expanding his analysis into a wider 'public sphere', Habermas has explored the place of communication as an integral part of social reality. Mapping its evolution in Europe from coffee houses to contemporary media, he has argued that a place for reasoned debate is a necessary precondition for democracy. Yet his analysis raises significant concerns with the 'public sphere' being subjected to erosion by the power of both the state and the market (Long, 2007, p. 915).

In France, thinkers like Roland Barthes, Michel Foucault and Pierre Bourdieu drew on the French fixation with linguistic culture to focus on how language is used to encode the 'cultural mythologies' of social domination, and how our own subjectivity is therefore shaped by the world around us (During, 1993, p. 10). Michel de Certeau is also a key thinker, especially with the insights from his influential work *The Practice of Everyday Life*, first published in French in 1980. He maintains that because of its unconscious and repetitive nature, everyday life is a distinctive dimension of social life when compared to the other elements of daily existence. What is especially revealing for him are the strategies of institutions and power structures, on the one hand, and the tactics of individuals who engage with them on the other. In his chapter 'Walking in the City' (Certeau, 1988, pp. 91–110) he demonstrates how the strategies of governments, corporations and other institutions in designing and mapping a city as a whole are subverted by the tactics people adopt as they regularly walk through it. As they walk, shortcuts are established and, at street level, a way of living develops that could never have been planned and, though influenced by the strategy, can never be wholly determined by it.

While cultural studies lacks the theoretical cohesion or methodological framework of its sister disciplines, there are identifiable strands of orientation and approach that have shaped its development and trajectory. The first of these can be found in an explicit affinity with the disenfranchised in society. A legacy of the influence of its German roots in the Frankfurt School, there is an underlying view that scholarship should be committed in its analysis to changing society by addressing real issues of power imbalance. To that end subaltern groups like 'teenage girls, punks, motorcycle gangs, skinheads and Rastafarians' are studied to give voice to their alternative 'readings' of their cultural experience. These 'readings' of the lives and experiences of those on the margins of society, it is observed, can be done 'in fun, in resistance, or to articulate their own identity' (During, 1993, p. 7; Cobb, 2005, p. 68). The recognition that such alternate 'readings' may legitimately exist side-by-side is based on an understanding of 'polysemy', where the same thing may carry two very different 'readings' depending upon the cultural location of the one doing the 'reading'. For example, the policing strategy of 'stop and search' in a context of response to gang violence and the proliferation of drugs may be seen as an appropriate strategy to uphold law and order; or, alternatively, as a flawed approach that is compromised by a disproportionate targeting of black and Asian people without lawful justification and is 'consistent with the evidence on racial prejudice and stereotyping' (EHRC, 2010, p. 58). Cultural studies then goes further in its analysis of each situation by adopting the concept of 'hybridization', which further layers complexity into what is revealed as a dynamic, multi-faceted and kaleidoscopic array of possibilities.

Such analysis then looks to uncover the process by which order is maintained within a culture between the dominant and subordinate groups and how this is accomplished without resort to coercive force. Drawing on the idea of 'hegemony' from the Italian Marxist Antonio Gramsci, cultural studies explores how consent is obtained for the ideas and worldview of the dominant class. The idea of hegemony suggests that below every cultural settlement between dominant and subordinate groups sits an ongoing dialogue of negotiation, compromise, retrenchment and resistance that are the necessary prerequisites for consent to be given (Cobb, 2005, pp. 54–6, 68; Vanhoozer et al., 2007, p.38). The history of the British royal family, for example, is a case in point. The constitutional monarchy of the United Kingdom has continued to evolve over the centuries and even over the decades of the reign of Queen Elizabeth II and must continue to do so under Charles III. When the House of Windsor has been perceived to be 'out of step' with the country, consent has been seen to swiftly ebb away. The 'give and take' involved in cultural accommodation means that cultural elements of the subordinate group are co-opted into the whole, as are the 'lived experiences' of the subordinate class into the institutions and structures of the dominant class. Thus the subordinate class has a vested interest in the dominant social culture. For Hall, when meaning is taken for granted, its settled-ness is part of the 'dead language' of cultural ideology. It is only when meaning is challenged and a conflictual discourse of struggle ensues that a given part of culture comes alive and part of a living 'social intelligibility' (Hall, 1982, p. 77).

The second strand that contributes to the orientation and approach of cultural studies lies with its links to literary studies in France and with the CCCS. At the latter, for example, the Centre was initially part of the English Department of the University because Richard Hoggart's own background was in English. It only became an independent department under the directorship of Stuart Hall. It was in this way that the process of analysing culture built a bridge between literary criticism and the 'texts' of popular culture. The gulf that exists between the literary and artistic works of the masters and the novels, music and movies of the contemporary mass market is vast. Yet Cultural Studies span the gap between Chaucer's fourteenth-century masterpiece, *The Canterbury Tales*, and Helen Fielding's 1996 best-seller, *Bridget Jones's Diary*, between Botticelli's *The Virgin and Child Surrounded by Five Angels* (c. 1470, in the Louvre, Paris) and Madonna's *Like A Prayer* album (1989, 15 million worldwide sales), by extending the methodologies of literary criticism to the more popular subject. Just as 'high' culture had been 'read' to distil its timeless wisdom, so now the products of mass culture that were loved by ordinary working people could be 'read' with the expectation of profound insight too (Cobb, 2005, p. 68; During, 2005, pp. 30–1).

A key element in this reading of cultural artefacts is the incorporation of the insights of semiotics into cultural studies. Emerging in the work of the Swiss linguist Ferdinand de

Saussure in the late nineteenth century, semiology is a field of study in its own right. With the objective of exploring what underpinned everyday speech and writing, Saussure differentiated between what is signified and the words we use as signifiers. This is semiology, or the study of signs.[5] Because of the rather arbitrary way that words become adopted as signifiers, it is only in relation to other words and in their combinations together that make up a sentence that meaning becomes apparent. A second level of meaning sits behind this 'linearity' and rests on what Saussure calls their 'associative relations'. Take, for example, the sentence: 'the person exploded a bomb in the city centre'. Substitute the word 'person' with soldier, terrorist, freedom-fighter or bomb-disposal expert and the different 'associative relations' of the words construct different meanings to the event. Semiologists have argued that all cultural products, whether seen, heard or felt, can be read in the same way (Baldwin et al., 1999, p. 32). Indeed, French literary theorist and philosopher Roland Barthes made the distinction between the denotive and connotative functions of cultural signs, symbols and images. If denotive meanings are like the definitions that could be looked up in a dictionary, connotative meanings are secondary and become attached to the original, creating wider fields of meaning. In this second level of signification, connotation deals with the subjective meanings and interpretations of the sign by those who encounter it. In *Mythologies*, written in 1957, Barthes famously illustrates his point:

> I am at the barber's, and a copy of Paris-Match is offered to me. On the cover, a young Negro in a French uniform is saluting, with his eyes uplifted, probably fixed on a fold of the tricolour. All this is the meaning of the picture. But, whether naively or not, I see very well what it signifies to me: that France is a great Empire, that all her sons, without any colour discrimination, faithfully serve under her flag, and that there is no better answer to the detractors of an alleged colonialism than the zeal shown by this Negro in serving his so-called oppressors. (Barthes, 1991, p. 115)

In cultural studies, then, any product of culture itself can be 'read' like any literary text. Three component parts of any communication make up the process of such a 'reading'. The intention gives way to what is produced, and then how what is produced is experienced and understood. In literary terms this is authorial intent, the published text and reader's response – technically speaking the illocution, the locution and the perlocution of the text.

What is significantly different in cultural studies to other approaches in analysing culture is the way that it fully embraces the subjectivity of personal experience (i.e., 'culture in relation to individual lives'). Such experience is shaped and then reinforced by the 'form-ful-ness' of the 'language, signs, ideologies, discourses, [and] myths' that surround us. The 'project' of cultural studies is therefore

> to abstract, describe and reconstitute in concrete studies the social forms through which human beings 'live', become conscious, sustain themselves subjectively. (Johnson, 1986, p. 45)

This frequently cited definition of the 'project' by Richard Johnson, another former Director of CCCS, locates cultural studies as a parallel endeavour to Marx's work on economic forms. Indeed, in the introduction to *A Contribution to the Critique of Political Economy* in 1859, Marx himself identified those subjective ideological forms through which the consciousness of the need to transform the economic means of production appear, and the fight for such transformation is nurtured (Marx, 1904, p. 12). Then this 'subjectivity' is understood as a distinguishing characteristic because it is to be an engaged form of analysis. An engaged analysis, that is, based on the fact that societies are structured unequally and that it worked in the interest of those with fewest resources (During, 1993, pp. 1–2).

Within cultural studies this interpretive analysis is conducted through qualitative ethnography that seeks to connect with everyday life in the real world outside the academy (During, 2005, p. 23; Highmore, 2016, p. 138). In summary, beyond its inception as a subject in 'a mix of left-wing sociology, adult education and literary criticism' (During, 2005, p. 1), its foundations laid in an inter-disciplinary working and its embrace of 'the whole of life' as its legitimate field of study, several key ideas are worth highlighting because they provide part of a common intellectual infrastructure for those committed to engaged research.

At the most basic level, cultural studies is about the continual interaction between how what we believe influences what we do, and how what we do shapes what we believe. It is 'the academic inquiry into this interaction of everyday life' (Morgan, 2008, p. 4). The approach has sought to navigate the path between freedom and responsibility on one side, and any kind of precast determinism on the other. For all that might be attributed to the forces of biology, history, economics or technology in conditioning our choices, preferences and predispositions, human agency with its freedom of choice and its consequence of personal responsibility must remain inescapable.

Fundamentally speaking, cultural studies is about description and analysis. Yet such a culturalist approach recognizes that the subjective nature of experience means that our social context and personal identity profoundly impact our perception of the world around us. This subjectivity of our personal identity thus provides the default lens through which our experience is conditioned. Our gender, sexuality, race and ethnicity can each provide the tools by which to engage in the analytical process. 'Whether celebrating popular culture or doing its bit to combat hegemony, cultural studies has always been at once an academic pursuit and a political movement' (Kuper, 2000, p. 230). Herein lies a significant issue to note. As an approach to interpreting culture, the strength of its subjective focus is probably also the greatest weakness of cultural studies. It is essentially a reductionist view that shrinks everything of note in popular culture to 'the political and economic power struggles that its production and consumption represents' (Cobb, 2005, p.70). Indeed, the repeated deconstruction of elements of culture inevitably leads to exposing the hidden conspiracy of power and knowledge to exercise oppression. Commenting on the 'paranoid misgivings' that this gives rise to, the American anthropologist Stefan Collini rather colourfully observes that the suspicion is that most forms of cultural activity are essentially a disguise for the fact that Somebody is Trying to Screw Somebody Else ... and in response it is the duty of those engaged in Cultural Studies to 'subvert,' 'unmask,' 'contest,' 'de-legitimize'. (Kuper, 2000, p. 230)

It is unsurprising that the subjective nature of this analytical approach shapes the worldview of the subject that is predominantly that of 'secular, middle-class, leftist, youngish (or wannabe young) more or less Eurocentric practitioners.' Progressivist by nature and resistant to a more conservative perspective, its practitioners can be clearly neglectful or excluding of different perspectives (During, 2005, pp. 7, 18). Yet that said, cultural studies makes a significant contribution to cultural self-awareness. Through its embrace of subjectivity and working with descriptions of 'lived experience', its use of the tools of literary criticism, semiology and postmodern deconstruction, its inter-disciplinary approach and its focus on power/hegemony, it has opened up new dimensions of insight into the contemporary condition of society.

Richard Rorty

That postmodern philosophy has impacted the study of culture is hardly surprising, given its focus and influence in the latter part of the twentieth century. The debates and conceptual maps that have been generated are particularly significant in sociology and cultural studies, with the latter also indicating a break with its Marxian roots (Barker and Jane, 2016, p. 213). Foucault and Barthes have been particularly influential, as has the work of Derrida and Rorty.

As an example of postmodern philosophers engaging with culture Richard Rorty is not an obvious choice. A controversial figure among his peers, who received his work 'with hesitance, a held nose, or indeed outright hostility' (Calder, 2007a, p. viii), yet the *New York Times* in 1990 could herald that he had 'become the most influential contemporary American philosopher ... turning himself into a philosophical maverick, a thorn in the academic establishment's side' (Klepp, 1990, p. 57). In the 1980s Rorty was happy to identify his approach as postmodern but by the early 1990s had stepped away from this as 'the word has become subject to such overuse that it ceases to signify anything particularly helpful' (Mambrol, 2017).

Educated at the University of Chicago and Yale, Rorty then taught at Wellesley College, Princeton, the University of Virginia and Stanford (Calder, 2003, p. 4). His progression through these institutions saw a fascinating migration that began with 21 years as Professor of Philosophy at Princeton (1961–82) to his appointment as a Professor of Humanities at Virginia (1982–98) and then as Professor of Comparative Literature at Stanford (1998–2007). The grandson of the Baptist theologian, pastor and social gospeller Walter Rauschenbusch, Rorty was himself an atheist, married to a practising Mormon, and believed that religion was a 'conversation stopper' (Gross, 2019, p. 16; Smith, 2020, p. 81). What is attractive in using Rorty as an illustrative thinker in reading culture is that he is identified as a Neo-pragmatist within the succession of American Pragmatism. Pragmatically speaking, it was usefulness that mattered. He believed that those who were privileged to be able to 'theorize' should seek to engage directly in concrete social issues (Calder, 2007a, p. 182). To that degree he carried on the social conscience of his parents and grandparents, but as a philosopher he was an anti-foundationalist – that is, he did not believe there to be any fundamental truths, principles or realities that provided a basis for our inquiries or our knowledge. All that was open to those seeking to read the world around them was the practice of 'redescription', a discipline that was central to his own approach and understanding. He was also convinced that philosophy was only one voice in the conversation, and that as a discipline it 'would be done better if more modest, piecemeal and low-falutin' (Calder, 2007b, p. 21).

For Rorty, the starting point of any deliberation was always that it was undertaken at a particular place and at a particular time (Calder, 2007a, p. 119). We cannot escape our context. In any moment we are constrained by the language we speak and the concepts that are available to us. More than that, our place and time shape and determine the issues that are current to us, what is accepted and goes without thinking and that which is contested and does not. With no 'foundational' truths or principles for evaluation, 'we live in story after story after story (Calder, 2003, p. 9). In this narrative, language acts as a mediator between our experience of the world and how we think about it. It is completely caught up by, and implicated in, the process of how we know things and 'we shall never be able to step outside of language, never be able to grasp reality unmediated by a linguistic description' (Rorty, 1999, p. 48). Indeed, our cultural narratives determine what has the right to be said and done in any specific cultural location (Calder, 2007a, p. 114). There may, of course, be better ways of describing and understanding our experience, but that takes someone using the 'tools' of language to describe things differently and for that 'redescription' to be discovered to work better (Calder, 2003, pp. 42–3). At the most fundamental of levels, Rorty observes, 'nobody was conscious of being conscious before we started talking about "consciousness"' (Rorty, 1998, p. 285).

While Rorty does not doubt that there is a real world that exists before we try to describe it, we can only know what this world is like through the descriptions we make of it. It is these competing descriptions that 'help us to see'. The world beyond these descriptions is what it is, it is the descriptions themselves that we find to be helpful or unhelpful, true or false, acceptable or unacceptable (Calder, 2003, p. 11). Our descriptions, of course, are limited by our own context, our language and ideas and indeed by the social reasons we have for undertaking the task of description of a particular thing in the first place. In that sense they may say more about us than they do of what we are seeking to describe. The intrinsic 'nature' of 'reality' is therefore beyond description. Our vocabularies and descriptions are tools and instruments that provide us with ways of 'coping with the world' (Calder, 2003, pp. 29–31), or more than that, of shaping the world and accomplishing our own intended ends. It is linguistic behaviour as tool-using, of language as a way of grabbing hold of causal forces and making them do what we want, altering ourselves and our environment to our own aspirations. (Rorty, 1991, p. 81)

For Rorty there is no 'goal of truth' that is to be discovered through inquiry; this vertical dimension is unavailable. It is only the horizontal line that exists through the practise of description and redescription. What enables the evaluation of any claim within a culture to be undertaken is the presence of concrete alternative suggestions about how things might be redescribed (Calder, 2003, pp. 55–7). Truth is thus not something that is discovered, but rather something that is made and remade through our description and redescription of what is held to be 'true'. This process is clearly observable and in evidence in the evolution of contemporary views regarding gender and sexuality. Here, appeals to vertical authorities such as biology and religious revelation sit alongside horizontal appeals to what works for individuals and how things are experienced as fundamentally 'true'. 'True', here is exactly how Rorty understands it, 'the sort of compliment that one pays to a proposition to which one consents' because it is understood to work and be 'good to steer by' (Calder, 2003, p. 65; 2007a, pp. 30–1). This is what locates Rorty within the tradition of American Pragmatism: the understanding that philosophy is about action and the outcomes of ideas in experience rather than merely refining the representation or mirroring of reality in philosophical discourse. In Rorty this is modified with his emphasis on it being regarded as an adaptive tool: a tool that is used to cope with life within the world and accomplish desired and pragmatic ends in better ways. As he says in a telling phrase, 'Time will tell, but epistemology won't' (Calder, 2007b, p. 21).

An underlying core theme of Rorty's work, and 'a key distinctive element' of his contribution to contemporary thought, is his emphasis on 'redescription' (Calder, 2007a, p. 1).

Our descriptions of the world, on this account, constitute (if not the world itself, then at least) the ways in which we interact with it. 'True' descriptions do not mirror the world, or 'represent' it, but rather make it comprehensible, useful, adaptable to human purposes. (Calder, 2007a, p. 63)

For Rorty, we cannot access the world beyond our descriptions of it. In fact, descriptions of the world that do not conform with what is accepted as normal can seem preposterous. However, progress and adaption only come for both societies and individuals when our redescriptions of the world provide us with new and useful ways of conceiving how things are. Our inherited descriptions of the world are replaced when these redescriptions function more successfully and prove themselves to be more useful in meeting our social needs:

> when Christians began saying 'Love is the only law', and when Copernicus began saying 'The earth goes round the sun', these sentences must have seemed merely 'ways of speaking'. Similarly, the sentences 'history is the history of class struggle' or 'matter can be changed into energy' were, at the first utterance, prima facie false. These were sentences which a simple-minded analytic philosopher might have diagnosed as 'conceptually confused', as false by virtue of the meanings of such words as 'law', 'sun', 'history', or 'matter'. But when the Christians, the Copernicans, the Marxists, or the physicists had finished redescribing portions of reality in the light of these sentences, we started speaking of these sentences as hypotheses, which might quite possibly be true. In time, each of these sentences became accepted, at least within certain communities of inquiry, as *obviously* true. (Rorty, 1991, p. 124)

In his first major book, *Philosophy and the Mirror of Nature* (1979), Rorty gives the name of 'edification' to this project of 'finding new, better, more interesting, more fruitful ways of speaking'. In it he recognizes that the task 'may consist in the hermeneutic activity of making connections between our own culture and some exotic culture or historical period, or between our own discipline and another discipline'. A clear commitment to an eclectic, interdisciplinary approach in developing conversations and partnerships. In this quest to find new, insightful and disruptive insights he identifies the significance of what he calls 'abnormal speech', the content of which takes us out of ourselves by the 'power of strangeness'. In so doing he advocates an 'inverse hermeneutic' which is a reinterpretation of what is familiar through 'the unfamiliar terms of our new inventions' (Rorty, 1979, p. 360). Of course, the value of any redescription is its usefulness. Rorty uses George Orwell to illustrate his point. Commenting on how Orwell 'broke the power of ... "Bolshevik Propaganda" over the minds of liberal intellectuals in England and America,' he wrote,

> Orwell's tricky way, in *Animal Farm*, was to throw the incredibly complex and sophisticated character of leftist political discussion into high and absurd relief by retelling the political history of this century in terms suitable for children. (Rorty, 1989, p.174)

Redescription is not only the province of academics, intellectuals and professional commentators. As with Orwell, writers, artists and broadcasters are also part of public discourse in this regard. All of this goes to indicate the haphazard way in which ideas and norms change in culture, society and politics. Orwell was successful because he wrote the right books at the right time (Rorty, 1989, p.170). Yet no-one can predict or plan for a new orthodoxy with any degree of certainty. The power to shape and influence culture is diffuse and fluid, carried along by unpredictable events in cultures and societies that have their own agendas, populated as they are by communities that are 'varied, multi-dimensional, and riddled with fragments of powerfulness' (Smith, 2020, p. 84). There is a significant contingency that must be factored into the perceived or acclaimed usefulness of any description or redescription.

Orwell's best novels will be widely read only as long as we describe the politics of the twentieth century as Orwell did. How long that will be will depend on the contingencies of our political future: on what sort of people will be looking back on us, on how events in the next century will reflect back on ours, on how people will decide to describe the Bolshevik Revolution, the Cold War, the brief American hegemony, and the role of countries like Brazil and China. (Rorty, 1989, p. 169)

This is an important reality to grasp. Redescriptions are just that, redescriptions. They are accepted as they prove useful, not because they embody some objective truth that is embedded in reality. They are not new theories to be embraced and they do not assume the elevated position of critical insight, neither do they dig below surface appearances to reveal eternal truths. 'They simply redescribe' (Calder, 2003, pp. 50-1). Of course, things are never so simple, and Rorty himself acknowledged all redescriptions are the property of the sentences that express them. Sentences, like language itself, are made rather than found and can be constructed so that 'anything could be made to look good or bad, important or unimportant, useful or useless, by being redescribed' (Rorty, 1989, p. 7).

Richard Rorty is a fascinating and illustrative example of how philosophy from within the broader school of postmodernism has engaged in seeking to 'read' culture. Gideon Calder, having studied and written about Rorty for over a decade, writes about how he finds him 'illuminating, thought-provoking and a joy to spend time with', and yet how he disagrees to some extent or other 'with most of his substantive claims' (Calder, 2007a, pp. viii–ix). Similarly, Graeme Smith, while acknowledging Rorty's uncomfortable fit as a conversation partner for a theologian, believes that Rorty's idea of edification can be a model for a reframing of public theology (Smith, 2020, pp. 81, 84).

Interrogating culture

Back in 1984, in the introduction to the book *Cultural Analysis*, the sociologist Robert Wuthnow lamented that 'little headway' had been made in the study of culture in contrast with the impressive pace of progress the social sciences had made in other areas. He feared that it was only 'slightly presumptuous' to contemplate the complete abandonment of this field of study altogether (Wuthnow et al., 1984, pp. 1–2). Wuthnow need not have feared: the 'cultural turn' was about to establish the reorientation of inquiry and research that he hoped for.[6]

Across the range of approaches to interrogating culture there are six takeaways that emerge as pertinent to a theological engagement in cultural hermeneutics. The first is that the subject of study is the 'whole of life'. From the micro to the macro; the lived experience of everyday life to the functioning of global institutions; the up-close focus on a single contemporary artefact like a movie or work of art to a wide-angled perspective on a social phenomenon like Black Lives Matter or cultural trends such as political popularism, all are legitimate subjects of interrogation. The beginning of which is the task of description.

Second, this descriptive process is itself only half the task. It is clearly foundational, and as with all foundations, is vitally important for what is to follow. Here it is the substantive work of analysis and interpretation. This is the substance of the discipline of hermeneutics. What is it that is really going on? The tools to accomplish the interpretive task come from across the board: literary criticism, semiotics, and any social, political, ideological, or indeed theological perspectives the interpreter chooses to embrace.

Third, subjectivity is inescapable. We come to the task with who and what we are and with what we believe, driven along by the reasons we have undertaken the task of interpretation in the first place. Objectivity may not be possible, but integrity and self-awareness are. We need to know ourselves, own our intentions and be transparent in our accounts. It even goes further than this. We need to comprehend the dynamics involved in how what we believe influences what we do, and how what we do then goes on to shape what we believe. This is what philosophers call 'the double hermeneutic effect' (Blakely, 2020, p. xxvi)

Fourth, the task to hand is about uncovering that which sits beneath the surface of things. It is about unmasking that which is hidden and revealing to the eye what is clear when you see it but invisible unless it is pointed out. This is especially pertinent in relation to the exercise of power, because visibility brings accountability and invisibility colludes with potential abuse.

Fifth, the principle of usefulness is helpful both in understanding why things are as they are and as a rationale for driving the interpretive process itself. What is the benefit? Why does it work? Who benefits? Why do they benefit? The pragmatics of an analysis are critical to understanding the internal dynamics of what is being studied.

Sixth, is the need for humility. Even the best, most detailed and 'thickest' description will only ever, at best, be partial. Even the most insightful interpretation will be limited by the lens through which the 'seeing' is enabled. And then, because we are people caught up in time and place, no attempt at understanding can escape the givenness of our location. We are context-bound in our life, our understanding and our forays into interpreting the world around us.

Seeking to understand our cultural location and experience will inevitably cause us to lean on, and draw from, the social sciences that have pioneered strategies for interrogating culture. However, Jason Blakely is keen to reiterate that the social sciences are not of the same substance as the natural sciences. They sit within the hermeneutical and interpretive traditions, with all that implies. While their 'methods and findings are too valuable to do without', they must be embraced only with an acceptance of their subjectivity, partiality, incompleteness and rootedness at a particular moment in time and space (Blakely, 2020, p. 126). A further good reason to properly embrace the humility of a seeker after truth.

Notes

1 Care must be taken not to confuse the 'cultural turn' with postmodernism. While in many ways they are intellectual siblings, with many similar family traits, they are separate and distinct. Whereas postmodernism is a movement in Western philosophy in reaction to modernism and is descriptive of what follows it, the 'cultural turn', by

contrast, has been a cross-disciplinary realization of the significance of the concept of culture in the development of theoretical understanding and methodological investigation. Victoria Bonnell and Lynn Hunt provide a helpful overview of the origins of the 'cultural turn' in their edited book, *Beyond the Cultural Turn: New Directions in the Study of Society and Culture* (1999, pp. 1–27).

2 In the United States archaeology is considered a branch of anthropology, while in Britain and Europe it is a separate discipline in its own right, hence the designation anthropological archaeology that seeks to bridge the differing designations.

3 Cultural anthropology (USA) and social anthropology (Britain) have different roots and historically different emphases. Today, however, the terms are largely interchangeable or are replaced by the portmanteau of sociocultural anthropology.

4 CCCS was an epicentre of the British approach to cultural studies until its closure in 2002 as part of a contentious restructuring process by senior managers within the University of Birmingham.

5 In the United States semiology is referred to as Semiotics.

6 Further to this, Wuthnow summarizes his thinking about cultural analysis by defining it as 'the study of the symbolic-expressive dimension of social life. As such, one of its chief aims is to identify empirical regularities or patterns in this dimension of reality and from these regularities to specify the rules, mechanisms, and relations which must be present for any particular symbolic act to be meaningful. The subject matter of cultural analysis is readily observable in the objectives acts, events, utterances, and objects of social interaction. The appropriate level of analysis is the patterns among these artifacts of interaction, rather than efforts to reduce culture either to the internal states of individuals or to the material conditions of societies. As a systematic body of inquiry, therefore, cultural analysis becomes distinct from related disciplines such as social psychology or sociology in that it concerns a unique aspect of human behaviour' (Wuthnow et al., 1984, p. 259).

5

Cultural Hermeneutics: Reading and Interpreting the World Through the Lens of Theology

Inculturated discipleship

> Go and make disciples of all *cultures*. (Matt. 28.19)

According to Ben Highmore the two fundamental questions to ask when engaging with culture are: first, what are we doing when we identify something as cultural? And second, what does this allow us to do (Highmore, 2016, p vii)? Historically speaking, Niebuhr's typology is illustrative of a sociological approach that seeks to describe and understand the relationship between culture and different theological expressions of Christian faith. Tillich, on the other hand, takes a more anthropological perspective and seeks to deploy a redefined Christian theology to identify deep-seated realities in the nature of human experience. Missiological strategies, by contrast, aim to understand the world outside the church that is to be reached and served by the Christian community. A thoroughgoing theology of culture will always fail if its *raison d'*être remains purely academic or merely a means to an end. There is something more elemental going on, by its very nature more essential and extending down into the deep structures of reality. A more fundamental question needs to be asked, one that requires a step further back.

Culture is an inescapable reality because it is a foundational element in our experience of existence. We live in a Theo-cultural creation. More than that, in Jesus we see God embracing culture as part of the redemptive strategy to realign humanity with the divine purpose, the Christo-cultural nature of the incarnation. However, it is the third strand, or Pneuma-cultural nature of discipleship, of a Theo-cultural understanding of the world, that provides the means to address Highmore's questions. Jesus called his followers to a life of discipleship. His 'great commission' was not one of going to 'make converts' in all cultures, but to 'make disciples' by 'teaching them to obey everything that I have commanded you' (Matt. 28.20). As Gerard Loughlin compellingly argues, 'Living the Christian life ... involves radically reimagining and resituating one's entire life within the story of Jesus', illuminated by its critically important centre, the resurrection (Loughlin, 1996, pp. 134, 202). There is no single template by which this can be accomplished. Culture is too complex and dynamic for that even to be a possibility. Thus, says Miroslav Volf, faith's stance towards culture ought to be 'defined by the centre of the faith itself, ... Christ as the divine Word incarnate and the Lamb of God who takes away the sin of the world' (Volf, 2011, p. xv). In this way, seeking to figure out what constitutes Christian discipleship at the time and place in which we find ourselves is the core of any devotion to Jesus. What does this inculturated discipleship look like for us as we seek to align ourselves with what Jesus embodied in who he was, what he taught and the path he took that led to the cross and then to his resurrection? This requires a 'bilingual' discipleship that both understands and is faithful to the biblical story while also properly understanding our cultural context and its influence over us (Tanner, 1997, p. 153; Graham, 2017, p.118; Vanhoozer et al., 2007, p. 8).

The need for such a bilingual approach is easier to identify than it is to accomplish because we are both naive about the formative role of culture upon us and gullible to its lure. We are naive because in the individuality of our thinking and rationality, our sense of autonomy and the personal exercise of choice, we fail to recognize how 'the forces of culture shape desire, vision, expectations, and the roles of one's subjectivity' (Fitch, 2022, p. 170). We are gullible because, in the instinctive and intuitive dimensions of our lives, we do not see how contagious culture is and how easily we catch it. We do not appreciate how we gravitate to those bits of culture that seem to 'fit' and confirm our convictions. And neither do we recognize how this culture then 'clings' to us because of the sense of meaning it gives us. A sense of meaning that is important because it provides our connection to the world and the navigational framework that helps us negotiate our lives. Tellingly, Justin Ariel Bailey observes that such gullibility is unsurprising in that stability of meaning is centred in the security of our personal and group identities (Bailey, 2022, pp. 20–5). It is difficult to underestimate the powerful nature of the connection that resides in such relationships and the gravitational pull they exert. If this is so, a critical question for every Christian disciple is 'What are you being formed by'? It is a sobering reality to acknowledge that even the way we think about God, engage in worship, read the Bible and practise the spiritual disciplines are culturally formed.

Such thinking is not new. Even back in the 1930s, the Austrian phenomenologist Alfred Schütz and others were exploring the concept of the 'lifeworld' within which everyday life is experienced and social reality is both created for each new generation yet under the constraints of the culture that has been inherited from those who have gone before (Ritzer, 2011, p. 219). Schütz was to prove especially influential because his ideas were then developed by the sociologist Peter Berger in his understanding of the 'plausibility structures' that exist in every society (Berger, 1990, p.192). Berger's ideas were in turn taken up and given wide circulation by the missiologist Lesslie Newbigin in his landmark work *The Gospel in a Pluralist Society*, where he defines them as 'patterns of belief and practice accepted within a given society, which determine which beliefs are plausible to its members and which are not' (1989, pp. 8–11). The implications of the prevailing plausibility structure for discipleship are obvious and profound. Historically, where Christianity has been deeply embedded in the institutions, life practices and thinking of a society it was considered normal and reasonable to be a person of faith. By contrast, in Western culture where Christianity is no longer the social force it once was, having been supplanted by the prevailing market economy, it is a different matter altogether. With the whole of life seemingly structured around consumer choice, the need to constantly reaffirm that choice produces social conditions that 'make faithfulness difficult and faithlessness almost natural (Hunter, 2010a, pp. 202–3).

The inescapable nature of the culture we inhabit is that we can only experience reality from within it. We can never step outside it. We can never accomplish objectivity. Our consciousness can no more exist outside its immersive embrace than can the proverbial fish out of water. In David Morgan's memorable phrase, 'People build their worlds, and their worlds build them' (Morgan, 2008, p. xiv).

For those pursuing discipleship this sets up what appears to be the age-old and unresolvable dilemma of being 'in the world' but not 'of the world'. This tension is intrinsic to a theology that understands the created order to be declared 'good' and yet under judgement because of 'the fall'. This is everything that is involved in teasing out the challenge to follow Jesus, who was quite clear when he prayed, 'I do not belong to the world' and yet goes on to intercede for his disciples: 'I am not asking you to take them out of the world, but I ask you to protect them from the evil one' (John 17.14–15). Added to which, earlier he had told them, 'If you belonged to the world, the world would love you as its own. Because you do not belong to the world ... the world hates you' (John 15.19–20). Bailey rightly observes that in every culture there is a struggle over whose perspective will prove to be normative (Bailey, 2022, p. 42). But it goes deeper and more personal than this. This struggle goes on within each disciple, both consciously and unconsciously.

James K. A. Smith highlights this quandary in exaggerated high relief with what he terms 'The Godfather problem'. In the bravura climax to the 1972 blockbuster movie *The Godfather*, mob boss Michael Corleone is seen taking his vows to be the godfather to his sister's baby. As he takes his solemn vows to serve Christ the movie repeatedly crosscuts to his life of violence and the murder of the heads of five rival mob families (Smith, 2017, pp. 166–8). The problem Smith identifies is that even when an individual is under the formative influence of the liturgy, it is possible to renounce the works of the devil while carrying them out at the same time. For Smith this is a visual parable of the challenge and critique that accompanies Christian discipleship. If we do not understand how our faith is affected by the world of which we are a part, and how we are to live our lives in that world, then our discipleship to Jesus is short-circuited and therefore cuts out (Vanhoozer et al., 2007, p. 16).

Culture forms us. We live within it. It provides us with the ability to perceive the world around us, the categories through which to understand it and the language to communicate what we see. We are held within its thrall. At one and the same time it both liberates us and holds us captive; it shapes us into the people we are becoming, but by the same process places limits on us. Because culture is in a perpetual motion through the choices and interactions of its subjects, what it enables and what it restricts are constantly changing too. This is the location of Christian discipleship. This is the context for the faithful obedience to everything Jesus commanded that is at the core of his call to 'go and make disciples' (Matt. 18.19–20). To fail to appreciate the active formative role of culture upon us is to leave us as passive and malleable subjects of the embedded structures of our surrounding culture and the shifting winds of its passing fads and fascinations. Added to which, as culture is the fruit of human activity it also reflects the fullness of human experience. Created by God and declared 'good', it is capable of producing a world that is rooted in truth, nobility, righteousness, purity, loveliness and excellence (Phil 4.8). Yet, at the same time, it also bears the marks of the 'fallenness' of humanity with all of its violence, greed, exploitation and abuse.

At the most fundamental level Christian discipleship must develop cultural self-awareness and cultural discernment. If it does not, it leaves itself prey to the cultural forces that surround it, vulnerable to being subverted as a cultural lackey rather than obedient to Christ. History is littered with examples of so-called Christian principles being used to justify the violence of the Crusades, the institutionalized racism of apartheid, or more recently the 'civilizational nationalism' of the Russian Orthodox Church that theologically underpins Putin's political ideology (Aridici, 2019, pp. 605–21), or the Christian nationalism in the United States that played a part in the 6 January 2021 attack on the United States Capitol (Gorski and Perry, 2022, pp. 1–2). From the grand scale of societal level issues like these into which individuals get caught up, to the more granular issues of everyday life, discernment is a prerequisite of discipleship. It is easy to look back at late Victorian ideas of holiness as quaintly of their time.

> They see no harm in such things as card-playing, theatre-going, dancing, incessant novel-reading, and Sunday-travelling, and they cannot in the least understand what you mean by objecting to them! (Ryle, 1956, p. 302)

It would perhaps be sobering to understand how future generations might look back to early twenty-first century expressions of faith. Will consumerism, individualism and a therapeutic approach to human need have led to a shallow and self-centred expression of faith, led and fed by churches and parachurch bodies run on principles imported from the 'successful' entrepreneurial enterprises of the business world? An expression of faith where the emphasis has been on the benefits gained in personal fulfilment, happiness and well-being. An embodiment of discipleship where the cost of discipleship in sacrifice, self-denial, perseverance and endurance has been neglected, if not lost altogether.

Now it is impossible for faith and culture not to mix. As John Stott wisely observed,

> Men and women, old and young, black and white, African and Asian, capitalist and socialist, waged and unwaged, middle-class and working-class, all read Scripture differently. (Stott, 1992, p. 190)

Indeed, contrary to the oft-quoted fifth-century Gallic monk, Vincent of Lérins, Christians have not everywhere and at all times believed the same things (Guarino, 2013, p. 2; Tanner, 1997, p. 124). The issue is not that Christianity always finds ways to contextualize itself into each successive culture, rather, it arises when elements of culture are taken up and either inappropriately modify faith or are themselves misconstrued as elements of the faith itself. When this happens and cultural norms are mistaken as 'theological non-negotiables', the result is syncretism because incompatible elements are blended into the practice of faith (Bailey, 2022, pp. 52–3).

The difficulty for the Christian disciple is that all this tension is wrapped up in issues of personal identity because of the way our cultural location plays a critical role in our own formation as a person. Then, sitting alongside identity, there are issues of belonging and purpose. This is a powerful and heady concoction that can easily assume control of our instinctive and intuitive faculties and our sense of self. What is required is nothing less than the discipling of our cultural imagination, but as Bailey wryly observes, this is easier said than done (Bailey, 2022, pp. 4–5; Wuthnow et al., 1984, p. 64).

If as disciples we are not to be merely unwitting stooges, domesticated by our cultural home, we need to develop our cultural nous. We need to be able to read the world around us and acquire skills in cultural literacy. But it also needs to go further than that. It has to be an applied discipline. It is about putting into practice the teaching of Jesus; it is about obeying all that he commanded in the circumstances of our lives. There is something deeper to be nurtured, an application of discernment that is rooted in a cultural savvy that understands practically what needs to be done, a cultural sagacity that consistently makes good and sound judgements upon which to act. Like the proverbial Israelite tribe of Issachar, 'who had understanding of the times, to know what Israel ought to do' (1 Chron. 12.32).

Trying to picture and conceptualize what this might look like is not easy. It is held in the tension between Walls' indigenizing and pilgrim principles.[1] We are thoroughly a part of our cultural home as indigenized people, yet our loyalty to Christ at the same time establishes a critical distance and, when required, a higher allegiance. Miroslav Volf also underlines this notion of 'critical distance' and suggests of Christian disciples, 'They are distant, and yet they belong' (Volf, 1996, p. 49). However, in seeking to establish a critical distance that safeguards Christian distinctiveness, the degree of separation significantly understates the intimate and powerful influence of a cultural home and the lived reality of day-to-day life. Help cannot be found in Hauerwas and Willimon's concept of 'resident aliens' because it is not fit for purpose in this regard, having been conceived to address an altogether different theological concern regarding the nature of the church. It would imply that disciples do not properly belong to their surrounding culture. Graham Cray's 'dual citizenship' idea of disciples belonging to both the Kingdom of God and a nation state is a more helpful idea, but it too falls short (Cray, 2007, pp. 9, 22). Culture is far more complex and multi-layered than the arrangement of contemporary geo-political boundaries or some idealized notion of a single, uniform Christian culture allow.

The theological understanding of the mutual indwelling of members of the trinity in perichoresis is probably a better conceptual analogy, and Jesus' use of the metaphors of yeast and salt can also stand scrutiny in this regard. We are both distinctively Christian and culturally immersed. These two realities constantly interrelate and interact with each other, producing an ever-changing, multi-dimensional life which is the life of faith in Christ. Steve Turner puts it like this: 'God entrusts culture to us – the ability to create it, enjoy it and critique it' (Turner, 2013, p. 56). Or, as William Edgar indicates, God has generously given us the world to enjoy and develop, which, while taking a sinister turn because of the fall, in Christ can be extended into God's shalom of goodness, justice and love (Edgar, 2017, p. 177).

It is 'radically reimagining and resituating one's entire life within the story of Jesus' (Loughlin, 1996, p. 134) that is the key to holding all this together. Through the public and private reading of the Scriptures, Christian disciples live within two narratives, that of their own life and alongside it the biblical arc viewed through the lens of devotion to Jesus. Whether by liturgical osmosis and the good offices of the lectionary or the personal discipline of Bible study, discipleship involves owning this biblical story as 'my story' and understanding each through the insights of the other. At the very heart of this is a process of mimetic learning as we copy in our own life what we see and understand from the Scriptures (Holmes, 2021, pp. 14–16).[2]

Faithful presence

'In searching for an answer ... one discovers endless complexity ... perplexing disparities [and] ...elements of irony and tragedy, but also assurance and possibility (Hunter, 2010a, p. ix). So wrote the American sociologist James Davison Hunter, famous for identifying and popularizing an understanding of the 'culture wars' in the United States in the 1990s – a work that proved to be particularly prescient (Hunter, 1991). In 2010 he recognized that in wrestling with how faith related to culture he was engaged in an issue of broadly academic interest that was also deeply personal. For the believer, the disciple, how to live out their faith, while simply expressed, needs to be made sense of among bewildering realities.

Writing from an American perspective where Christian cultural engagement was highly politicized, Hunter wanted to argue for a very different vision, a different paradigm altogether. He saw both the conservative right and progressive left as being 'functional Nietzscheans', with their campaigning and action fuelled by 'ressentiment' – Nietzsche's term for a hostility directed toward the cause of perceived problems and frustrations – as they sought to win people to their cause, adopt their Christian worldview and accomplish a bottom-up democratic transformation of society. Such a view of cultural change, supposedly exemplified by individuals like William Wilberforce, held that 'If you have the courage, hold to the right values ... with an adequate Christian worldview, you too can change the world.' For Hunter, such an approach is 'almost wholly mistaken' and certainly 'deeply flawed' (Hunter, 2010b,). This is because it does not take account of how culture is formed by, and deeply embedded in, 'elites, networks, technology, and new institutions'. When ideas and values do move history, it is not so much because they are inherently truthful or obviously correct but rather that they are advantageous to a culture's institutional

CULTURAL HERMENEUTICS

infrastructure and to some degree already embedded within it (Hunter, 2010a, p. 17).

For Hunter, Christians need to stop talking about 'redeeming the culture', 'building the kingdom' and 'transforming the world' and recover instead what it means to be a 'faithful presence'. The point is not to change the world so much as to serve the world faithfully as individuals and as a community of faith, in all our relationships, tasks and spheres of influence. If the former carries with it a sense of conquest, control and power through the coercive means provided by the state, the latter models itself on Jesus. His use of power was derivative, in that it came from his intimacy with his Father and submission to his will; it was humble because he rejected status and reputation; it was compassionate and served the good of all; and it was noncoercive, blessing rather than cursing 'the other' (Hunter, 2010a, pp. 187–93, 280; Hunter, 2010b).

Looking at how an understanding of 'faithfulness' has been used by Christians in relation to wider culture, Hunter identifies three general orientations or paradigms of 'defence against', 'relevance to' and 'purity from'. With the 'defence against' response, Protestant Fundamentalists, mainstream Evangelicals and conservative Catholics look to create a defensive enclave to the wider secular world with parallel institutions in music, education and the like. They feel displaced from the centre of society's life and live in hope of the time when a Christian worldview will again hold sway, underpinned by Christian values and moral understanding. Those aspiring for a 'relevance to' the wider culture were historically drawn from theological liberalism, though more recently they have been joined by a variety of 'seeker church' and 'emerging church' movements. For Hunter, they take their cues almost exclusively from the contemporary world around them yet offer very little in return. Those pursuing 'purity from' cultural engagement have given up on an irredeemable world and seek to preserve the historic truths of Christian faith in authentic and distinctive communities that withdraw from a full-on cultural engagement. The focus of concern for purity may differ: for example, Pentecostals and Evangelicals may be more focused on sexual sin while neo-

Anabaptists focus on the violence built into contemporary capitalism and political processes. The common outcome is an 'us and them' view of the world. All three approaches carry something important about Christian life and witness, though each makes a significant sacrifice too. The objective of relevance does so by inversely losing its distinctiveness, while defending distinctiveness can become confrontational and aggressive, often about trivialities. Purity from the world is most often accompanied by having disengaged, withdrawn and given up on the world altogether (Hunter, 2010a, pp. 213–19, 223–4). And so Hunter poses the leading question:

> How can one be authentically Christian in circumstances that, by their very nature, undermine the credibility and coherence of faith? What is an authentically biblical way of existing in a pluralistic world in which Christianity will never be anything other than one culture among others ... What does it mean for a believer to be faithful in this generation? (Hunter, 2010a, p. 224)

For Hunter, his advocacy of Christians rediscovering their vocation to be a 'faithful presence' is grounded in the character of God who is 'fully and faithfully present' to us. Not merely in terms of the suggested proximity of immanent omnipresence, but in *'Pursuit, identification, [and] the offer of life through sacrificial love* – this is what God's faithful presence means' (Hunter, 2010a, p. 243). Though estranged, we are sought out and pursued. In 'being born in human likeness' (Phil. 2.7) incarnation seals God's identification with us in Christ and the divine knowledge of our humanity is intimately internalized. Jesus then proclaims and demonstrates the offer of 'abundant life' (John 10.10) 'marked by goodness, peace, truth, beauty, joy, fruitfulness ... the shalom of flourishing'. And all is made possible by sacrificial love, 'not that we loved God but that he loved us and sent his Son to be the atoning sacrifice for our sins' (1 John 4.10). This understanding of the faithful presence of God is taken up and underlined by David Fitch as he further draws attention to God's active presence throughout the whole of the biblical narrative, but especially after Pentecost through the body of Christ, the church (Fitch, 2016, pp. 19–26). For Fitch, taking up Hunter's vision in the practice of 'faithful presence' is essential for the life of discipleship in the world.

Exploring the contours of a 'shalom of flourishing' towards which the Christian community should strive, Hunter suggests that faith, hope and love can be seen as corresponding to meaning, purpose and the intimacy and affection of belonging. These qualities of life then begin to indicate the kind of substance that 'faithful presence' brings to the wider community as disciples seek to 'nurture and cultivate' the world of which they are a part. This kind of whole-life or public discipleship is then the lived embodiment of the Kingdom of God and Jesus' call to 'love your neighbour as yourself' (Matt. 22.39). Indeed, Hunter goes so far as to suggest that a theology of 'faithful presence' places disciples under an 'obligation' to shape patterns of life, work and relationship towards a shalom that seeks the welfare of everyone (Hunter, 2010a, pp. 254, 262–3; Cray, 2007, pp. 9, 22).

In conversation with James K. A. Smith, Hunter was asked to speculate what the American church would look like in fifty years if the present generation became committed to the principles of 'faithful presence'. Hunter replied:

> Needless to say, it is important not to be utopian. Christians would be far from perfect but the church would be at the center of their lives, for worship and formation. These churches would be multiethnic but also multiclass; their population, not unlike the population of the larger community. They would ... [engage] in their creative care for the dispossessed, but their engagement with the world would not end there. They would be active and productive in every sphere of life – the service industry, skilled labor, education, business, philanthropy, science, medicine, law, the arts, academia, and, yes, politics too, and at every level, for there would not only be theologies to support them but resources to prepare, launch, and sustain them ... they pursue excellence in all spheres of life, they would be engaged in the most difficult problems of

the day. The church would likely be smaller than it is today but only where the acids of modernity would further dissolve the residues of cultural Christianity ... In fifty years, there is no question in my mind that Christians would be considered even more odd than they are today by virtue of what they believe and the morality by which they live, and yet because they are fully engaged in each sphere of life as individuals and communities of character, they would serve as a credible and creditable conscience of the overlapping communities they inhabit. Odd, to be sure, but no one would deny that they do extraordinary good in the world.

In looking forward Hunter is quite clear that Christians must understand the unique and evolving nature that culture presents to them. 'If the context for faithfulness has changed, then it means the challenge to faithfulness ... has changed as well' (Hunter, 2010a, p. 199). This constant shifting of the cultural context, along with his admission that 'faithful presence' must not be portrayed as a utopian solution and that Christians, even at their best, will not create a perfect world, led to modest claims for the fruit of such living. He concluded, 'through the practice of faithful presence, it is possible ... that they will help to make the world a little bit better' (Hunter, 2010a, p. 186).[3]

So, to return to Highmore's questions, what are we doing when we identify something as cultural and what does this allow us to do? For the Christian disciple, understanding the nature of the cultural world in which they live and its theological implications is vitally important. It means that they are not passive actors who have been blindly inculturated by their host society. Understanding their cultural context restores their agency to practise 'inculturated discipleship', discipleship that is attuned to their context while maintaining their fidelity to Christ. A practice of 'faithful presence' liberates them to live life in all its fullness by discerning thoughtfully, engaging wisely and serving selflessly.

Theological chutzpah

> From one ancestor he made all *cultures* to inhabit the whole earth and he allotted the times of their existence and the boundaries of the places where they would live. (Acts 17.26)

If we are to properly inhabit our world, understanding the all-embracing cultural nature of our reality that extends from its Theo-cultural creation to the Eschato-cultural vision, theology must engage with culture. The last century profoundly opened up our comprehension of the complex, shifting and powerfully influential forces of which culture itself is comprised. It is therefore vitally important for theology to properly engage with culture. Theology too must fully take its 'cultural turn'. This will not be accomplished by merely baptizing the cultural disciplines into a Christianized version of themselves. It has to be a much more thoroughgoing endeavour than that. Neither can it be achieved by a missiological push to understand culture and construct a bridge for missional engagement. It has to go much deeper than this. This is not to set aside the knowledge, analysis and insight of the cultural disciplines, because in the paraphrased maxim of St Augustine, 'all truth is God's truth'. Such understanding is of vital importance. Neither is it to downplay the significance of Christian mission, because to cite another oft-quoted maxim, 'the church exists by mission as a fire exists by burning'. The full observation of Emil Brunner from which this is drawn goes on to highlight how, in the absence of mission, both the church and faith cease to exist (Brunner, 1931, p. 108).

To fully engage its own 'cultural turn' theology needs to properly embrace it in the process of Christian formation, both of individual believers and the communities of which they are a part. Of course, theology already infuses such formation from a whole variety of directions and a number of different theological 'voices' are readily identifiable. Looking to make sense of the complex and dynamic processes involved in Christian practice, the Action Research Church and Society (or ARCS) team, an ecumenical and interdisciplinary research group, helpfully highlighted four such voices. Normative theology, formal theology, espoused theology and operant theology each contribute to the ongoing experience of 'faith seeking understanding' that shapes discipleship and informs action (Cameron et al., 2010, pp. 53–6). In this, normative theology provides the theological authority for a practising Christian group and can include Scripture, liturgy and official church teaching; formal theology is located in the academy with 'professional' theologians and also embraces interdisciplinary dialogue; espoused theology is that embedded within a given group's articulation of its own beliefs; while operant theology is what is actually expressed by being embedded in its actions. The ARCS team offer this heuristic and hermeneutical framework as a device to make the complex layers of theology at work in Christian communities manageable. In doing so they freely acknowledge its limitations as a device that does not claim to be exhaustive in its analysis or that other approaches might be equally useful. In addition, they recognized that the voices, while distinct, are far from being discrete and are better understood as interrelated and overlapping while in a constant process of interacting evolution.

While the ARCS framework is particularly insightful, any recognition and inclusion of the cultural issues in play only emerge when derived through one of the four voices. This highlights the need to

> develop the theoretical basis and practical tools for a properly theological analysis of cultural contexts, with a view to equipping the church to be able to engage contemporary realities with theological truth. (Holmes, 2008, p. x)

What is needed is for theology to develop a new voice, an interpretive voice, a voice of the theology of cultural hermeneutics. This is the description and analysis of culture through a theological lens. While there have been some notable exceptions over the years, these have most frequently been issue-based theological treatments of wider social campaigns, from nuclear disarmament and inner-city poverty to the environmental concerns of the climate crisis. These forays into a theological engagement with culture tend themselves to be led by wider movements in contemporary culture to which the church is playing an internal game of 'catch up'. The reverse of this is the cultural angst that is generated by a culture that is perceived as moving away from its inherited Christian norms. Here the church is engaged in what appears to be a rearguard action of resistance to change that it seems impotent to affect. The truth is that society was probably never as 'Christian' as, in hindsight, it is perceived to have been. It is fascinating that the influential Wesleyan commentator and preacher, Hugh Price Hughes, writing at the height of Victorian religiosity, could complain that the nation's educated elite had been 'consciously or unconsciously, dominated by the social ideals of Plato, Aristotle, Cicero, and Horace [but] ... have never studied either Isaiah or St. John' (Hughes, 1894, p. 1).

Having been largely on the back foot during the wider 'cultural turn', theology now needs to find its place more firmly and clearly if it is to find its new interpretive voice of cultural hermeneutics. If Christ is indeed 'Lord of all', if in Kuyper's words, 'there is not a square inch in the whole domain of our human existence over which Christ, who is sovereign of all, does not cry: "Mine!",' Christians have every right to engage with culture, to analyse and interpret it. Indeed, if religion is a part of culture, those engaged in the study and analysis of culture must grant a place to theology's account of things. If culture is always an aspect of our contact with reality and any form of cultural enquiry is a quest in search of 'the real' that lies behind it (Highmore, 2016, p. 119), then theology is particularly experienced and well-equipped to join the search. It has a long history of seeking to make sense of life across the centuries and the cultures that inhabited them. So those who share in the task from other disciplines must embrace the commitment of theology to speak truthfully about present realities (Marsh, 2004, pp. 129–30; Holmes, 2008, p. x). Indeed, there is a certain 'brazenness' in theology's persistence in believing that there is truth that lies behind appearances, a reality that when seen can become a revelation (Cobb, 2005, p.71). This places theology in a strong position to fully engage with its own 'cultural turn'.

Now Kathryn Tanner makes an obvious point in recognizing the significance of an anthropological understanding that suggests theology to be a form of cultural activity. It is clearly a human product that bears the marks of its historical and social context like any other human activity (Tanner, 1997, p. 63). However, this is what makes the task of voicing a cultural hermeneutic a 'slippery' endeavour for theology. As cultural beings, any theological reading of culture immediately runs the risk of confirming our own theological predispositions as authentic (Bailey, 2022, p. 9). The danger of syncretism is always knocking at the door. Yet we can never even begin such an engagement with culture without already having a location that triangulates against our faith, our spiritual experiences and our theological convictions. We can do no other than read culture in this way if our description is to be both genuine and faithful to our discipleship. Theology has to have the confidence to own its place in the cultural conversation. This will involve it not only in offering its own critique, but also in being open to scrutiny from the other direction, where its own internal convictions and presuppositions can be tested for coherence, fidelity and inappropriate cultural contamination. A certain degree of theological chutzpah is an advantage in this regard.

A theological engagement in cultural hermeneutics has a dual function. Inwardly it both enables and resources the process of reflection and self-awareness. This knowledge of self, place and context is vital for an inculturated discipleship that remains true to Jesus, the outward expression of faith. This outward expression also has a further dimension. When faith understands its context and why it does what it does, it also has something to say to the wider world. At one level this is what Elaine Graham has called the 'apologetics of presence', comprised of a threefold hermeneutic of discernment, participation and witness (Graham, 2017, pp. 124–5). Further to this is the exercise of a relevant and comprehensible prophetic engagement. Such a role might come as something of a surprise to those who consider theology to be 'little more than the curator of a museum of heritage. [Tending] to the relics of western "civilization"'

(P. Fletcher, 2009, p. xi). Indeed, it pushes back against the unquestioned cultural quarantining of religious discourse in public life that has come to typify contemporary Western culture with a misconstrued, and misapplied, understanding of the separation of church and state. In doing so it also responds to the unexpected evolution in the thinking of Jürgen Habermas, the Marxist atheist sociologist, in which he advocates the participation of people of faith in the public square to help refine societies' 'moral intuitions' (Portier, 2011, p. 426; Habermas et al., 2010). A further consequence of the cultural quarantining of religious discourse in the West has been an increasing lack of religious literacy and theological understanding. In a world where God has not gone away and religion has a 'new visibility', many disciplines are ill-equipped to properly understand what they see and to articulate an appropriate response (Berger, 1999; Hoelzl and Ward, 2008; Micklethwait and Wooldridge, 2009; Graham, 2017, pp. 1–2, 5).

In a very real sense, the acquisition of an interpretive voice of cultural hermeneutics is theology in a different mode. This is not theology providing the normative touchstone of orthodoxy or a formal theology from the academy with its intellectual expression of faith. It is not the internally embraced understanding of an espoused theology or the lived reality of an operant theology; it is of a different order. It will, of course, embody elements of each of these, but it is different to all of them. It is inquisitive of the world around it and wants to understand what is going on. It knows no boundaries to the range of its investigative activities and is interrogative of what it discovers. It wants to comprehend the world around it on its own terms before it begins any theological engagement. However, it does have the audacity to engage culture theologically and seeks to identify its theological nature, whether that is explicitly articulated or unconsciously implied. It is the resources of faith that shape the lens to bring everything into focus as the Scriptures, theological tradition and the experience of the people of faith provide the theological means to see. And the 'everything' also includes theology's own cultural embeddedness which, when addressed by the truth of the subject it is exploring, may find that this truth also has its own liberating power that sets it free in new and unexpected ways from its own cultural bondage.

Reading culture through a theological lens

> Do not be conformed to this *generation,* but be transformed by the renewing of your minds, so that you may discern what is the will of God – what is good and acceptable and perfect. (Rom. 12.2)

Interpreting Scripture has been foundational for Christian faith from the very beginning. Indeed, to start at the very beginning, when Jesus sits down to explain the Jewish Scriptures to his disciples, the discipline of biblical hermeneutics in the Christian tradition is born. By the Middle Ages this discipline had developed, through the insights of the early church fathers, into the four-fold method of interpretation known as *the Quadriga.* Classically expressed by John Cassian (*c.* 360–435) it provided a guiding framework for interpreting the text of the Bible for a thousand years. First, the text had to be understood literally before it could then, secondly, be opened up allegorically, 'in faith', to produce spiritual understanding. The third move, 'in love', led to the tropological revelation of moral insight that leads to action. Then, with Cassian's own contribution, the text could be addressed anagogically, 'in hope', to bestow a foretaste and anticipation of heaven itself (Johnston, 2007, p.305–6).

While, then, hermeneutics is hardly new to Christian theology, it has almost wholly been centred on understanding and interpreting the biblical text. Yet the contemporary use of hermeneutics in the wider world now spans and embraces philosophy, literary studies and semiology alongside its deployment in more general contexts. Fascinatingly, this broader use of the discipline can itself be tracked back, through Schleiermacher, to the earliest modern use of the term that appeared in J. C. Dannhauer's *Sacred Hermeneutics, or the Method of Expounding the Sacred Scriptures* of 1654 (Bühler, 2000, p. 295). It is, of course, fitting to note that after two centuries of development as an autonomous discipline, the application of hermeneutical insights has come full circle with the tools of the discipline now thoroughly incorporated into contemporary biblical studies.

Through missiology and contextual, intercultural and philosophical theology the wider 'cultural turn' has already had an impact. Missiology seeks to better understand its cultural setting and therefore more effectively bridge the gap between the Christian community and those beyond its boundaries. In counterpoint to this outward reach, developments in contextual, intercultural and philosophical theology have facilitated an inward-facing theological reflection that explores how culture shapes theology. Yet if Christianity is to fully embrace its own 'cultural turn' it must take one further step and learn how theology can more adequately 'read' culture. Its understanding of the hermeneutical or interpretive task needs to be outwardly deployed as well as inwardly engaged. In doing so it will discover that this is not wholly unfamiliar terrain, and that many of the necessary skills have already been acquired over many centuries of faithful interpretation of the biblical material. As Paul wrote to the Romans, it is about engaging, renewing and transforming the mind in the process of discerning the will of God. And to do so not merely in social acquiescence and conformity to the world around us, but in understanding what it means for the daily life of a disciple to be an act of worship through being a 'living sacrifice' (Rom. 12.1–2).

In some senses the models of theological reflection that have been developed within the sphere of Practical Theology have been helpful in shifting attention outwards by focusing reactively on the issues thrown up by Christian living and ministry in real-life situations. The widespread use of the 'Pastoral Cycle' model and its variants is illustrative of this. Popularized by the Latin American liberation theologians of the late 1970s, the innovation of this approach to theological reflection was to begin and end with lived experience. The process of identifying live issues and analysing them before then introducing theological elements into the reflection and swiftly moving on to determine an appropriate response was quickly and widely taken up around the world. The departure from using the Bible or doctrine as the starting point for theological reflection was its primary, if at times strongly contested, contribution to late twentieth-century Christian thinking. However, this is still a long way from a fully engaged theological immersion in cultural hermeneutics. Some of the steps to help us get there can be gleaned from the insights of the other disciplines that seek to read and interpret the culture around them. To these can be added the fruit of missiological reflections that have sought to understand the cultural location of the community to which the gospel is to be demonstrated and shared.

From Geertz's 'thick description' to Rorty's 'redescription', the ability to capture what something is like is clearly the essential component that makes its interpretation possible. However, with the insight of cultural studies, Ben Highmore states the obvious, that this is not an objective, rationalistic or scientific process. Rather it is a creative and inventive endeavour that seeks to illuminate the essence of experience. The end result needs to be the articulation of 'experiential maps' that move between the anecdotal evidence and systematic observation, and from the microscopic to a macro view (Highmore, 2016, pp. 102–3). All this goes to the relationship between language and reality, between words and what our words represent that is beyond them.

Samuel Hayakawa and the 'ladder of abstraction'

These ideas are elegantly captured by the American semanticist, Samuel Hayakawa, as he popularized the idea of the 'ladder of abstraction' with reference to the case of 'Bessie the Cow'. His account is rendered like this. Recognizing how extremely limited our senses are, we have to acknowledge that how we see and feel things is constrained by the 'peculiarities of our nervous systems'. It is therefore absurd to think that we perceive anything as it really is. Enter Bessie, who is identified as a cow. She has a life from the microscopic level to her life on the farm and in the herd, of which we only see a small fraction. Then, of course, she is not some static 'object' but a living, breathing animal whose life is a dynamic process. However, from the small fraction of what we experience of Bessie in how she looks, moves, sounds and feels, from our past experience we can identify her as 'a cow'.

'Bessie the cow', as the object of our experience, is an abstraction by our own perceptions of something outside ourselves. In the process we disregard all the differences between Bessie and other cows, indeed between Bessie as she was in the past and will be in the future. Ignoring too the gulf between the relatively static idea of a cow and the 'whirl of eventfulness' that is Bessie's life. The 'Ladder of Abstraction' then progresses as we move from Bessie the animal to the category of cow that itself leaves out the specifics of different breeds of cows and the individual peculiarities of individual cows. Further abstractions up the ladder see Bessie categorized as 'livestock', 'farm assets', 'an asset' and finally as 'wealth'.

In looking to unpick the mystery of how we know what we know, Hayakawa makes the observation that all we know is such abstractions. They may be low-level abstractions like 'Bessie', or high-level ones like 'wealth'. They are a necessary shorthand that enables us to navigate the reality they represent. The test of any abstraction is not whether it is 'high' or 'low', or that they are referrable to lower levels. Accurate thinkers, like interesting writers, informative speakers and well-adjusted individuals, need to be able to move 'quickly and gracefully' between the levels 'with minds as lithe and deft and beautiful as monkeys in a tree' (Hayakawa, 1952, pp. 165–80).

Michael Polyani and 'tacit knowledge'

Michael Polyani was also fascinated by how we know what we know. A Hungarian born refugee from Hitler's Berlin in 1933, he was to hold professorships at the Victoria University of Manchester successively in chemistry and the social sciences. A friend and colleague of computer pioneer Alan Turing and correspondent with Albert Einstein, Polyani considered his greatest discovery his work on 'tacit knowledge'. As a scientist he came to believe that the role of the imagination and intuition in our knowing was far greater than was acknowledged or accepted. For him all knowledge is personal and rests upon our personal judgements and personal commitments (Johnston, 2007, pp. 163–5). These in turn are shaped and informed by our mental life that is sustained by 'works of art, morality, religious worship, scientific theory and other articulate systems that we accept as our dwelling place'. When we overlook the contribution that these make to our knowing we falsify our conception of truth (Polanyi, 1964, p. 286). Undergirding it all, we believe more than we can prove and know more than we can say, like riding a bicycle (Polanyi, 1964, pp. 49–50). It is at this level of 'tacit knowledge' that our intuitional and imaginative life is also at work, enabling us to 'see' when two distinct and separate ideas or experiences come together and make a connection. This is how discoveries are made, knowledge is deepened and insight gained.

Believing that a purely scientific description of the world was sterile and empty, Polanyi maintained that the real goal of humanity was meaning – a sense of meaning that was itself pursued through humanity's passion for discovery and sustained by a faith in 'the hunch' that sought to test and reveal its truth (Johnston, 2007, p. 163).

Poststructuralism and the emergence of cultural analysis

In many ways Polanyi anticipated some of the emphases that were to enter into the popular domain in the latter decades of the twentieth century through the intellectual fascination with postmodernism. As Steve Holmes observed, 'the postmodern turn in recent Western cultures has made cultural analysis central to almost all forms of public discourse; to not be engaging with culture is to be cut off from most intellectually serious people' (Holmes, 2008, p. 19). As early as the inter-war years Virginia Woolf and George Orwell had begun to offer readings of popular postcards and posters that critics had long felt lacked the substance and gravity to be worth bothering with (Childs, 2006, p. 2).

As postmodernism and its sibling poststructuralism[4] gained ground, the whole of culture increasingly became open to scrutiny. Not only the artefacts of popular culture from music and the cinema to advertising and fashion, but events, movements and social processes too (Cobb, 2005, p. 22). Indeed, it would be simplistic to view culture as just about ideas and things because it is very much about experience and feelings as well. The place of memory and the senses as an integral part of culture make it 'a semantically dense object' (Highmore, 2016, pp. 108–11). Ultimately, a central element of poststructuralist thinking is that culture in all its forms can be 'read' like the text of a book. Thus, just as literary criticism can take the text of a book and examine it in its cultural context, so culture and its artefacts can be taken and 'read' according to literary approaches (Baldwin et al., 1999, p. 40).

John Austin and speech/act theory[5]

Looking to understand the component parts of reading culture, the *speech/act theory* introduced by British philosopher John Austin is particularly useful. In his 1955 William James lectures delivered at Harvard and later published in his classic *How To Do Things With Words* (1962), he suggests a three-fold understanding of illocutionary, locutionary and perlocutionary acts. These are the component parts of communication and discourse: the illocutionary acts that sit behind what we say or write, informing, ordering and shaping them; the locutionary act itself in which we express ourselves; and the perlocution, the acts or effects the communication has on those who hear or read it (Austin, 1962, p. 108). Thinking in terms of reading culture, Vanhoozer helpfully suggests that the triad of illocution-locution–perlocution can also be viewed alongside the parallel triads of author-text-reader and 'the world behind, of, and in front of the text, a three-world approach (Vanhoozer et al., 2007, p. 49).

This tri-focus approach is more readily obvious in cultural hermeneutics when looking at a particular artefact of culture such as a book, a movie, a piece of architecture and so forth. However, it is also useful in more nebulous cultural phenomena from Brexit to American Christian nationalism, or K-pop to wokeness. In this regard the triad explores the context behind the cultural trend, the phenomena themselves and then the impact or effect they have.

The world behind ...

In exploring the world, or context, that sits behind any cultural expression, its illocution, the prevailing worldview is significant. For example, the wholesale Americanization of Korean culture following the Korean War (1950–53) will have contributed significantly to the development of K-pop and its embrace of the Western music industry. By contrast, the legacy of empire led to the contrasting attitudes to those of other cultures that Zygmunt Bauman highlighted as mixophilia and mixophobia (Bauman, 2007, pp. 87–93), with the latter winning the 2016 Brexit referendum by 51.9% to 48.1% among the highly divided 33.5m who registered their vote (Uberoi, 2016, p. 3). Exploring through 'thick description' what shapes and drives a cultural expression also requires what Paul Ricoeur termed the 'hermeneutics of suspicion'. This is an approach that, in its act of interpreting, is asking the telling questions of who benefits and where power resides. The 'hermeneutics of suspicion' looks to identify and unmask that which is hidden or disguised.

> The 'hermeneutics of suspicion' is the name usually bestowed on this technique of reading texts against the grain and between the lines, of cataloging their omissions and laying bare their contradictions, of rubbing in what they fail to know and cannot represent. While suspicion can manifest itself in multiple ways, in the current intellectual climate it often pivots on a fealty to the clarifying power of historical context. What the literary text does not see, in this line of thought, are the larger

circumstances that shape and sustain it and that are drawn into the light by the corrective force of the critic's own vigilant gaze. (Felski, 2011, p. 574)

Ricoeur himself was inspired by the three 'masters of suspicion', Marx, Freud and Nietzsche. Of course, their own respective ideological preoccupations would each have resulted in very different hermeneutical frameworks and interpretive conclusions, most of which would have been reductionist in their outcomes, distilling the substance of their insight into Freudian psychodynamics, Marxist economics or Nietzschean nihilism. Such ideologically informed interpretation is not necessarily a bad thing. Feminist, black, queer and postcolonial approaches illustrate this well as having a proven track record in exposing injustice, prejudice and the hidden tentacles of cultural power as they reach into the fabric of our lives. The mistake is for any single ideological approach to be seen as the only pathway to enlightenment. The truth is that there are a great many approaches that can be taken, each of which, in Edward Said's observation, will result in an interpretive reading that is more of a 'production than an excavation of meaning'. To illustrate this Peter Childs takes sixteen subjects (from the ethics of Harry Potter to Amazonian democracy) to be interrogated by sixteen different critical approaches (from trauma theory to historicism) and observes that even within his small book 256 different readings are possible. Indeed, with Terry Eagleton he acknowledges that it is even more complicated than that. As we interpret, we are reading and thinking backwards and forwards at the same time, predicting and recollecting, while being aware of other possibilities that we have not pursued (Childs, 2006, pp. 8–9).

> Where 'the world behind ...' sits more on one individual, the author of a book or the director of a movie, a series of questions about authorial intent, the individual's wider body of work or, indeed, the psychological and psychoanalytical questions around their formative experiences. (Lynch, 2005, p. 120)

The world of ...

The second world to explore is the one that the cultural artefact or expression inhabits, the locution or its tangible articulation. It is vitally important that it is understood on its own terms rather than merely to be a foil for the readers' already pre-formed convictions, judgements and prejudices. If we are to be able to 'read' it, we need to know where it is located and what 'language' it is expressed in. To read a written text we literally need to be able to read the language in which its written, but to be able to 'read' a painting, an advertisement or a movie we need to be able to 'speak' the language of art, advertising or the cinema. How does each respectively go about embodying and expressing what they seek to communicate? What are the rules and conventions by which they abide? What does their essence stand for? The same is also true for anything that might become the focus of cultural scrutiny. The world of sports and leisure, politics and social movements and religion and belief systems can all be similarly scrutinized. Take the world of cricket and the controversy that broke with Yorkshire County Cricket Club in 2020, when the club was accused of institutional racism by their former player and sometime captain Azeem Rafiq. Here the worlds, languages and identities of cricket, race and Yorkshire all come into play to properly understand and read this cultural moment (Fletcher, 2021).

Taken to the next level, the prospective reader of culture needs to understand what 'kind', or genre, of cultural text or expression they are seeking to read. The written word, for example, can be poetry or prose, fiction or non-fiction, news reporting, propaganda, or a personal journal, a social media posting and so on. The kind of text you read subtly, or not so subtly, changes your manner of reading and significantly advances your chances of understanding what it is all about. Having established this the analysis can begin. What is being said and embodied? How is that being pursued or accomplished – by logical argument? By emotional engagement? By positive association? Is its purpose clearly stated and transparently acted upon or is it more implicit, if not hidden or misleading? What are the mechanics and dynamics in play? How does it work, and to what end? What does it mean to live in the world of this cultural artefact or expression? Cultural texts, expressions and movements provide the rubric of the world we live in. They provide us with metaphors, examples and aphorisms that enable us to comprehend the life we live, and a vision of what we aspire for it to be or the nightmare we desperately want to avoid. During the Brexit debate it was the slogans of 'Take Back Control', 'We Want Our Country Back', 'Believe in Britain' and 'Global Britain' that expressed the deeper-lying dis-ease with the European Union that led to the success of the Leave Campaign. Beneath each of these clarion calls is a narrative of commentary on what was then perceived to be the state of the nation and the direction to be taken to address it.

The world in front ...

The third world of exploration is the world in front of the cultural artefact or expression, the perlocution, the realm of the response. Vanhoozer makes the point that every time we are addressed by a cultural artefact or expression we have to make a choice (Vanhoozer et al., 2007, pp. 52–3). Where will we live? In Ricoeur's scheme, do we *appropriate* the offer of a new way of seeing and living that is offered to our imagination, or do we not? Then the next step, rather than just projecting ourselves into the imagined world presented to us, do we apprehend the substance of it into our life and thereby enlarge our life as a result (Ricoeur, 2016, pp. 145–6).

In microcosm it is the world of advertising that offers a focused and accelerated example of the world in front of the cultural expression and the immediacy of its call for a response. Advertising generates vast sums of revenue for broadcasters, social media platforms and any other medium that can carry its messages to a desired audience. It does this because it works. By creating a visceral link to its targeted demographic, it acts as a mirror that reflects back to society what it holds most dear

(Vanhoozer et al., 2007, p. 54). Indeed, it can act as an echo chamber that perpetuates the status quo, which is always the danger in any response to a cultural artefact or expression: that it merely becomes an exercise in confirmation bias as we reinforce the ideas and values that we already hold most valuable. However, every cultural artefact and expression that we engage with provides us with a choice. Does it confirm our present convictions as we accept and re-embrace it, or do we acknowledge its challenge and incorporate its insight and essence into the way we live our lives? From the ubiquitous memes of social media to the evolving mores of our wider culture, and from the cutting-edge ideas of high fashion and the academy to the values embodied in *Strictly Come Dancing* and *The Great British Bake Off*, the persistent question is what we allow to shape us.

Moving between the worlds

When looking to engage in cultural analysis it is almost impossible to treat each of the three worlds as hermetically sealed spheres of engagement. They freely bleed into one another and make the task altogether more messy and seemingly chaotic than ordered minds are naturally comfortable with. Literary and film studies provide a good example of what this looks like when engaging in the analytical task. The approaches they take necessarily inhabit a variety of dimensions and perspectives and therefore require a deftness and agility to navigate.

Connected since the birth of cinema if not before, with Eisenstein and others identifying a 'film sense' in art long before the emergence of cinema (Goodwin, 1979, p. 227), literary and film studies together bridge the gap between old art and new. While film studies is a very young discipline that has paralleled the growth of interest in cultural analysis, literary criticism's pedigree stretches back to the classical era and Aristotle's *Poetics*. Together they also straddle written and visual expression with a proliferation of exchanges between literary works and films, with one estimate identifying 30% of films deriving from novels and 80% of best-sellers being adapted for the big screen. Those within the disciplines see them as having a particular contribution to make to the wider study of culture (Corrigan, 2012, pp. 2–3). If culture is to be 'read', then the disciplines that 'read' literature and cinema clearly have experience and insight to be drawn upon to inform any such 'reading' that embraces both language-based and visual embodiment.

In their heralded introduction to literary theory and criticism, Andrew Bennett and Nicholas Royle are keen from the outset to demonstrate how different approaches and schools of thought interrelate and overlap. Siloed thinking in this regard can be as restricting as it is intimidating. Thus when a more fully creative, fluid and cross-fertilizing approach is taken, the insights of any given school of thought are more clearly accessible to being grasped. It is only in the interaction between, for example, a biographical and historical analysis that seeks to understand the author through a detailed study of the text itself and how its structure, plot and characterization work, and interpretive filters like those of psychoanalytical or ideological theory, that new, distinctive and stimulating insights can emerge (Bennett and Royle, 2016, pp. ix–x, xiii).

The *New York Times* review of Hemingway's first novel, *The Sun Also Rises*, demonstrates this freedom to move adroitly between the worlds as it addresses the phenomenon of 'the lost generation' that emerged between the two world wars:

> Mr. Hemingway makes his characters say one thing, convey still another, and when a whole passage of talk has been given, the reader finds himself the richer by a totally unexpected mood, a mood often enough of outrageous familiarity with obscure heartbreaks ... No amount of analysis can convey the quality of 'The Sun Also Rises.' It is a truly gripping story, told in a lean, hard, athletic narrative prose that puts more literary English to shame. Mr. Hemingway knows how not only to make words be specific but how to arrange a collection of words which shall betray a great deal more than is to be found in the individual parts. It is magnificent writing, filled with that organic action which gives a compelling picture of

character. This novel is unquestionably one of the events of an unusually rich year in literature. (*New York Times*, 1926)

Or, more recently, its review of Douglas Stuart's *Shuggie Bain* that went on to receive the 2020 Booker prize:

> He's lovely, Douglas Stuart, fierce and loving and lovely. He shows us lots of monstrous behavior, but not a single monster – only damage. If he has a sharp eye for brokenness, he is even keener on the inextinguishable flicker of love that remains. The book is long, more than 400 pages, but its length seems crucial to its overall effect. Like Agnes, we're all doomed to our patterns. How often we repeat the same disastrous mistakes, make the same wrong turn again and again. And yet, like Shuggie, how often we rise, against all odds, to stumble forward once more. The book leaves us gutted and marveling: Life may be short, but it takes forever. (Cohen, 2020)

Film theory and criticism are a younger expression of their literary siblings and add to the available range of analytical tools those that are peculiar to the cinematic experience. In analysing how a film works, visual and aural aesthetics become vitally important. Framing, editing, special effects and a movie's score all contribute to the viewers' experience. A film's narrative is experienced through the senses and is intuitively absorbed in a manner that is vastly different to reading a book. It is also far more likely to be a shared or communal experience than the more solitary pursuit of withdrawal from company to read. Yet the same need still exists to be able to nimbly navigate between the worlds when seeking to 'read' a film alongside being sensitive to the unique features that are inherent in the medium. For example, 'genre criticism' needs to be aware of the filmic conventions that sit with any given genre such as a horror, science fiction, romantic comedy or road movie. Or again, while 'auteur criticism' normally looks to a movie's director as its focus, the array of creative contributions from producers, writers, composers, actors, editors, film crew and the rest means that it is almost always a collaborative endeavour (Johnston, 2006, pp. 186–201). Commenting on director James Cameron's

2022 movie *Avatar: The Way of the Water* reviewer Clarisse Loughrey observes:

> The dialogue is either filled with faux-spiritualism or Cameron-typical quips such as 'it's called a punch, bitch'. The two extremes never blend in a way that feels convincing. But these are exactly the same criticisms lobbed at the first Avatar and, often, the rest of the director's filmography. Cameron, at this point, seems interested less in being an artist than a cinematic frontiersman. That's the point of The Way of Water – it's not about what the film has to offer us now, but what it tells us about the future. (Loughrey, 2022)

Or, on Stephen Spielberg's 2021 remake of *West Side Story*, Richard Brody wrote in *The New Yorker*:

> The story of the original "West Side Story" is that of white Jewish artists (Leonard Bernstein, Arthur Laurents, and Jerome Robbins, later joined by Stephen Sondheim) who planned to make a musical play about Jewish and Irish gangs and then, worrying that they were heading for cliché, shifted their focus to people they knew nothing about. The result was a big stage and screen hit that has always been diminished by the blind spots of its script and its casting. Spielberg didn't open up the story to involve new ideas and experiences, nor did he reckon with the cultural and political forces that gave rise to 'West Side Story' in the first place ... Dismayingly, Spielberg didn't have the courage or the insight to imagine it. (Brody, 2021)

These more popular critiques of literature and film are illustrative of the fluidity of approach that is required when seeking to effectively 'read' a product of culture like a novel or a movie. A fluidity that understands the significance of the world a cultural text embodies, alongside the worlds behind and in front of it. Being able to move freely between them, holding them together as a whole while simultaneously interrogating them for their explicit and implicit substance, is the essence of the interpretive task.

Theology's outward 'cultural turn' towards hermeneutics

In fully embracing its own outward 'cultural turn' Christianity is not doing something completely alien. Over the centuries Christianity has thrived because it has proven to be a successful transcultural movement. It has found ways to migrate from one cultural home to another, frequently when these new locations are dramatically different from what it has encountered before. Beginning in a culturally distinct Judaism, the Jesus movement successfully transitioned into the Hellenistic culture of the Roman empire alongside also establishing small communities of believers in the surrounding cultures of Mesopotamia and the Parthian and Sasanian empires, and the north-east African Kingdom of Aksum. Over the centuries this ability to culturally transition was demonstrated chronologically in the West through the Dark Ages and into the Medieval, Renaissance, Enlightenment and Modern worlds, and around the world geographically in an expansion that was substantially accelerated by the modern missionary movement.

From an imperial census at his birth to a legally sanctioned execution at his death, Jesus' life was lived intimately and intricately enmeshed in a particular cultural moment, just like everyone else who has ever lived. This is an inescapable reality. For those seeking to live as Jesus' disciples this has always thrown up questions with an immediacy of importance and carrying an imperative urgency. 'What does faithfulness to Christ look like in these pressing circumstances?' 'What does the gospel require of us as we are confronted by war, famine, injustice, the climate crisis and all shades of social evil?' Christian discipleship, therefore, has always been fully immersed in, and engaged with, its host culture. Whether that experience has been perceived as positive and affirming where a culture has self-identified as 'Christian', or at the other extreme, one of conflict and persecution, the cultural locatedness of lived faith cannot be denied.

Theological reflection has equally been an integral part of this cultural encounter. From Thomist 'Just War' theory to Anabaptist pacifism, and medieval notions of the 'divine right of kings' to Latin American 'liberation theology' inspired by Marxist analysis, it has always been there.

Frequently ethical and most often responsive in nature, Christianity has a long track record of thinking about what it means to live a life of faithfulness to the gospel of Christ. However, if it is to fully embrace the outward dimension of its own 'cultural turn' it must take a further step. Learning from the insights of the cultural disciplines, it must mature in its ability to 'read' and interpret the culture of which it is a part. This is more than developing a theological appreciation and sensitivity that understands how the wider culture influences and shapes its theological responses. Indeed, it is more than its traditional ethical responsiveness and missiological imperative. This is developing a discipline of theological interpretation that is culturally savvy, contextually self-aware, spiritually attuned and confessionally authentic. Being culturally savvy means an attentiveness to the what and why of all that is going on in the surrounding culture. Contextual self-awareness is understanding the shaping forces exerted by a host culture and their impact on you. Being spiritually attuned and confessionally authentic is recognizing that if theology does not have a basis in living faith it dissolves into merely being a religious dimension of anthropology, sociology or cultural studies.

In such an endeavour perhaps the most attractive temptation for those embracing an inherited tradition of faith is the lure of inhabiting a small 'c' conservative orientation to life. As Kevin Vanhoozer observes,

> We don't simply read cultural texts but we read *through* them. In short: the cultural texts we love best come to serve as the lens through which we view everything else and as the compass that orients us toward the good life. (Vanhoozer et al., 2007, p. 36)

The danger is to merely replicate and reinforce our existing convictions rather than placing them under rigorous and detailed consideration. A significant dimension of this is the instinctive inclination to what 'feels' right. This is the comfortable position that can short-circuit a more thoroughgoing examination because everything seems obvious. This is where unconscious bias hides and conclusions are prematurely presumed. Such cultural conditioning, when challenged, can also provoke a response ranging from mild discomfort and awkwardness to an intense, unreasoned and visceral reaction. Developing the ability to engage in an inward debate and dialogue between heart and mind, ideas and emotions is the only real antidote. It is understanding that when our personal intuitions and inclinations are disturbed in this way, this should trigger a quest to understand why, and whether this stands scrutiny or not.

While seeking to interpret culture through deploying a theological lens may have its own challenges, it also has a distinctive contribution to make. As Gordon Lynch compellingly argues, because of its concern with the 'nature of truth, what constitutes a meaningful view of life, what it means to live good and fulfilling lives and to build just and peaceable communities' it should be seen as a 'normative' discipline (Lynch, 2005, p. 184). A discipline that demonstrates how culture should be interpreted because it has a long history of exploring and developing the necessary categories and tools to aid such interpretation. Tillich would agree. While this is certainly a valuable contribution to the wider cultural discourse, it is of vital importance for those within the community of faith.

Normative it may be, but infallible it is not, 'neither as objective as geometric proof nor as arbitrary as a statement of one's personal preferences' (Vanhoozer et al., 2007, p. 36). Once again it underlines the vital need for humility in the task of interpretation. Justin Ariel Bailey probes more deeply and offers three postures to adopt that might be used to underpin this hermeneutical humility. First, he advocates a 'non-reductive' curiosity that resists the urge to oversimplify. Faith seeks understanding, not an uncomplicated formula or an explanation reduced to memorable sound-bites or the bullet-points of a PowerPoint presentation. Second, he urges a 'non-dismissive' discernment that resists overconfidence in one's own convictions. Rather, in humility and openness to God, it is willing to listen and learn from anyone, in good faith, recognizing the dignity of all who bear God's image. Third, he adopts the call of Rabbi Edwin Friedman to be a 'non-anxious presence'. The ability to be present for others without the need to control or be controlled by the actions of others (Bailey, 2022, pp. 141–7).

At its most fundamental this is John Stott's principle of 'double listening': the 'difficult and even painful task' that seeks to be attentive to the 'ancient Word' and the modern world, relating them together with 'fidelity and simplicity' (Stott, 1992, pp. 13, 28–9; Wright, 2020, p. 68). In this Stott echoed the earlier exhortation of theological students by the Swiss theologian Karl Barth to 'take your Bible and take your newspaper, and read both. But interpret newspapers from your Bible' (*Time*, May 31, 1963).

Interpretive frameworks

If the task is to read theologically the various texts, artefacts and elements that contribute to the cultural whole, the question is how do you do that? To avoid a superficial exercise in biblical 'proof-texting' or a meandering and indulgent process of theological 'wool-gathering', various frameworks have been suggested to support a 'reading' of culture in the literary style. Perhaps the most widely used is a theological overview of the epochs of human history divided by the Bible into creation, fall, redemption and consumption (Holmes, 2008, p. xiii; Stott, 1990a, pp. 34–5; Turnau, 2012, pp. 41–77; Vanhoozer et al., 2007, pp. 41–3). John Stott links this theo-historical framework with the qualities of 'the good' creation, 'the evil' fall, 'the new' in redemption and 'the perfect' with the end of the age. Kevin Vanhoozer tags this as the 'theodrama' of God's presence and activity in the world and maintains that alongside this the doctrines of the incarnation, general revelation, common grace and the *imago Dei* have a particular bearing on a theology of culture.

Expanding on the work of Vanhoozer, Justin Ariel Bailey sees the benefits of seeking to read culture in the style of a literary text; however, he attempts to build a multi-dimensional model of five metaphors and their corresponding practices in life. In doing this he is keen to dispel the illusion of critical distance that is inherent in the approach of literary criticism, because no-one is culturally neutral. He also seeks for the analysis to be grounded in the 'lived dimension' of everyday life. In this approach theology becomes an integrative discipline that opens and hosts space for others while protecting that space from being dominated by any one voice. His five cultural dimensions are:

- The Meaning Dimension: *Culture as Immune System.*
  An investigative mode that seeks to understand what connects and why.
  The cultural practice is 'hosting'.
- The Power Dimension: *Culture as Power Play.*
  A diagnostic mode that identifies the sources and uses of power.
  The cultural practice is 'iconoclasm'.
- The Ethical Dimension: *Culture as Moral Boundary.*
  A normative mode that determines what is good and right.
  The cultural practice is 'servanthood'.
- The Religious Dimension: *Culture as Sacred Experience.*
  An immersive mode that is about where we are anchored and pulled.
  The cultural practice is 'discernment'.
- The Aesthetic Dimension: *Culture as Poetic Project.*
  An imaginative mode that explores what could be through desire and delight.
  The cultural practice is 'making'.
  (Bailey, 2022, pp. 15–17 and 140)

Others have looked to systematic theology, narrative, identity and other categories to provide a consistent structure and method with which to interrogate the elements of culture.[6] It was with this in mind that while teaching cultural hermeneutics at Spurgeon's College I developed an approach based on biblical genres to help those preparing for Christian mission and ministry to think critically about understanding the world

CULTURAL HERMENEUTICS

through the insights of Scripture, and the Bible through the eyes of contemporary life. Called 'Engaging with the Word of God' the model used five biblical genres to help structure their cultural analysis and reflection.

- The Law – matters of right and wrong (personal morality).
- The Prophets – issues of justice and compassion (social morality).
- The Psalms – experience of lament and thanksgiving (spirituality).
- The Gospel – good news of grace and peace (engaging Jesus).
- The Apocalypse – trajectory and destiny (eternity).

Analysing culture is often described as an interrogative discipline and it should be no surprise that having a range of appropriate questions to pose is vitally important.[7] An interesting example of this is provided by Ted Turnau in what he describes as a five-step process of diagnostic questioning that blends imagination and intellect in seeking to penetrate beyond the surface of things.

- *What's the story?* What is the plot? How does the plot serve to develop characters? Or in the absence of a coherent plot, what mood does this text project?
- *Where are we?* What sort of imaginative world is projected by the text? Look for the style and structure, the ethics and aesthetics of this imaginative world.
- *What is good and true and beautiful here?* How does this imaginative world reflect God's grace to human beings? How would you connect it to God's creation and redemption story?
- *What is false and evil and perverse here, and how can I subvert it?* How does the worldview of the text capture the grace in idolatry? How does this world lie about reality, and how can you expose the lie? How can you reveal the weak and crumbling foundations of its chosen idols?
- Finally, *how does the gospel apply?* How does the Christian worldview respond to the desires and questions stirred by the

imaginative world of the text? How does God's redemption, the new life and new creation that he achieved for us, answer and silence the idols? How is God's mercy and excellence unveiled as the answer to these desires raised by popular culture. (Turnau, 2012, pp. 245–6, 313–14)

The necessity of humility: the starting point of hermeneutics is discipleship

As theology has made its own outward-looking 'cultural turn' towards hermeneutics it has undertaken an impossible task. The whole of cultural reality is too vast to comprehend. While there are immense commonalities of shared understanding and belief, culture is not uniform. Around the world there are countless differences, some large and others small. Then, within the differences, there are variations on deviations and modifications on alternatives that make culture into a kaleidoscopic array. But then, of course, culture is not a static entity. It changes over time, sometimes rapidly, sometimes slowly and imperceptibly. Yet like the best kaleidoscopes the slightest turn brings a whole new, colourful pattern into view. However 'thick' the description and pertinent the analysis, any attempt at cultural hermeneutics will always be vastly incomplete, always provisional and constrained by the subjectivity of the 'hermeneutical baggage' we have brought to the task.

Such a vision of the task to hand, however, should not be a discouraging one. Rather, it lays an important foundation of humility that recognizes our necessary limitation. Professor of Cultural Studies Ben Highmore rightly wants a more 'modest sense' in the subject that admits the limitations of a 'culturistic perspective'. Yet at the same time he also advocates an ambitious form of study that addresses reality (Highmore, 2016, p. 138). If the outward 'cultural turn' for theology is in essence about discipleship, it too should embrace the spiritual grace of humility while ambitiously pursuing the agency that cultural understanding provides to practise inculturated discipleship. That we will never comprehend it all or understand it fully should not deter us. Speaking to a previous generation of Christian discipleship in terms of being 'perfected in love', the seventeenth-century founder of Methodism, John Wesley explored the appropriate limitations of the quest:

> They are not perfect in knowledge. They are not free from ignorance, no, nor from mistake. We are no more to expect any living man to be infallible than to be omniscient. They are not free from infirmities; such as weakness, or slowness of understanding, irregular quickness or heaviness of imagination ... impropriety of language, an ungracefulness of pronunciation, to which one might add a thousand nameless defects, either in conversation or behaviour. (Wesley, 1976, p.16)

Wesley would agree with the apostle: 'Not that I have already obtained this or have already reached the goal; but I press on to make it my own' (Phil. 3.12).

For all the complexity, qualifications and limitations when seeking to interpret the culture around us, for theology to enter the world of cultural hermeneutics is a further dimension of Anselm's 'faith seeking understanding'. Or again, inspired by Dietrich Bonhoeffer, speaking of biblical hermeneutics rather than cultural interpretation and yet strangely still apposite:

> The starting point of hermeneutics is not philosophy or translation but discipleship – the relationship of the interpreter to the Lord in prayer discipline and action for others. (Stassen et al., 1996, p. 296)

Cultural hermeneutics 'in the Spirit'

> When the Spirit of truth comes, he will guide you into all the truth; for he will not speak on his own, but will speak whatever he hears, and he will declare to you the things that are to come. (John 16.13)

For the earliest community committed to following Jesus, the implications of their discipleship were very clear. First, they were on a journey to 'the ends of the earth'. With all that they knew and could not anticipate about the forthcoming transcultural migration of their message, whatever it might mean, they also had Jesus' promise of the coming of the Holy Spirit. The Spirit was the one who would come alongside them as an accompanist, helper, teacher, empowerer and guide. Theirs was to be an inculturated discipleship, a Pneuma-cultural discipleship that would enable a strong and robust connection with the spiritual reality at the heart of their faith and a deep rootedness in the substance of the culture they called home.

As they wrestled with the implications of this journey, the role of the Spirit would not have surprised them. 'Jesus's movement widely recognized the Spirit as the chief agent of divine wisdom and revelation' (Keener, 2016, p. 161). That Jesus had told them to wait and not begin their mission until they received the spiritual power of the Holy Spirit, at the same time as making clear its global reach, is no coincidence. 'The significance of the day of Pentecost for theology and culture cannot be overstated' (Bailey, 2022, p. 35). Theology's outward 'cultural turn' for the sake of discipleship can be understood in no other way. It has to be 'in the Spirit' because this is how Christian discipleship and culture have been in relationship since the very beginning. In this vibrant and dynamic engagement, theology needs to map the spaces of human activity and creativity, identify limits (Holmes, 2008, pp. 18–19), affirm achievements and provide a constructive and insightful commentary on what it considers. Yet this must never fall into the trap of being a purely intellectual exercise that plays creatively with ideas and fails to connect with the lived realities of day-to-day life. Neither should it succumb to the allure of a purely speculative theology that is full of imaginative richness and yet detached from the real world in which people live. It is a hermeneutic of the Spirit who stands with, guides and enables disciples in place of Jesus himself and, as Jesus promised, 'he will take what is mine and declare it to you' (John 16.14).[8]

Spirit-filled – the epistemology of faith

all of them were filled with the Holy Spirit. (Acts 2.4)

When New Testament scholar Craig Keener was seeking to explore what he identified as a 'Spirit hermeneutic' for addressing the biblical text, he saw it as helping 'to articulate how the experience of the Spirit that empowered the church on the day of Pentecost can and should dynamically shape our reading of Scripture' (Keener, 2016, p. 4). While the tasks of biblical hermeneutics and cultural hermeneutics are clearly different in their focus, they are not unrelated undertakings.[9] At the heart of Keener's work is the articulation of the believing community's faith as an epistemic commitment. All of its interpreting, understanding and knowing builds on the basis of this faith commitment about the nature of reality:

> Epistemically, Christians need be no more reticent about their starting convictions than are others. Everyone has starting premises that are difficult to justify on their own terms – for example, epistemologies that are empiricist, rationalist, or existential. We may explore the options, but ultimately when we decide to follow Christ, or to the extent that we commit ourselves to follow him, this entrusting ourselves to him, and so staking the direction of our lives on him, involves an epistemic commitment. (Keener, 2016, p. 163)

As with cultural studies, fully embracing our subjectivity is an important dimension of understanding. Such a commitment does not preclude being able to engage subjects honestly and openly, neither does it imply an uncritical and unchallengeable commitment to the Christian tradition. In naming faith as an epistemological commitment Keener goes further than a mere acknowledgement of subjectivity. Faith in Jesus Christ as Lord shapes our way of experiencing and knowing the world around us in all its dimensions. In this sense it is very clearly a Christocentric epistemology rather than something more nebulous and ill-defined as a generalized category of 'faith' (Keener, 2016,

p. 157). This Christocentric commitment is also that which anchors the epistemology. While a 'Spirit hermeneutic' is an experiential approach that is rooted in the practice of discipleship, the spiritual formation of the Spirit-filled disciple is deeply shaped by the inner witness of the Spirit and the Spirit's unbreakable fidelity to Christ (John 14.26; 16.13–14; 1 John 2.20, 27).

Spirit-led – hermeneutical proximity and fluidity

> a sound like the rush of a violent wind ... filled the entire house where they were sitting. (Acts 2.2)

As helpful as interpretative frameworks are in focusing thinking and providing a strategy by which theology can engage in exploring culture, ultimately they fall short. Given the complex and dynamic nature of culture, any such stylized approach will discover that the depth of its description and the scope of its analysis are limited by the structure it adopts. Any attempt at hermeneutics will always be rooted in a moment of time, but a standardized format of theological engagement will further tend towards a homogenization of outcomes that seriously limits the range of its useful insight. As Clive Marsh poignantly observes, life is not lived in theory, and 'unsystematic living' is full of interruptions, contradictions and 'impurities' that confound the theoretical purist (Marsh, 2004, p. 132). And because discipleship is about the shape of lived experience, such observations from the random interruptions, contradictions and 'impurities' of living are vital if the outcomes of any cultural hermeneutics are to have real-life traction. Yet even here the need for a more fluid adaptability is necessary. 'As to a strategy for engaging the world, perhaps there is no single model for all times and places' (Hunter, 2010a, p. 276).

What is needed is for theology to have a free-form style of theological engagement. While drawing on the insights of all methodologies, frameworks and approaches, it retains a case-by-case autonomy to respond to the subject or situation under

CULTURAL HERMENEUTICS

consideration. Conceived as a function of Christian discipleship, such a freestyle theology fits very well with an understanding of the Spirit of God that Jesus maintains, like the wind 'blows where it chooses', and goes on to affirm it in terms of discipleship by adding, 'So it is with everyone who is born of the Spirit' (John 3.8). To be Spirit-led provides what Keener identifies in interpreting the Bible as a 'hermeneutical proximity' because the disciples' experience ties in with their hermeneutical reading. The experiential dimension of the interpreter's faith is an integral part of the hermeneutical process. Given the Spirit's teaching role within the believing community and the commitment in Christ to be guided by the Spirit, an understanding of being 'Spirit-led' provides exactly the correlation that enables the hermeneutical task to mirror the complexity and fluidity of culture. Inasmuch as cultural hermeneutics is an activity of faith, 'ideally the omniscient Spirit can guide us in showing us at least what we need to see for what he is calling us to do' (Keener, 2016, pp. 24, 42).

As disciples, our response to the culture around us roughly falls into two forms. The first is an almost instantaneous and instinctual reaction. Without thinking, we have a perception of whether something is right or wrong, in harmony with Christ or out of kilter with him. It could be said that this is a form of 'spiritual intuition' rooted in the believer's inner relationship with the Spirit, or the 'witness', inner light or sense of shalom/peace that the Spirit bequeaths. Indeed, this relationship with God 'in the Spirit' brings with it a deep, intimate and experiential knowledge of the divine that transcends a purely cognitive understanding. If the Spirit does indeed dwell within a believer, '[h]ow can the presence and activity of the Third Person of the Trinity living inside us not make a difference?' (Keener, 2016, pp. 41, 285).

Such an understanding does beg the question of how to distinguish between a 'spiritual intuition' that is 'in the Spirit' and some other intuition that merely reflects our own experiences, preferences and prejudices and their cultural conditioning. Does it stand scrutiny against the message of Jesus, the biblical witness, Christian tradition and our knowledge of the world through secular disciplines? Further to this, Keener recommends the insight of those who are culturally different from us. Here perspectives of neo-Western liberalism or old-style colonialism dressed in the clothes of traditional conservativism are swiftly 'outed' (Keener, 2016, pp. 77–87).

The second form of response to culture 'in the Spirit' is the more cognitive, reasoned and intellectual engagement with the truth. Justin Ariel Bailey maintains that it is helpful to view these two dimensions of our cultural interpretation in terms of what psychologists call 'system 1' and 'system 2', thinking that Daniel Kahneman epitomizes as 'thinking fast' and 'thinking slow' (Bailey, 2022, pp. 138–9). Given that this is how our brains seem to be wired, it should be no surprise that the 'Spirit of truth' engages disciples as 'teacher' in the conscious recollection and application of the words of Jesus (John 14.26) as well as with 'sighs too deep for words' (Rom. 8.26–7).

The Spirit of truth – thick description and redescription

> a sound like the rush of a violent wind … tongues, as of fire … amazed and astonished … filled with new wine … it is only nine o'clock in the morning. (Acts 2.2–15)

Theology has nothing to fear from truth. With the Spirit identified as the 'Spirit of truth' the die is cast. Nothing that is true can be considered out of bounds, to be ignored or beyond the scope of theology's interest and embrace. In dealing with pagan culture Augustine advocated two norms. The first is summed up in the adage 'all truth is God's truth'. Whatever its origin, Christians should have no hesitation in plundering it for their own use. The second is the norm of charity, where he simply says, 'Knowledge which is used to promote love is useful' (Cobb, 2005, pp. 84–5). Theology is then clearly an interdisciplinary discipline before it ever begins to engage with analysing culture. But when it does, it needs to learn from and deploy all the insights of cultural disciplines. The 'thick description' of anthropology, the principle of redescription in Rorty, understanding the dynamics of subjectivity from cultural studies and the benefits of the 'cultural turn' in sociology and other disciplines lay a solid foundation from which theology can benefit and contribute to ongoing dialogue.

In this light it is fascinating to observe that in 2022 the London Interdisciplinary School, which was founded in 2017 and granted degree-awarding powers in 2021, was advertising its polymath approach as 'the most radical new university to open in decades' with theology as a centrally placed hub in its network of subject connections (Benson, 2023). Theology itself needs to be both eclectic and synthetic in its approach, finding new ways to benefit from Augustine's insight just as Calvin did. In his commentary on Titus he wrote, 'All truth is from God; and consequently, if wicked men have said anything that is true and just, we ought not to reject it; for it has come from God' (Calvin, 1856, pp. 300–1).

With the accelerated nature of cultural change in the contemporary world, there is no doubt that the discipline of redescription becomes ever more important. So the skill of being able to read the surrounding cultural context becomes increasingly important too. This is underlined by Kathryn Tanner as she seeks to explore how differences in theological judgement can suggest conflicting notions of discipleship among practising Christians. Thus she writes,

> The theologian has to be creative when redescribing in Christian terms the shifting worlds of different times and places, when giving a Christian meaning to new domains of human existence, when figuring out how to reinterpret a Christian outlook in contemporary terms or how to reconstitute it in ways that meet current challenges. (Tanner, 1997, p. 160)

The Spirit of discernment – hermeneutics, perspicacity and praxis

> repent, and be baptized ... save yourselves from this corrupt generation. (Acts 2.38–40)

Cultural hermeneutics in the service of discipleship has a two-fold function of discernment when it is 'in the Spirit'. First, it develops an appreciation of culture's formative action, a kind of cultural self-awareness, a discernment of how the elements of life shape and orient us to the world around us and in our relationship with God. In his 'farewell discourse' Jesus told the disciples that the Spirit would come to them and act as an Advocate, like a legal counsel, exposing and laying bare the truth about 'sin, righteousness and judgement', truth that is understood only in relation to Jesus himself. The truth about sin is that it demonstrates its unbelief by not aligning itself with Jesus and the message of the Kingdom of God he proclaimed. The truth about righteousness is Jesus himself, the Word of God made flesh, the embodiment of everything that expresses oneness with the heart, character and purposes of God. In his physical absence from the world it is the Spirit who actively witnesses to what substantive righteousness looks like in love, mercy, grace, justice, compassion, patience, shalom and so forth. In the light of this truth about sin and righteousness, judgement is clear and is already clear to be seen. As his disciples go about negotiating their way through issues of sin and righteousness, seeking to understand how to live faithfully, Jesus reassures them that the Spirit 'will guide you into all the truth' (John 16.8–13).

This cultural savvy or self-awareness, then, needs, second, to inform and shape real-life application in the attitudes, decisions and actions of regular life, the active life of Christian discipleship, of learning to be a 'faithful presence' in the circumstances of our lives. As such, discernment is a quality of spiritual maturity. It is a key trait of 'those whose faculties have been trained by practice to distinguish good from evil' (Heb. 5.14). In a very real sense, being able to name something implies knowing about it and discerning something of its nature and identity (Bailey, 2022, p. 54).

It would be a misconception to envisage the life of faith to be something fragile that needs to be protected and nurtured far away from the overwhelming power of cultural forces that have no time for Christ and his Kingdom (Bailey, 2022, p. 37). Rather, it is in the bustle, pressures, quandaries and conflicts of living that the gospel is unleashed as a powerful and robust presence. Cultural hermeneutics 'in the Spirit' promises the potential for competence in discernment that in turn informs Christian discipleship: cultural perspicacity and praxis.

The Spirit of prophecy – articulating the partial

> this is what was spoken through the prophet Joel. (Acts 2.15)

There are as many definitions of what is meant by prophecy as there are commentators, hucksters, futurologists and click-bait entrepreneurs on social media platforms. Biblically, at its most basic level, it has far more to do with speaking God's Word into a present situation than more popular ideas of predicting what is to come like some present-day Nostradamus or Mother Shipton. The Old Testament scholar Walter Brueggemann helpfully wrote:

> It is the task of prophetic ministry to bring the claims of the tradition and the situation of enculturation into an effective interface. That is, the prophet is called to be a child of the tradition, one who has taken it seriously in the shaping of his or her own field of perception and system of language, who is so at home in that memory that the points of contact and incongruity with the situation of the church in culture can be discerned and articulated with proper urgency. (Brueggemann, 2001, p. 2)

In this sense, cultural hermeneutics, when pursued 'in the Spirit' as a component of Christian discipleship, is a prophetic activity.

Brueggemann goes on to show that such 'prophetic ministry consists of offering an alternative perception of reality and in letting people see their own history in the light of God's freedom and his will for justice', not only in the great issues of contemporary life, but also wherever people 'try to live together and show concern for their shared future and identity' (Brueggemann, 2001, pp. 116–17).

Such prophetic ministry must, however, recognize its limitations. First, it is limited by its knowledge. Even the anthropologist Clifford Geertz insisted that cultural analysis was 'guessing, as intelligently and educatedly as one can, at meanings' that could give rise to 'wildness' and 'dimness' (Inglis, 2000, p. 114) – a reality that the apostle Paul was only too well aware of: 'For we know only in part, and we prophesy only in part' (1 Cor. 13.9). Yet, for Craig Keener, the fact that there are also such wild and dim abuses of prophecy does not invalidate it. 'The existence of counterfeits or worn currency does not require us to abandon money, and witnessing shabby structures does not invite us to throw away our tools and quit building' (Keener, 2016, p. 289).

Second, it is limited by its embeddedness in its own cultural context. Kathryn Tanner explores this as our 'culturally conditioned theological imagination' (Tanner, 1997, p. 168). This is the view that is also highlighted by James K. A. Smith's 'The Godfather problem', which draws attention to how everyday culture always rivals the gospel for hegemony in the formation of Christians (Fitch, 2022, p. 172). For Christopher Watkin it is the explanation of the uncritically embraced Marxist Christ of the 1960s, the hippie Christ of the 1970s and the postmodern Christ of the 1990s:

> the real Christ, who comes in grace and truth to confront, complete, and console every culture ... should not fit comfortably in any culture, and if he nestles snugly into our own, then we have almost certainly lost sight of the biblical Christ. (Watkins, 2022, p. 30)

Third, it is limited by its own 'hermeneutical proximity' as Keener calls it. And while reading culture in an experiential yet responsible way may be profitable, the implications of a purely subjective reading make the 'testing' of such insight essential (Keener, 2016, pp. 24–7, 118). As the apostle Paul advises the church at Corinth,

> Let two or three prophets speak, and let the others weigh what is said. If a revelation is made to someone else sitting nearby, let the first person be silent. For you can all prophesy one by one, so that all may learn and all be encouraged. And the spirits of prophets are subject to the prophets, for God is a God not of disorder but of peace. (1 Cor. 14.29–33)

The Spirit of Jesus – empowered missional witness

> But you will receive power when the Holy Spirit has come upon you; and you will be my witnesses in Jerusalem, in all Judea and Samaria, and to the ends of the earth. (Acts 1.8)

Across Luke's two-volume account of the origins of Christianity the role of the Holy Spirit is a common theme. In his Gospel, prior to Jesus' arrival to be baptized, John the Baptist preaches about the one who would follow him and baptize 'with the Holy Spirit and fire' (Luke 3.16). The baptism itself is sealed by Jesus' reception of the Holy Spirit in the form of a dove and the affirmation of the divine voice 'You are my Son ... with you I am well pleased' (3.33). Then 'full of the Holy Spirit' Jesus is led into the wilderness to his temptations (4.1), returning 'filled with the power of the Spirit' to commence his ministry in the Galilee (4.14). Then, summarizing the early stages of Jesus' ministry, the first full story that Luke records is of him choosing to read from the scroll of Isaiah at his home synagogue in Nazareth, beginning with the words 'The Spirit of the Lord is upon me, because he has anointed me'. The prophet's message of 'good news to the poor', 'release to the captives', 'recovery of sight to the blind', freedom for the oppressed and the celebration of Jubilee is concluded with Jesus' statement, 'Today this scripture has been fulfilled in your hearing' (4.18–21). Widely now referred to as Jesus' 'manifesto sermon', it clearly establishes the role of the Holy Spirit in the mission of Jesus. Indeed, in missiology the prominence of the Nazareth sermon frequently eclipses Matthew's 'Great Commission' as the key biblical text (Bosch, 2003, p. 84). The role of the Spirit in the mission of Jesus is clearly established.

Between Jesus' ascension and the events of the day of Pentecost the disciples follow Jesus' instruction and wait for the arrival of the Spirit (Luke 24.49 and Acts 1.8). His instructions have been clear, the Spirit's coming is about their empowerment for a mission 'to all nations', 'in Jerusalem, in all Judea and Samaria, and to the ends of the earth' (Luke 24.48–9; Acts 1.8). Thus, in both the ministry of Jesus and at the birth of the church, the coming of the Spirit is explicitly connected with mission. 'Luke's primary emphasis regarding the Spirit involves mission, and most scholars acknowledge empowerment for mission as the Spirit's most prominent activity in Acts' (Keener, 2016, p. 43).

Taking his lead from Barth, that no theological construction is complete until it issues in an imperative address to human action, Stephen Holmes maintains that no theological analysis of culture is complete until it moves to engagement and acting for social transformation (Holmes, 2008, p. xiv). It should therefore be no surprise that cultural hermeneutics conducted 'in the Spirit' will have a missional focus and impetus as an authentic fruit of the gospel of Jesus.

Cultural hermeneutics that is 'in the Spirit' is an integral part of a 'Pneuma-cultural discipleship'. That is, understanding the God-given nature of our cultural experience and recognizing our cultural home as the context in which we live as a 'faithful presence' aligned to the teaching of Jesus.

Justin Ariel Bailey suggests that it is helpful to think of discipleship in two movements. In the first, 'living from culture' is where we seek to understand why we resonate with or resist a particular expression of culture in the way that we do. Because we are so embedded in our host context this is an act of discernment that examines what is going on in our own hearts and why. The second movement is how we live 'for culture':

> Another way to say this is,' Your interpretation is your life.'
> ... we are all cultural interpreters. We are already engaged in countless acts of interpretation as we navigate the world. The best way to know my interpretation of a ... cultural trend is to watch how I live with it, how I live it out in my daily life with others. (Bailey, 2022, pp. 11–14)

Living 'for culture' is the fruit of reading our context 'in the Spirit' and could be seen as an expression of the Pauline idea of 'being led by the Spirit' (Rom. 8.14 and Gal. 5.18). Speaking of discipleship, Craig Keener is right to remind us that 'we must live in daily dependence on the Holy Spirit'. Then he continues that in this sense the 'Spirit's role of illumination thus focuses on the ... perlocution ... The Holy Spirit is largely involved at the perlocutionary level as we are enabled to understand' (Keener, 2016, pp. 288, 13). Ultimately, it is as the nineteenth-century American writer Henry David Thoreau reflected in his journal, 'The question is not what you look at, but what you see' (Johnston, 2006, p. 23).

Notes

1 Walls' indigenizing and pilgrim principles are explored more fully on page 88.

2 While Holmes' article is specifically addressing issues of Baptist identity and what he discerns as a distinctively Baptist approach to the New Testament, I am convinced that his insights with regard to a mimetic reading of Scripture are also more widely practised among Christians of differing denominational and theological convictions. 'This is my story, and so I am called to act the way that Jesus and the apostles acted – this is mimesis' (Holmes, 2021, p. 16).

3 While Hunter's work on 'faithful presence' has been generally well received, two critiques are worth noting as illustrative of the conversations spawned by his ideas. David Fitch believes that the ideas needed fleshing out in two main, and related, areas. He felt that the thesis too easily dissolved into individualism and did not properly stress the

significance of the believing community in resourcing and supporting collective action. Further to this he felt that more space should have been given to the 'how to' of forming disciples who could exercise 'faithful discipleship' (Fitch, 2016, pp. 12–14). His book addresses these issues with the main content based around seven suggested disciplines that might help to form disciples for 'faithful presence'. Daniel Strange is more hard-hitting in his critique. He sees the concept as too nebulous, too passive and conceding, and lacking the punch, drive and vision to be culturally fit-for-purpose. Writing from the Reformed tradition, he explores a more full-blown, old-style Calvinist approach to the cultural mandate, embracing what dominion, the Reformation *solas* and military metaphors can bring to help establish Schilders' vision of the church as 'the greatest indirect cultural force' (Strange, 2015, pp. 47–56).

4 Postmodernism and poststructuralism are broad brushstroke terms that are deployed in a variety of ways, and sometimes interchangeably. They inherently challenge modernist and structuralist ideas, are suspicious of reason and are characterized by scepticism and relativism. They are particularly sensitive to the role of ideology in attaining and retaining power in the public sphere. It is perhaps easiest to consider poststructuralism to be an aspect of postmodernism that is particularly concerned with the nature of discourse and language patterns because they relate to subjectivity and identity with writers like Roland Barthes, Jacques Derrida, Michel Foucault and Jean Baudrillard from continental philosophy of the second half of the twentieth century.

5 There is some debate over the relationship between J. L. Austin's Speech Acts Theory and the Hermeneutics of Symbols of Paul Ricoeur, and how far Ricoeur was influenced by Austin. For a fuller account see Alexis Deodato S. Itao's *Of Words, Meaning, and Hermeneutics: J. L. Austin and Paul Ricoeur on the Art of Making Sense of Things* (Itao, 2021).

6 Appendix 2 contains an illustrative sample of other frameworks that have been suggested to aid the reading of culture. Theology's encounter with film studies and popular culture has been a particularly fruitful source of approaches in this regard.

7 Appendix 3 contains examples of interrogative questions suggested by Crouch, Lynch, Bailey and Benson.

8 Having already begun to develop a hermeneutic of the Spirit in relation to a theological reading of culture, I discovered Craig Keener's *Spirit Hermeneutics* (2016). While Keener is a New Testament scholar and was specifically looking at biblical hermeneutics, I was struck by the complementarity between our ideas, alongside benefitting deeply from his insights and critical reflection. Taking as read the foundational importance of literary and historical context in understanding the text of the Bible, Keener defines his approach in these terms: '*Spirit Hermeneutics* is primarily designed to function as biblical theological reflection

supporting a dynamic, experiential reading of Scripture.' His justification in this was to be faithful to the Spirit-inspired biblical text and the experience of the Spirit within a believer or among believers as an interpreting community (Keener, 2016, p. 1). The thrust of his work is guided by six core principles:

1 Following the model of biblical interpretation offered in the New Testament, Scripture is read 'experientially, eschatologically and missionally'.
2 Given the transcultural nature of the task of biblical interpretation, 'the gifts and voice' of the global church should be welcomed for the significant contribution they can make in further opening-up insights into the biblical text.
3 'A disciplined reading that understands what biblical texts meant in their ancient contexts and thus a reading that can better empathize with those to whom these texts were first directed.'
4 A 'distinctively Christian, and thus distinctively Spirit-directed, epistemology' of 'Word and Spirit' provides both a foundation alongside a potential corrective function for a 'Spirit hermeneutic'.
5 A 'Spirit hermeneutic' will necessarily be a Christocentric reading of the text.
6 Not 'all purported Spirit readings equally reflect the mind of the Spirit. Some in fact can be fairly amiss ... [this reinforces] the importance of testing readings by their consistency with the Spirit's already-established message in Scripture.' (Keener, 2016, pp. 286–7)

9 Clearly, for Keener the 'Spirit hermeneutic' involves not only the activity of the Spirit in the interpretative action of hermeneutics, but also in the inspiration of the biblical text, whichever model of inspiration is adopted by the interpreter. For a 'Spirit hermeneutic' approach to reading culture the role of the Spirit changes, but as the creator Spirit from whom everything that is has come, and the omnipresent and omniscient Spirit to whom everything within the world of culture is open, a parallel theological dynamic is at work.

Conclusion:
Evangelizing our Culture

It was a paragraph at the beginning of Gerard Loughlin's *Alien Sex: The Body and Desire in Cinema and Theology* that proved to be a startling eye-opener to me. Seeking to illustrate how movies are the result of 'strange complicities between art and science, the poetic and the technical' he wrote:

> Toward the end of Alfred Hitchcock's *Saboteur* (USA, 1942), the Fifth Columnist Frank Fry (Norman Lloyd) is pictured in a taxi. He looks to his right, out of its window. In the next shot we see what he sees: a large ocean liner, capsized by its pier. It is the *SS Alaska* that Fry had sabotaged in a preceding scene. The ship has clearly been photographed from a moving car, and when the next shot cuts back to Fry in the taxi, we know that he – and we – have witnessed the results of his sabotage. He turns away from the window with a vague smile of satisfaction on his face. But the actor Norman Lloyd never saw the ship through the window of his taxi. He was photographed at the Universal film studios in California, seated in a stage taxi, while the ship was several thousand miles away in New York, being the *SS Normandie* that had capsized at its berth. But when the shot of the ship is spliced between those of Fry looking out of the film frame, the *Normandie/Alaska* finds itself in the same narrative space as its saboteur; or rather we, the viewers, find it there ... The cinematic effect would have little power if it were not for the craving of its viewers to find relationships, to see connections. (Loughlin, 2004, p. xi)

CONCLUSION

While it was beyond what I think Loughlin was intending to say, I was making a number of connections. First, there were the issues about the relationship between the facts of what happened in the making of the movie, the narrative that was being told and the location of truth. Second, I could see that it was not only about finding relationships and seeing connections, it was also about embracing the narrative and being immersed in the world of the story. To accomplish this a third issue arose, the fascinating insight that to fully enter into and understand the power of Hitchcock's storytelling, it was necessary to exercise faith in the storyteller and the fruit of their giftedness. 'Conversely, if someone cannot suspend disbelief (note: it's a question of belief) ... then the cinematic effect collapses' (Vernon, 2004, p. 14).

We live our own lives in narrative form. We each have a lifestory and we mostly know how all the various parts fit together to get us to arrive at where we find ourselves today. Instinctively we are interpreters, attributing significance to some events and neglecting others, discerning reasons why things happened, constructing meaning and shaping our identity. It is not only those with a hyper-active social media presence who are curating their lives. Then, our understanding of the cultural tapestry against which our lives are lived is similarly stitched together into this as a seamless whole. We do not have to be taught to do this, we do it naturally. In another insightful image conjured up by Gerard Loughlin that can be reapplied here, we do not need to stand 'waiting for a theological Miss Marple to investigate and reveal who did what, when and where' (Loughlin, 1996, p. 201).[1] Developing skills in cultural hermeneutics 'in the Spirit' is therefore about improving this innate and intuitive ability. It is about liberating us from the twin dangers of slavish conformity to our inherited culture and the seductive allure of our cultural present. It is about personal and spiritual agency.

Of course, this then begs the question, what does this cultural hermeneutics 'in the Spirit' look like? Such an illustration would need to be rich in description/redescription, drawing on the wealth of interdisciplinary analysis and immersed in biblical and theological insight. Such work would, of necessity, need to resist the temptation to oversimplify or silo its analysis, yet at the same time ensure its rootedness in application and the lived-experience of Christian discipleship. It must be accessible, comprehensible and practically applicable. While such a task is beyond the scope of what is possible here, the kind of subjects that might be profitably explored in the context of Christian discipleship could be:

- Secularization, post-secularization, a genuinely secular society and faith in the public square.
- Christendom, post-Christendom and 'the next Christendom'.
- Consumerism, surveillance capitalism, wealth and the nature of the principle of choice.
- Religious literacy, inclusion, mutual understanding and social cohesion.
- Spiritual experience, neurotheology and faith in the inner space.
- The nature of truth in the light of 'fake news', conspiracy theories and a 'post-truth' society.
- The media and the impact of 24-hour news in an entertainment culture, commercial ownership and political oversight.
- Popular culture, entertainment, social media, celebrity, gaming and streaming.
- Artificial intelligence with algorithms, smart home devices, 'the internet of things', driverless cars and smart weapons.
- Political idealism in a consumer culture with radicalization, populism, cancel culture, environmentalism, immigration et al.
- Liquid identity with curated online personas, gender identity and fluidity, and the influence of consumer choice in personal and social construction.
- Health and well-being with regard to personal fulfilment, mental health, obesity, the pandemic and death as the last taboo.

Of course, there are as many variations in the composition and inclination of such a list as there are attempts at constructing it. Then, each of these subjects can be approached at broad brushstroke or granular level. Secularization, for example, could be addressed as the full sociological theory, or at a more specific level the National Secular Society's campaign to disestablish the Church of England.[2] Events like the 'storming of the capitol' in Washington DC on 6 January 2021 or the Lying-in-State and State Funeral of Queen Elizabeth II could be a focus, as could social movements like Black Lives Matter and the Campaign for Nuclear Disarmament. More classical readings, after the literary analysis approach, could be made of any work of literature, from Margaret Atwood's *The Handmaid's Tale* (1985) to J. K. Rowling's *Harry Potter and the Philosopher's Stone* (1997), or of music from Puccini's *La Bohème* (1895) to Queen's *Bohemian Rhapsody* (1975). Indeed, any work of creative art or any kind of cultural artefact, however common or ordinary, is open to scrutiny. Nothing is beyond the scope of description, analysis and interpretation 'in the Spirit', though their relative significance can vary greatly as can their implications for discipleship.

A vision of evangelizing our culture with a 'faithful presence'

> 'But I say to you that listen, love your enemies, do good to those who hate you, bless those who curse you, pray for those who abuse you. If anyone strikes you on the cheek, offer the other also; and from anyone who takes away your coat do not withhold even your shirt. Give to everyone who begs from you; and if anyone takes away your goods, do not ask for them again. Do to others as you would have them do to you ... But love your enemies, do good, and lend, expecting nothing in return. Your reward will be great, and you will be children of the Most High; for he is kind to the ungrateful and the wicked. Be merciful, just as your Father is merciful ... Forgive, and you will be forgiven; give, and it will be given to you. A good measure, pressed down, shaken together, running over, will be put into your lap; for the measure you give will be the measure you get back.' (Luke 6.27–38)

Evangelizing our culture[3] is when the good news of the Kingdom of God that animated Jesus is embodied and articulated by those who follow him. It is the content of the Nazareth manifesto from Isaiah (Luke 4.16–30), the distillation of the Mosaic Law into loving God and loving our neighbour as ourselves (Matt. 22.37–40), the Beatitudes and the content of the Sermon on the Mount (Matt. 5–7) and the other revelations of a life well-lived in harmony with God that provide the real life substance of discipleship. Evangelizing our culture is seeding it with the values that undergird the Kingdom of God and the actions that express it. Cultural hermeneutics that is 'in the Spirit' enables such discipleship to culturally understand itself and its context and therefore more adequately to be the 'faithful presence'.

What this evangelizing of our culture is not is some preconceived and misguided plan to transform society. 'Culture is too complex, dynamic, and unpredictable to change as a result of intentional action' (Mladin, 2021, p. 8). While Christian action may transform a situation or a life, moment by moment, such actions only ever anticipate the coming of the Kingdom, they never inaugurate it. Grandiose visualizations of recapturing a lost past or creating a new future where Christian values are translated into law and the structures of society are a form of neo-colonialist imperialism. From the Christian nationalism of the American political right to the Christian Socialism of the European political left, they can owe as much to culturally inherited ideological convictions as they do to a biblically inspired vision of the Kingdom of God. Indeed, as James Davison Hunter has convincingly demonstrated, when cultural change does occur it is generally top down and serves the interests of the networked elites (Hunter, 2010a, pp. 41–3). More than this, while he sees the activity of 'culture-making' as having its own validity before God, he underlines that it is, strictly speaking, neither redemptive or salvific in character. Indeed, where it views such work 'as "kingdom-building" this side of heaven ... [it] tends to lead to one version or another of the Constantinian project' (Hunter, 2010a, pp. 232–3).

CONCLUSION

> But love is also about grace, mercy, and justice, without which we are left with malice and humiliation, cruelty and coercion, and injury and injustice. The practice of faithful presence, then, generates relationships and institutions that are fundamentally covenantal in character, the end of which are the fostering of meaning, purpose, truth, beauty, belonging, and fairness – not just of Christians but for everyone. (Hunter, 2010a, p. 263)

It is intriguing in this regard that when Jesus seeks to find metaphors with which to liken his understanding of the Kingdom of God he comes up with salt, yeast and light. 'Salt is good; but if salt has lost its taste, how can its saltiness be restored' (Luke 14.34). Unsalty salt is clearly pretty useless, but when salt is sprinkled on a meal it is dissolved into the whole and, in losing its own substance, materially impacts the whole. Similarly with yeast: 'To what should I compare the kingdom of God? It is like yeast that a woman took and mixed in with three measures of flour until all of it was leavened' (Luke 13.20–21). Bread is the result of yeast being taken up into the mix of the whole. Or again with light, 'You are the light of the world. [On its lampstand] it gives light to all in the house' (Matt. 5.14–16). It is not the light source, but its presence enables others to 'see', not the light but everything else. In Jesus' profound summary statement, 'For those who want to save their life will lose it, and those who lose their life for my sake, and for the sake of the gospel, will save it' (Mark 8.35).

> So the challenges and opportunities morph with time, which means that Christians who are going to be 'faithfully present' to the society into which they're sent need to be attentive students of history, readers of the zeitgeist, ethnographers of their present ... Christian cultural analysis and social engagement must be rooted in a deeply *historical* posture, a sense of our embeddedness in time, and a healthy attention to the specifics of the moment in which we find ourselves. (Smith, 2017, p. 125)

In this way Christianity is incarnated into whatever culture it finds itself. As Lamin Sanneh joyfully observed, 'Christianity helped Africans to become renewed Africans, not re-made Europeans' (Sanneh, 2003, p. 43). Cultural hermeneutics 'in the Spirit' enables us to steer a path between the twin dangers of slavish conformity to our inherited culture and the seductive allure of our cultural present. It sets us free to exercise our agency as disciples of Jesus to be a 'faithful presence' that embodies and articulates the good news of God's love and our commitment to 'love our neighbours as ourselves' because people matter, have value, dignity and worth. That is discipleship, an art of living in which followers of Jesus are apprenticed for a lifetime.

Notes

1 In this instance Loughlin is considering how to read the biblical narratives of the resurrection, in the light of conflicting evidence, to discover the integrity of the biblical witness.

2 For more information see https://www.secularism.org.uk/religion-and-state/ (accessed 09.02.2023).

3 I am conscious that in using the phrase 'evangelizing our culture' it already has some life within Roman Catholic thinking as a part of 'The New Evangelization' and Pope John Paul II's call to counter the absence of Christian values in contemporary culture in seeking to generate 'a cultural alternative that is fully Christian.' Not a homogenous single whole as in the past, but nonetheless with the accompanying implication that cultures needed to be challenged to change and be transformed by being converted (Gallagher, 1997, pp. 54, 85; Gorringe, 2004, p. 201). A profound, lengthy and ongoing process, 'The normal consequence of successful evangelization is that Christianity becomes "at home" in the evangelized culture. It becomes "customary"' (Shorter, 2006, p. 62). The Catholic author and editor Stratford Caldecott expresses it in the following terms:

> the evangelization of culture is not a superficial 'baptism' of society, but implies a radical transformation of it. The Popes speak of a 'civilization of love' or a 'culture of life'. This can only be achieved, in any degree, by living out the Commandments and Beatitudes in our communities, and thus by creating a more just and humane society. That, in fact, is the goal and message of Catholic social teaching, which is

CONCLUSION

founded on the dignity of the individual person as an image of God. As human beings we achieve our personal fulfilment only through the worship of God and the service of our neighbour ... So, teaching the Church's social doctrine is an important part of evangelization. But that does not mean we do it only to win converts! A 'civilization of love' is not a civilization in which every person HAS to be a Christian. It is a civilization in which love is the supreme value, and where the 'logic' of love somehow shapes the structures of society. It is quite possible to have people of many different beliefs working and living together in such a society. We are working for the common good of humanity, and there are many people who would agree with us on the nature of the common good who do not recognize (we would say, do not YET recognize!) the divinity of Christ. (Caldecott, 2004)

Appendix 1

Representative Reflections on Defining the Concept of Culture

Anthropology

Culture can be loosely summarized as the complex of values, customs, beliefs and practices which constitute the way of life of a specific group. It is 'that complex whole', as the anthropologist E. B. Tylor famously put it in his *Primitive Culture* [1871], 'which includes knowledge, belief, art, morals, law, custom, and any other capabilities and habits acquired by man as a member of society.' (Eagleton, 2000, p. 34)

The new idea he [Geertz] has to hand is the idea of culture itself, but noting just how unusably all-inclusive the concept often is (by now it has swollen to embrace any manifestation of a society as well as becoming a synonym for 'society' itself), Geertz limits its meaning to the still extensive as well as suggestively delicate definition as those 'webs of significance' humankind spins for itself. Catching hold of the web without crushing it is a matter of 'thick description', which is how Gilbert Ryle directs us to distinguish between a boy whose eyelid twitches, a boy who is winking, and a boy imitating another boy's clumsy attempt at winking. A bit less contrivedly, it is by thick description that we decide, as chair of a political meeting, that the man with his arm up is waving to a friend, easing the pain in his shoulder, or voting. (Inglis, 2000, p. 113)

APPENDIX 1

[S]*ignifying* practices, a semiotic definition of culture which was ephemerally popular in the 1970s. Clifford Geertz, for example, sees culture as the webs of signification in which humanity is suspended. Raymond Williams writes of culture as 'the signifying system through which ... a social order is communicated, reproduced, experienced and explored ... All social systems, then, involve signification, but not all of them are signifying or "cultural" systems.' (Eagleton, 2000, p. 33-4)

Human beings, says Clifford Geertz ... are animals suspended in webs of significance that they themselves have spun. 'Culture' is the name for these webs. It is *what we make of the world*, materially, intellectually and spiritually. These dimensions cannot be separated: the Word is necessarily flesh. In constructing the world materially we interpret it, set values on it. To talk of values is to talk of a culture's self-understanding, its account of its priorities. (Gorringe, 2004, p. 3)

But perhaps we can combine this notion of culture as a 'web of meaning' which human beings create for themselves – the stories, myths and constructions which shape our understanding of the world – with a more materialist understanding of culture as essentially the realm of human fabrication, a systematic outworking of the achievements of *homo faber* – humanity the tool-maker, the builder of worlds. So 'culture' reflects something of our innate abilities for making, building and imagining worlds, both metaphysical and material, as well as our capacity to move adroitly between the two. (Graham, 2007, p. 77)

Clifford Geertz combines succinctness and clarity: '[T]he culture concept ... denotes an historically transmitted pattern of meanings embodied in symbols, a system of inherited conceptions expressed in symbolic form by means of which men communicate, perpetuate, and develop their knowledge about and attitudes towards life.' (Carson, 2008, p. 2)

In explanatory importance and in generality of application it is comparable to such categories as gravity in physics, disease in medicine, evolution in biology. (Kroeber and Kluckhohn, 1952, p. 3)

Culture consists of patterns, explicit and implicit, of and for behavior acquired and transmitted by symbols, constituting the distinctive achievements of human groups, including their embodiment in artifacts; the essential core of culture consists of traditional (i.e., historically derived and selected) ideas and especially their attached values; culture systems may, on the one hand, be considered as products of action, on the other hand as conditioning elements of further action. (Kroeber and Kluckhohn, 1952, p. 357)

Robert Redfield: 'shared understandings made manifest in art and artifact.' (Carson, 2008, p. 2)

On another view, culture is the implicit knowledge of the world by which people negotiate appropriate ways of acting in specific contexts ... more know-how than know-why, ... in John Frow's words, 'the whole range of practices and representations through which a social group's reality (or realities) is constructed and maintained'. (Eagleton, 2000, p. 35)

Culture is not only what we live by. It is also, in great measure, what we live for. Affection, relationship, memory, kinship, place, community, emotional fulfilment, intellectual enjoyment, a sense of ultimate meaning: these are closer to most of us than charters of human rights or trade treaties. (Eagleton, 2000, p. 131)

Although less than one hundred years old, the modern anthropological mention of 'culture' now enjoys a remarkable influence within the humanistic disciplines of the academy and within commonsense discussions of daily life. (Tanner, 1997, p. ix)

APPENDIX I

This ends our overview of the way the English word *culture* gains its anthropological sense as a group-differentiating, holistic, nonevaluative and context-relative notion. (Tanner, 1997, p. 24)

Sociology and cultural studies

Man cannot exist apart from society. The two statements, that society is the product of man and that man is the product of society, are not contradictory. They rather reflect the inherently dialectic character of the societal phenomenon. Only if this character is recognized will society be understood in terms adequate to its empirical reality. The fundamental dialectic process of society consists of three moments, or steps. These are externalization, objectivation, and internalization ... Externalization is the ongoing outpouring of human being into the world, both in the physical and the mental activity of men. Objectivation is the attainment by the products of this activity (again both physical and mental) of a reality that confronts its original producers as a facticity external to and other than themselves. Internalization is the reappropriation by men of this same reality, transforming it once again from structures of the objective world into structures of the subjective consciousness. It is through externalization that society is a human product. It is through objectivation that society becomes a reality *sui generis*. It is through internalization that man is a product of society. (Berger, 1990, p. 3–4)

Berger defines culture as 'the totality of man's products' ... as material artifacts and non-material socio-cultural formations that guide human behavior (what we call society is a segment of culture), but the *reflection* of this world as it is contained within human consciousness. The subjective side of culture must be emphasized, for these products on the individual level serve as more or less lasting measures of human subjectivity. In different words, these products manifest the subjective meanings or intentionality of those who produced them. The fabric of culture then is the intersubjective meanings individuals hold concerning the world in which they live. Culture exists, 'only as people are conscious of it' ([Berger] 1966:78). (Wuthnow et al., 1984, p. 35)

In an essay published in 1980, Stuart Hall offered a reflection on the historiography of cultural studies, focusing on the work of Raymond Williams, in which he found formulated two different emphases in the definition of culture (Hall, 1980). The first was 'the sum of the available descriptions through which societies make sense of and reflect [on] their common experiences' (1989: 50). The second, Hall summarized as 'those patterns of organization, those characteristic forms of human energy which can be discovered as revealing themselves ... within or underlying all social practices' (60). For Hall, cultural studies does right to engage both emphases in 'the dialectic between social being and social consciousness' (63). Culture, in other words, is both: the meanings that are embodied in the practices. Or, to push their dialectical relation to the logical end: culture is the meanings and the practices that produce one another in the three-fold dialectical process described by Peter Berger as externalization, objectivization, and internalization (Berger, 1969, p. 4). This means that culturalism regards culture not simply as the effect of human activity but as the constructive activity that makes social reality. Culture is what people do to negotiate their relationship to natural, social, and economic realities. Cultural studies is the academic inquiry into this interaction of everyday life. (Morgan, 2008, pp. 3–4)

Stuart Hall offers a similarly generous view of culture as the 'lived practices' or 'practical ideologies which enable a society, group or class to experience, define, interpret and make sense of its conditions of existence'. (Eagleton, 2000, p. 34)

In the 1980s and 1990s academics and intellectuals often signalled their dedication to complexity and difference by pluralizing words like 'culture'. You could see the point when history showed you that culture was often assumed to be the preserve of white middle-class men. So instead of American culture people would write about the 'cultures' of the United States. One unfortunate effect of this was that the plural of culture led to a myriad of isolated, singular 'cultures' – football culture, gay culture, women's culture, music culture and so on. I want to avoid the effect by assuming that culture is the word we give to the plurality and contradiction of meanings, feelings and practices that circulate in the world and, crucially, to their circulation. (Highmore, 2016, p. viii)

definition of culture ... by James Taylor in 1949: 'Culture can be briefly characterized as a stream of ideas flowing between individuals through the medium of symbolic activities, verbal teaching, or imitation.' (Bauman, 2018, p. 8)

All definitions of culture ... share the fact that they objectivize culture – beyond all discussion, it is a human creation, existing in people and through people as an object in and of itself, exterior to the individual, and therefore a potential object of study. Such an intellectual objectification of the cultural sphere, though it seems natural and obvious to us today, certainly did not stem from an innate capability of the human species, or from the particular 'nature' of cultural phenomenon. (Bauman, 2018, p. 9)

It is, as one sociologist [Bauman] puts it, the belief that human beings 'are what they are taught.' (Eagleton, 2000, p. 34)

Theology and Christian apologetics

What we have in view when we deal with Christ and culture is that total process of human activity and the total result of such activity to which now the name *culture*, now the name *civilization*, is applied in common speech. Culture is the 'artificial, secondary environment' which man superimposes on the natural. It comprises language, habits, ideas, beliefs, customs, social organization, inherited artifacts, technical processes, and values. This ... the New Testament writers frequently had in mind when they speak of 'the world'. (Niebuhr, 1951, p. 32)

Niebuhr goes on to state that while he cannot venture to define the 'essence' of this culture he can highlight seven of its chief characteristics. It is:

1 always *social*
2 *human achievement*
3 *a world of values*
4 dominantly those of the *good for man*
5 concerned with the *temporal and material realization of values*
6 concerned with the *conservation of values*
7 directed to the *pluralism* that is characteristic of all cultures. (See Niebuhr, 1951, pp. 32–9)

The essence of culture is found in the *hearts and minds of individuals* – in what are typically called "values". Values are, simply, moral preferences; inclinations toward or conscious attachment to what is good and right and true. Culture is manifested in the ways these values guide actual decisions we individuals make about how to live ... By this view, a culture is made up of the accumulation of values held by the majority of people and the choices made on the basis of those values.' (Hunter, 2010a, p. 6)

This book views culture as a work and world of meaning. Better, *culture is made up of 'works' and 'worlds' of meaning*. Culture is a *work* because it is the result of what humans do freely, not a result of what they do by nature to produce something significant. Let us call the products of such work *cultural texts*. (Vanhoozer et al., 2007, p. 26)

Vatican II, in which 'culture' is described both as the sum of human achievement and the milieu in which Christian faith in necessarily proclaimed and practiced. (Lynch, 2007, p. 67)

APPENDIX 1

We will define culture as 'more or less integrated systems of ideas, feelings, and values and their associated patterns of behavior and products shared by a group of people who organize and regulate what they think, feel, and do.' (Hiebert, 1985, p. 30)
Hiebert further then identifies three foundational dimensions of culture that relate to ideas, feelings and values – the cognitive (knowledge, logic and wisdom), affective (feelings and aesthetics) and evaluative (values and allegiances) dimensions of culture. (See Hiebert, 1985, pp. 30–4)

In its most general sense it means the whole web of interpretative strategies by which human beings make sense of their experience. (Marsh and Ortiz, 1997, p. 24)

There is one more piece of introductory material that is necessary: a definition of 'culture'. This is a notoriously difficult task. Nonetheless, we need a working definition, and so let me offer one, not my own, which at least brings out those aspects of the concept which I presently regard as most theologically interesting, 'a culture is a particular collection of socially learned ways of living found in human societies' [Marvin Harris, 1999, p. 19]. (Holmes, 2008, p. 4)

Culture is the accumulation of behaviors and beliefs that characterize a group of people. It is comprised of the attitudes, symbols, language, rewards, expectations, customs, and values that define the experience and context of those people. (Barna, 2005, p. 108)

Today, 'culture' has become a fairly plastic concept that means something like 'the set of values broadly shared by some subset of the human population.' (Carson, 2008, p. 1)

A culture is an ecosystem of institutions, practices, artifacts, and beliefs, all interacting and mutually reinforcing. Cultures are rarely entirely homogenous or consistent, but generalizations about specific cultures are nonetheless possible. Despite their complexity, cultures can have an overriding ethos. (Myers, 1989, p. xi)

They begin 'making something of the world'. This phrase which I have adapted from the Christian cultural critic Ken Myers, distills what culture is and why it matters: *Culture is what we make of the world.* Culture is, first of all, the name for our relentless, restless human effort to take the world as it's given to us and make something else. (Crouch, 2008, p. 23)

Appendix 2

Frameworks for Interrogating Culture

Kelton Cobb's systematic theology as a loose organizing principle

Focusing on popular culture Cobb sees following a traditional approach to systematic theology as a helpful way of identifying theological topics of interest. He starts with:

- God.
- Human nature.
- Sin.
- Salvation.
- Eschatology.

But then he suggests that the theological tools that can be particularly helpful within this framework as a beginners' set are:

- Ultimate concern.
- The holy.
- Ontological and moral faith.
- Revelation and ecstasy.
- Religious symbols.
- Myth.
- Liminality.
- Religion.

Cobb also uses H. Richard Niebuhr's categories of 'broken faith' (defiance, fear and escape), along with William James' 'once-born healthy-minded souls' and 'twice-born sick souls' and the analytical rubric of cultural studies such as hegemony, style, *bricolage*, memes, simulacra (Cobb, 2005, pp. 12–24, 132).

Dave Benson's six modes of cultural engagement

Benson uses the biblical narrative as one coherent metaphor to guide a missional understanding of secular education and direct a 'simple and sufficient' posture for engagement with it.

1   Creation: Garden Together/Direct.
2   Fall: Expose Error/Challenge.
3   Israel: Seek Wisdom/Partner.
4   Jesus: Redeem Life/Sacrifice.
5   Church: Foster Wholeness/Unite.
6   New Creation: Pre-empt Praise/Celebrate.
    (Benson, 2020, pp.114–27)

James Davison Hunter's dialectical tension between affirmation and antithesis

Christian discipleship is carried out in an inevitable and irresolvable tension, between our cultural context and the call of God, between history and revelation. Following Miraslov Volf's observation of this tension in 1 Peter, where on one hand the church is described as 'aliens and exiles' in the world (1 Pet. 1.1; 2.11) and yet are also exhorted to 'For the Lord's sake accept the authority of every human institution' (1 Pet. 2.13). In its beliefs, ideals and institutions the church is distinct from the rest of society, while also being instructed to accommodate to the reality of the world around them.

For Hunter herein lies the 'call' for Christians to live within this tension of affirmation and antithesis. Everything in the world is part of that which was created by God and declared good. This is not negated by the fall. Goodness, beauty and truth are an integral part of the fallen creation. Indeed, people of every creed and none can possess knowledge, wisdom, goodness, justice and morality. Of course, herein also is the paradox that nonbelievers can sometimes demonstrate these qualities more than believers, who because of the universality of the fall, can prove themselves to be unloving, unjust and displaying wholly inappropriate qualities of character. However, in the realm of 'common grace' the task of world-making is an expression of humanity being made in God's image and the 'cultural mandate' of Genesis. Insofar as this anticipates the shalom of the Kingdom of God it is merely a foretaste of what is to come and a witness to the nature of God.

By contrast with the affirmation is that antithesis that is rooted in the totality of the fall. All human effort falls short and stands under judgement and all human achievement is measured by the standards of the coming Kingdom. The church exists as a 'community of resistance' that challenges structures that dishonour God, dehumanize people and do harm to the creation. Such resistance is not destructive but is rather creative and constructive. From metaphysical, epistemological and anthropological assumptions down to individual behaviours it opposes that which undermines human flourishing and offer positive alternatives that might enhance lived lives. And, of course, 'the time has come for judgment to begin with the household of God' (1 Pet. 4.17).

For Hunter, interpreting culture has to be undertaken through this critical duality because it defines the present state of history in the divine purpose and affects everything. He quotes Volf, 'Christian difference is ... not an insertion of something new into the old from outside, but a bursting out of the new precisely within the proper space of the old' (Hunter, 2010a, pp. 230–6).

Marsh and Ortiz and theology's critical dialogue with culture

Exploring the subject of theology and film, Marsh and Ortiz condense H. Richard Niebuhr's five 'Christ and culture' categories to three. They see three possible accounts for the relationship between Christian theology and culture.

- Theology against culture.
- Theology immersed in culture.
- Theology in critical dialogue with culture.

They maintain that there are five 'theological hallmarks' or commitments that are the fruit of their third category, which they adopt for their exploration of film:

- God present and active in creation, in the world beyond the church.
- The importance of the church.
- Human beings made in the image of God.
- The creativity of God's Spirit.
- The concreteness of Christianity caused by Christianity's Christological concentration.

To this they adapt and add Tillich's 'theology of correlation' to complete their exploratory strategy, which they describe as an interdisciplinary dialogue engaged in a quest for truth (Marsh and Ortiz, 1997, pp. 28–30).

Steve Nolan and 'Understanding Films: reading in the gaps'

As with Justin Ariel Bailey and culture as a whole, Nolan has serious reservations about taking a literary approach when interpreting films. He maintains that films are much more than 'visual stories' and prefers the description of 'signifying practices'. This he believes enables films to be understood on their own terms and interpreted more easily in regard to their cultural significance. He believes that borrowing from structuralist film theory offers a more profitable way to produce culturally informed theological reflection. That is, in exploring the way films invite viewers to construct a certain identity for themselves, to ask why they do this and to assess the results of this process. He suggests adopting three specific ideas to develop an interpretive frame through which theology can engage with film:

- *The spectator's pseudo-identification* – in viewing the film the spectator forges a fictional or pseudo-identification with the

screen character-actor-star, thus assuming an ego assigned or signified by an 'other'.
- *The spectator is sutured into the narrative space* – the desire to identify with the character-actor-star joins the spectator into the film's narrative space and therefore enters into the film as the narrative unfolds.
- *The spectator becomes a participant in a constructed reality* – individuals readily inhabit the reality constructed by the film-maker, a cinematic impression of reality that repositions the spectator within its own story. Such a cinematic impression is always ideological and the spectator situates themselves within it.

(Nolan, 2005, pp. 34–6, 43–4)

Gerard Loughlin and narrativist theology

With an academic background in literature and literary studies as well as theology, Loughlin seeks to bring them together with film in an interdisciplinary encounter. Convinced of the power of narratives, he views the biblical story as containing an invitation not so much to 'get inside the text, as to let the text get inside us, so that we are nourished by its word and enabled to perform its story' (Loughlin, 1996, p. 139). Following Ricoeur, he happily embraces Gadamer's idea of the 'fusion of horizons', where in the readers' imagination the horizon of the world of the text merges with their own. In this process the reader refigures their own world in an act of completing the narrative work (Loughlin, 1996, p. 146).

Taking these ideas, he uses film, literature and theology as conversation partners where narratives are allowed to stand alongside one another and, following Barth, owns that 'there can be other true words alongside the Word of God'. In being attentive to the voice of Christ in that which is alien, 'we may discover that all our comforts and satisfactions are turned upside-down, and we are challenged to look again, to see the world remade' (Loughlin, 2004, pp. xii–xiv).

Appendix 3

Interrogative Questions

Andy Crouch

Crouch's 'diagnosing culture' seeks to understand how a given cultural artefact fits into its wider cultural context. As the following summary shows, in doing this Crouch has found it helpful to begin and end with something tangible.

- *What does this cultural artefact assume about the way the world is?* What are the key features of the world that this cultural artefact tries to deal with, respond to, make sense of?
- *What does this cultural artefact assume about the way the world should be?* What vision of the future animated its creators? What new sense does it seek to add to a world that often seems chaotic and senseless?
- *What does this cultural artefact make possible?* What can people do or imagine, thanks to this artefact, that they could not before?
- *What does this cultural artefact make impossible (or at least very difficult)?* Almost every cultural artefact, in small or large ways, makes something impossible – or at least more difficult – that was possible before.
- *What new forms of culture are created in response to this artefact?* Because culture inevitably begets culture ... what is cultivated and created that could not have been before? (See Crouch, 2008, pp. 29–30)

APPENDIX 3

Gordon Lynch

Lynch's criteria for helping to form an aesthetic judgement with the texts and performances of popular culture:

- Does it demonstrate an impressive level of *technical skill*?
- Does it exemplify *originality, imagination, or creativity*?
- Does it offer a satisfying *reflection of human experience* or provide a means for empathizing with a range of different experiences?
- Does it offer a valuable *vision of the meaning of our lives*?
- Does it provide us with *genuinely pleasurable experiences*, whether emotional, sensual, or intellectual?
- Does it *encourage constructive relationships* between people or make certain *useful and enjoyable forms of social interaction* possible?
- Does it make possible a *sense of encounter with 'God,' the transcendent, or the numinous*?
- Does it successfully *serve the function* for which it has been created?
- Is it *authentic*?

(See Lynch, 2005, pp. 190–1)

Justin Ariel Bailey

Bailey's five lenses to look through to view a cultural artefact.

The Meaning Dimension

- Is this 'a thing'? In other words, does this cultural artefact represent something shared by many people rather than being peculiar to a few people? Why is this 'a thing'?
- How does this thing connect? Why do people find this meaningful?
- Why do I resonate with or resist this thing? What does it mean to me, and why?

- How does it connect with Christian accounts of the world? Does it emerge from within or outside Christian cultures? How have Christians embraced or resisted this thing?
- Where do we see glimmers of beauty, goodness, and truth?
- How does this cultural artefact fit into and express the movements of the biblical story (created goodness, pervasive fallenness, or hope of redemption)?

The Power Dimension

- What are the interests of those in power when it comes to this cultural artefact?
- Who benefits from the success of this cultural artefact? Who does not benefit? Who does it place in the centre? Who does it push to the margins?
- How could this artefact be used to exercise influence, constrain desire, serve as propaganda, or support the status quo?
- Should/can we resist? What makes resistance difficult?
- Where do we see cultural idolatry – a good thing that has been made into an ultimate thing? Is there a connection to be made between the cultural idolatry and occasions of cultural injustice?
- What would iconoclasm (confronting idolatry) look like? What, if anything, needs to be rejected or replaced? What needs to be complicated? What critique does the gospel bring?

The Ethical Dimension

- What boundaries are provided by the people who participate in this cultural phenomenon? What is deemed acceptable, normal, desirable, or virtuous behaviour?
- What is the implicit vision of human flourishing (what it means to be a good human) according to this cultural artefact? Where is the moral high ground?
- How does this artefact's vision of flourishing fit the Christian vision of righteousness, peace and joy?

- How does this cultural artefact lead us to relate to those on the other side of the moral boundary, and how does this compare with how Scripture leads us?
- What do we make of this artefact if we are ultimately answerable to God?
- How can we participate in this cultural phenomenon in a way that leads to the organic flourishing of others?

The Religious Dimension

- When it comes to this cultural artefact, what deserves attention as 'sacred'? What is worthy of our ultimate concern?
- How does this cultural artefact help people cope with the difficulties of life? How does it organize life into a consistent rhythm, even ritual behaviour?
- How does this cultural phenomenon form a community of support, and what are the common things in the centre?
- How might it offer transcendence of self-interest, even moments of ecstasy?
- What are those who participate in this cultural phenomenon doing with God? Is it a way to avoid God? Where are there 'cracks' to let God's light in?
- What challenge, critique, or completion does the gospel bring to the religious vision of this cultural artefact? How does the gospel offer fuller meaning that could not be found apart from Christ?

The Aesthetic Dimension

- How does this cultural artefact elicit desire and delight?
- What is the implicit vision of the beautiful and worthwhile life?
- How do appearances play into the felt experience of the cultural trend? What are the 'branding' elements that associate this cultural artefact with what is desirable?

- How is this cultural artefact generative, and what does it generate? What are some ways that participants have taken this in surprising ways? Does it include a layer of excess, 'just for the heaven of it'?
- How does Christian faith direct the desire and delight this cultural artefact elicits? What are we being trained to love, and how can the love of God reorient these desires?
- What will I make of this cultural phenomenon? How will this be integrated into my life? What will I make in response to this cultural phenomenon? (See Bailey, 2022, pp. 150–2).

Dave Benson

Benson's 'six piercing questions' that we should ask of our own cultural context:

- What partial good is evident, which I can direct to its transcendent source?
- What idolatry distorts life, which I must challenge, prophetically speaking truth to power?
- Where do I see the possibility of coalition building for the common good, and how may I partner?
- How has violence enslaved [us], and how might sacrifice break its hold over the system as a whole?
- How might we become a community of character capable of healing deep division? And what would it look like to unite polarized parties, nurturing integration through diversity?
- What is truly excellent [here], a sign of new creation, which we can affirm and celebrate?

(See Benson, 2020, pp. 124–5)[1]

Note

1 Benson was reflecting specifically on an educational context and his questions have been generalized in this account of his thinking.

Bibliography

Alexander, Jeffrey C., 2003, *The Meanings of Social Life: A Cultural Sociology*, Oxford: Oxford University Press.
Archbishops' Council, 2004, *Mission-Shaped Church: Church Planting and Fresh Expressions of Church in a Changing Context*, London: Church House Publishing.
Aridici, Nuray, 2019, 'The power of civilizational nationalism in Russian foreign policy making' in *International Politics* 56.5, available at https://link.springer.com/article/10.1057/s41311-018-0159-8 (accessed 04.11.2022).
Austin, J. L., 1962, *How To Do Things With Words*, Oxford: The Clarendon Press.
Baasland, Ernst, 1997, 'The Contextualized Witness of the Apostles', in *World Evangelization 80*.
Bailey, Justin Ariel, 2022, *Interpreting Your World: Five Lenses for Engaging Theology and Culture*, Grand Rapids, MI: Baker Academic.
Baldwin, Elaine, Brian Longhurst, Scott McCracken, Miles Ogborn and Greg Smith, 1999, *Introducing Cultural Studies*, Harlow: Prentice Hall.
Banks, Robert, 1999, *Reenvisioning Theological Education: Exploring a Missional Alternative to Current Models*, Grand Rapids, MI: William B. Eerdmans.
Barker, Chris, and Emma A. Jane, 2016, *Cultural Studies: Theory and Practice* (5th edition), London: Sage.
Barna, George, 2005, *Revolution: Finding Vibrant Faith beyond the Walls of the Sanctuary*, Wheaton, Ill: Tyndale House.
Barrett, C. K., 1978, *The Gospel According to St. John* (2nd edn), London: SPCK.
—— 1979, *A Commentary on the First Epistle to the Corinthians* (2nd edn) *(Black's New Testament Commentaries)*, London: Adam and Charles Black.
Barthes, Roland, 1991, *Mythologies: Selected and translated from the French by Annette Lavers*, New York, NY: The Noonday Press.
Bassnett, Susan, 2014, *Translation Studies (New Accents)* (4th edn), Abingdon: Routledge.

Bauman, Zygmunt, 2000, *Liquid Modernity*, Cambridge: Polity Press.
—— 2005, *Liquid Life*, Cambridge: Polity Press.
—— 2007, *Liquid Times: Living in an Age of Uncertainty*, Cambridge: Polity Press.
—— 2011, *Culture in a Liquid Modern World*, Cambridge: Polity Press.
—— 2018, *Sketches in the Theory of Culture*, Cambridge: Polity Press.
Beasley-Murray, George R., 1987, *John (Word Biblical Commentary)*, Waco, TX: Word Books.
Bennett, Andrew, and Nicholas Royle, 2016, *An Introduction to Literature, Criticism and Theory* (5th edn), Abingdon: Routledge.
Benson, Dave, 2020, 'Why we need the world: musings from the interface of theology and education', in Michael Frost, Darrell Jackson and David Starling (eds), *Not in Kansas Anymore: Christian Faith in a Post-Christian World*, Eugene, OR: Wipf and Stock/Morling Press.
—— 2023, 'The London Interdisciplinary School advert' on Facebook, available at https://www.facebook.com/photo?fbid=10159584737451758andset=a.10153456534926758 (accessed 30.01.2023).
Berger, Peter L., 1990, *The Sacred Canopy: Elements of a Sociological Theory of Religion*, New York, NY: Anchor Books.
—— (ed.), 1999, *The Desecularization of the World: Resurgent Religion and World Politics*, Grand Rapids, MI: William B. Eerdmans Publishing Company.
Bevans, Stephen B., 2002, *Models of Contextual Theology* (2nd edn), Maryknoll, NY: Orbis Books.
Blakely, Jason, 2020, *We Built Reality: How Social Sciences Infiltrated Culture, Politics and Power*, Oxford: Oxford University Press.
Bonnell, Victoria E. and Lynn Hunt (eds), 1999, *Beyond the Cultural Turn: New Directions in the Study of Society and Culture*, Berkeley, CA: University of California Press.
Bosch, David J., 2003, *Transforming Mission: Paradigm Shifts in Theology of Mission*, Maryknoll, NY: Orbis.
Bourdieu, Pierre, 1977, *Outline of a Theory of Practice*, Cambridge: Cambridge University Press.
Brody, Richard, 2021, 'Steven Spielberg's "West Side Story" Remake Is Worse Than the Original', in *The New Yorker* (14 December), available at https://www.newyorker.com/culture/the-front-row/review-steven-spielbergs-west-side-story-remake-is-worse-than-the-original (accessed 24.12.2022).
Brown, Delwin, Sheila Greeve Davaney and Kathryn Tanner, 2001, *Converging on Culture*, Oxford: Oxford University Press.
Brown, Raymond E., 1985, *Biblical Exegesis and Church Doctrine*, New York, NY: Paulist Press.
Bruce, F. F., 1980, *I and II Corinthians (The New Century Bible Commentary)*, London: Marshall, Morgan and Scott.

—— 1984, 'The church of Jerusalem in the Acts of the Apostles', in *Bulletin of the John Rylands Library* 67.2.

Brueggemann, Walter, 2001, *The Prophetic Imagination* (2nd edn), Minneapolis, MN: Fortress Press.

Brunner, Emil, 1931, *The Word and the World*, London: SCM Press.

Bryan, Steven M., 2022, *Cultural Identity and the Purposes of God: A Biblical Theology of Ethnicity, Nationality and Race*, Wheaton, IL: Crossway.

Bryant, Clifton D., and Dennis L. Peck, 2007, *21st Century Sociology: A Reference Handbook*, Volumes 1–2, Thousand Oaks, CA: Sage Publications.

Bühler, Pierre, 2000, 'Hermeneutics', in Adrian Hastings, Alistair Mason and Hugh Pyper (eds), *The Oxford Companion to Christian Thought: Intellectual, Spiritual, and Moral Horizons of Christianity*, Oxford: Oxford University Press.

Caldecott, Stratford, 2004, 'The evangelization of culture and Catholic social teaching', in *Second Spring*, available at https://archive.secondspring.co.uk/spring/lazu.htm (accessed 10.02.2023).

Calder, Gideon, 2003, *Rorty and Redescription*, London: Weidenfeld and Nicolson.

—— 2007a, *Rorty's Politics of Redescription*, Cardiff: University of Wales Press.

—— 2007b, 'Obituary: Richard Rorty (1931–2007)' in *Philosophy Now* (62, July/August), available at https://philosophynow.org/issues/62/Richard_Rorty_1931-2007 (accessed 23.09.2022).

Calvin, John, 1856, *Commentary on the Epistles to Timothy, Titus, and Philemon: translated from the original Latin by the Rev. William Pringle*, available at https://biblicalstudies.org.uk/book_pastoral-epistles_calvin.html (accessed 30.01.2023).

Cameron, Helen, Deborah Bhatti, Catherine Duce, James Sweeney and Clare Watkins, 2010, *Talking About God in Practice: Theological Action Research and Practical Theology*, London: SCM Press.

Caputo, John D., 2007, *What Would Jesus Deconstruct? The Good News of Postmodernism for the Church*, Grand Rapids, MI: Baker Academic.

Carson, D. A., 2008, *Christ and Culture Revisited*, Grand Rapids, MI: Wm Eerdmans Publishing Co.

Carter, Craig A., 2006, *Rethinking Christ and Culture: A Post-Christendom Perspective*, Grand Rapids, MI: Brazos Press.

Cartledge, Mark J., and David Cheetham, 2011, *Intercultural Theology: Approaches and Themes*, London: SCM Press.

Certeau, Michel de, 1988, *The Practice of Everyday Life*, London: University of California Press.

Chang, Jonah, 2012, *Shoki Coe: An Ecumenical Life in Context*, Geneva: WCC Publications.

Chatraw, Joshua D., and Karen Swallow Prior, 2019, *Cultural Engagement*, Grand Rapids, MI: Zondervan Academic.
Cheney, Kristen, 2012, 'Locating Neocolonialism, "Tradition," and Human Rights in Uganda's "Gay Death Penalty"', in *African Studies Review* 55.2 (September 2012).
Childs, Peter, 2006, *Texts: Contemporary Cultural Texts and Critical Approaches*, Edinburgh: Edinburgh University Press.
Clark, Terry Ray and Dan W. Clanton, Jr. (eds), 2012, *Understanding Religion and Popular Culture: Theories, Themes, Products and Practices*, London: Routledge.
Cobb, Kelton, 2005, *Theology and Popular Culture*, Oxford: Blackwell.
Cohen, Leah Hager, 2022, 'In 1980s Glasgow, a World of Pain Made Bearable by Love', in *New York Times* (11 February) available at https://www.nytimes.com/2020/02/11/books/review/shuggie-bain-douglas-stuart.html (accessed 24.12.2022).
Cook, Ian, David Crouch, Simon Naylor and James R. Ryan (eds), 2000, *Cultural Turns/Geographical Turns: Perspectives on Cultural Geography*, London: Routledge.
Corrie, John, 2002, 'Contextualization Revisited', in *Missiologic* 3 (September 2002).
Corrigan, Timothy (ed.), 2012, *Film and Literature: An Introduction and Reader* (2nd edn), Abingdon: Routledge.
Coupland, Douglas, 1991, *Generation X: Tales for an Accelerated Culture*, New York, NY: St. Martin's Press.
Cray, Graham, 2007, *Disciples and Citizens: A vision for Distinctive living*, Nottingham: Inter-Varsity Press.
Crouch, Andy, 2008, *Culture Making: Recovering Our Creative Calling*, Downers Grove, IL: IVP Books.
Datema, David Earl, 2022, 'The universal particularism of *panta ta ethne*: A biblical case for the continued viability of the people group concept in mission', in *Missiology* 50.2 (April 2022).
de Graft, Joe, 1977, *Muntu*, Kampala, Uganda: East African Publishers.
Dunn, James D. G., 2003, *Paul the Apostle*, London: T&T Clark.
During, Simon, 1993, *The Cultural Studies Reader*, London: Routledge.
—— 2005, *Cultural Studies: A Critical Introduction*, London: Routledge.
Eagleton, Terry, 2000, *The Idea of Culture*, Malden, MA: Blackwell Publishing.
Edgar, William, 2017, *Created and Creating: A biblical theology of culture*, London: Apollos.
Eliot, T. S., 1948, *Notes towards the Definition of Culture*, London: Faber and Faber.
EHRC (Equality and Human Rights Commission), 2010, *Stop and think: A critical review of the use of stop and search powers in England and Wales*, available at www.equalityhumanrights.com/sites/default/files/ehrc_stop_and_search_report.pdf (accessed 10.09.2022).

BIBLIOGRAPHY

Felski, Rita, 2011, 'Context Stinks!', in *New Literary History* 42.4 (Autumn 2011).

Fitch, David E., 2016, *Faithful Presence: Seven Disciplines that Shape the Church for Mission*, Downers Grove, IL: IVP Books.

—— 2022, 'The way worship works in mission: Proposing an alternative to the standard account', in *Missiology* 50.2 (April 2022).

Fletcher, Paul, 2009, *Disciplining the Divine: toward an (im)political theology*, Farnham: Ashgate.

Fletcher, Thomas, 2021, 'The ECB must launch a national inquiry into racism at all levels of cricket', in *The Guardian* (20 November 2021), available at https://www.theguardian.com/sport/blog/2021/nov/20/ecb-national-inquiry-racism-cricket (accessed 18.12.2022).

Foucault, Michel, 1970, *The Order of Things: An Archaeology of the Human Sciences*, New York, NY: Random House.

—— 1977, *Discipline and Punish: the Birth of the Prison*, New York, NY: Pantheon Books.

Gallagher, Michael Paul, SJ, 1997, *Clashing Symbols: An introduction to Faith and Culture*, London: Darton, Longman and Todd.

Geertz, Clifford, 1973, *The Interpretation of Cultures: Selected Essays*, New York, NY: Basic Books, Inc.

Gilliland, Dean S. (ed.), 1989, *The Word Among Us: Contextualizing Theology for Mission Today*, Dallas, TX: Word Books.

Godley, A. D. (trans.), 1921, *Herodotus II, Books III-IV*, London: William Heinemann.

Goodwin, James, 1979, 'Literature and film: A review of criticism', in *Quarterly Review of Film Studies*, 4:2.

Goodwin, Richard Vance, 2022, *Seeing Is Believing: The Revelation of God Through Film*, Downers Grove, IL: IVP Academic.

Gorringe, T., 2004, *Furthering Humanity*, London: Ashgate.

Gorski, Philip S., and Samuel L. Perry, 2022, *The Flag and the Cross: White Christian Nationalism and the Threat to American Democracy*, New York, NY: Oxford University Press.

Gould, Paul M., 2019, *Cultural Apologetics: Renewing the Christian Voice, Conscience, and Imagination in a Disenchanted World*, Grand Rapids, MI: Zondervan.

Graham, Elaine, 2007, 'What We Make of the World: The Turn to "Culture" in Theology and the Study of Religion', in Gordon Lynch (ed.), *Between Sacred and Profane: Researching Religion and Popular Culture*, London: I.B. Tauris.

—— 2017, *Apologetics without Apology: Speaking of God in a World Troubled by Religion*, Eugene, OR: Cascade Books.

Grimshaw, Mike, 2018, 'The future of the philosophy of religion is the philosophy of culture – and vice versa', in *Palgrave Communications* 4.72, available at https://www.nature.com/articles/s41599-018-0129-1 (accessed 12.03.2022).

Groh, Arnold, 2020, *Theories of Culture*, Abingdon: Routledge.
Gross, Neil, 2019, *Richard Rorty: The Making of an American Philosopher*, Chicago: The University of Chicago Press.
Gruber, Judith, 2018, *Intercultural Theology: Exploring World Christianity After the Cultural Turn*, Göttingen: Vandenhoeck and Ruprecht.
Guarino, Thomas G., 2013, *Vincent of Lérins and the Development of Christian Doctrine*, Grand Rapids, MI: Baker Academic.
Guhin, Jeffrey, Jessica McCrory Calarco and Cynthia Miller-Idriss, 2021, 'Whatever Happened to Socialization?', in *Annual Review of Sociology* 47, pp. 109–29.
Gümüşay, Kübra, 2022, *Speaking and Being: How Language Binds and Frees Us*, London: Profile Books.
Habermas, Jürgen, et al., 2010, *An Awareness of What is Missing: Faith and Reason in a Post-secular Age*, Cambridge: Polity Press.
Hall, Stuart, 1973, *Encoding and Decoding in the Television Discourse: Paper for the Council of Europe Colloquy on 'Training in the Critical Reading of Television Language*, available at https://www.birmingham.ac.uk/Documents/college-artslaw/history/cccs/stencilled-occasional-papers/1to8and11to24and38to48/SOP07.pdf (accessed 13.09.2022).
——1982, 'The rediscovery of "ideology": return of the repressed in media studies', in Michael Gurevitch, Tony Bennett, James Curran and Janet Wollacott (eds), *Culture, Society and the Media*, London: Methuen.
Harris, Marvin, 1999, *Theories of Culture in Postmodern Times*, London: Altamira Press.
Harvey, Lincoln, 2014, *A Brief Theology of Sport*, London: SCM Press.
Hauerwas, Stanley, and William H. Willimon, 1989, *Resident Aliens*, Nashville, TN: Abingdon Press.
Hawthorne, Gerald F., 1983, *Philippians (Word Biblical Commentary)*, Waco. TX: Word Books.
Hayakawa, S. I., 1952, *Language in Thought and Action*, London: George Allen and Unwin Ltd.
Hesselgrave, David J. and Edward Rommen, 1989, *Contextualization: Meanings, Methods, and Models*, Grand Rapids, MI: Baker Book House.
Hiebert, Paul G., 1985, *Anthropological Insights for Missionaries*, Grand Rapids, MI: Baker Book House.
——2009, *The Gospel in Human Contexts: Anthropological Explorations for Contemporary Missions*, Grand Rapids, MI: Baker Academic.
Highmore, Ben, 2009, *A Passion for Cultural Studies*, Basingstoke: Palgrave Macmillan.
——2016, *Culture*, Abingdon: Routledge.
Hoelzl, Michael, and Graham Ward, 2008, *The New Visibility of*

Religion: Studies in Religion and Cultural Hermeneutics, London: Continuum.

Hofstede, Geert, and Gert Jan Hofstede, 2005, *Cultures and Organizations: Software of the Mind*, New York, NY: McGraw-Hill.

Hoggart, Richard, 1957, *The Uses of Literacy: aspects of working-class life with special reference to publications and entertainments*. Harmondsworth: Penguin Books.

Holmes, Stephen R. (ed.), 2008, *Public Theology in Cultural Engagement*, Milton Keynes: Paternoster.

—— 2021, 'Baptist Identity, Once More', in *Journal of Baptist Theology in Context*, Issue 3 (2021), available at https://www.jbtc.org.uk/issue-3 (accessed 06.11.2022).

Howell, Brian M., and Jenell Williams Paris, 2011, *Introducing Cultural Anthropology: A Christian Perspective*, Grand Rapids, MI: Baker Academic.

Hughes, Hugh Price, 1894, 'Social Evolution', in *The Methodist Times: A Journal of Religious and Social Movement*, Vol. 10, No. 485, April 12, 1894, London.

Hunsberger, George R., 1998, *Bearing the Witness of the Spirit: Lesslie Newbigin's Theology of Cultural Plurality*, Grand Rapids, MI: William B. Eerdmans Publishing Company.

Hunter, James Davison, 1991, *Culture Wars: The Struggle to Define America*, New York, NY: Basic Books.

—— 2010a, *To Change the World*, Oxford: Oxford University Press.

—— 2010b, 'Faithful Presence', in *Christianity Today*, available at https://www.christianitytoday.com/ct/2010/may/16.33.html (accessed 16.12.2021).

Hunter, James Davison, and James K. A. Smith, 2010, 'Neither Triumphalism nor Retreat: A Conversation about Faithful Presence with James Davison Hunter', in *The Other Journal: An Intersection of Theology and Culture*, 18, The Seattle School of Theology and Psychology, available at https://theotherjournal.com/2010/09/22/neither-triumph alism-nor-retreat-a-conversation-about-faithful-presence-with-james-davison-hunter/ (accessed 08.11.2022).

Inglis, Fred, 2000, *Clifford Geertz: Culture, Custom and Ethics*, Cambridge: Polity Press.

Itao, Alexis Deodato S. 2021, 'Of Words, Meaning and Hermeneutics: J. L. Austin and Paul Ricoeur on the Art of Making Sense of Things', in *Meta: Research in Hermeneutics, Phenomenology, and Practical Philosophy*, Vol. XIII, No. 2 (December), available at http://www.metajournal.org/download.php?id=461andtype=articles (accessed 09.01.2023).

Jacobs, Mark D., and Lyn Spillman, 2005, 'Cultural sociology at the crossroads of the discipline', in *Poetics* 33.1.

Jenkins, Philip, 2011, *The Next Christendom: the Coming of Global Christianity*, Oxford: Oxford University Press.
Johnson, Richard, 1986, 'What is Cultural Studies Anyway?', in *Social Text*, 16, available at https://doi.org/10.2307/466285 (accessed 06.09.2022).
Johnston, Robert K., 2006, *Reel Spirituality: theology and film in dialogue* (2nd edn), Grand Rapids, MI: Baker Academic.
—— (ed.), 2007, *Reframing Theology and Film: New Focus for an Emerging Discipline*, Grand Rapids, MI: Baker Academic.
Keener, Craig S., 2003, *The Gospel of John: A Commentary*, Grand Rapids, MI: Baker Academic.
—— 2016, *Spirit Hermeneutics: Reading Scripture in Light of Pentecost*, Grand Rapids, MI: William B. Eerdmans Publishing Company.
—— 2020, *Acts (New Cambridge Bible Commentary)*, Cambridge: Cambridge University Press.
Keller, Timothy, 2012, *Center Church*, Grand Rapids, MI: Zondervan.
Klepp, L. S., 1990, 'Every Man a Philosopher-King', in *The New York Times Magazine* (Dec. 2), available at https://www.nytimes.com/1990/12/02/magazine/every-man-a-philosopherking.html (accessed 23.09.2022).
Kraft, Charles H., 2005, *Christianity in Culture*, Maryknoll, NY: Orbis.
Kroeber, A. L., and Clyde Kluckhohn, 1952, *Culture: A Critical Review of Concepts and Definitions (Papers of the Peabody Museum of American Archeology and Ethnology Vol. XLVII, No. 1)*, Cambridge, MA: Harvard University Press.
Kuper, Adam, 2000, *Culture: The Anthropologists' Account*, Cambridge, MA: Harvard University Press.
Labadi, Sophia (ed.), 2019, *The Cultural Turn in International Aid: Impacts and Challenges for Heritage and the Creative Industries*, Abingdon: Routledge.
Ladd, George Eldon, 1982, *A Theology of the New Testament*, Guildford: Lutterworth Press.
Larkin, William J. Jr., 1995, *Acts (The IVP New Testament Commentary Series)*, Downers Grove, IL: Inter-Varsity Press,
Lash, Nicholas, 1973, *Change in Focus*, London: Sheed and Ward.
Lienemann-Perrin, Christine, 1981, *Training for a Relevant Ministry: A study of the contribution of the Theological Education Fund*, Madras: The Christian Literature Society.
Long, D. Stephen, 2008, *Theology and Culture: A Guide to the Discussion*, Eugene, OR: Cascade Books.
Long, Elizabeth, 2007, 'Cultural Studies', in George Ritzer (ed.), *The Blackwell Encyclopedia of Sociology*, Oxford: Blackwell Publishing.
Long, Thomas G., 1989, *Preaching and the Literary Forms of the Bible*, Philadelphia: PA: Fortress Press.

BIBLIOGRAPHY

Loughlin, Gerard, 1996, *Telling God's Story: Bible, Church and narrative theology*, Cambridge: Cambridge University Press.

—— 2004, *Alien Sex: The Body and Desire in Cinema and Theology*, Oxford: Blackwell Publishing.

—— 2005, 'Cinéma Divinité: A Theological Introduction', in Eric S. Christianson, Peter Francis and William R. Telford (eds), *Cinéma Divinité: Religion, Theology and the Bible in Film*, London: SCM Press.

Loughrey, Clarisse, 2022, 'Avatar: The Way of Water review – You probably still won't care, but at least it's very pretty', in *The Independent* (13 December), available at https://www.independent.co.uk/arts-entertainment/films/reviews/avatar-2-review-way-of-water-b2244433.html (accessed 24.12.2022).

Luzbetak, Louis J., 1988, *The Church and Cultures: New Perspectives in Missiological Anthropology*, Maryknoll, NY: Orbis.

Lynch, Gordon, 2005, *Understanding Theology and Popular Culture*, Oxford: Blackwell Publishing.

—— (ed.), 2007, *Between Sacred and Profane: Researching Religion and Popular Culture*, London: I.B. Tauris.

—— 2007, 'Film and the Subjective Turn: How the Sociology of Religion Can Contribute to Theological Readings of Film', in Robert K. Johnston (ed.), *Reframing Theology and Film: New Focus for an Emerging Discipline*, Grand Rapids, MI: Baker Academic.

—— 2012, *The Sacred in the Modern World: a Cultural Sociological Approach*, Oxford: Oxford University Press.

Malinowski, Bronislaw, 1922, *Argonauts of the Western Pacific: An Account of Native Enterprise and Adventure in the Archipelagoes of Melanesian New Guinea*, London: George Routledge and Sons.

Mambrol, Nasrullah, 2017, *The Philosophy of Richard Rorty*, available at https://literariness.org/2017/06/06/the-philosophy-of-richard-rorty/ (accessed 23.09.2022).

Marsh, Clive, 2004, *Cinema and Sentiment: Film's Challenge to Theology*, Milton Keynes: Paternoster.

—— 2018, *A Cultural Theology of Salvation*, Oxford: Oxford University Press.

Marsh, Clive, and Gaye Ortiz (eds), 1997, *Explorations in Theology and Film*, Oxford: Blackwell Publishing.

Marshall, I. Howard, 1981, 'Culture and the New Testament', in John R. W. Stott and Robert Coote, *Down To Earth: Studies in Christianity and Culture, the papers of the Lausanne Consultation on Gospel and Culture*, London: Hodder and Stoughton.

—— 1998, *Acts (Tyndale New Testament Commentaries)*, Leicester: Inter-Varsity Press.

Martin, Ralph P., 1986, *2 Corinthians (Word Biblical Commentary)*, Waco, TX: Word Books.

Marx, Karl, 1904, *A Contribution to the Critique of Political Economy: translated from the Second German Edition by N.I. Stone*, Chicago, IL: Charles H. Kerr and Company.
McGrath, Alister E., 1998, *Historical Theology: An Introduction to the History of Christian Thought*, Oxford: Blackwell Publishing.
—— 2001, *Christian Theology: An Introduction*, Oxford: Blackwell Publishing.
McKinney, Richard W. A. (ed.), 1976, *Creation, Christ and Culture: Studies in Honour of T. F. Torrance*, Edinburgh: T&T Clark.
Mead, Margaret, 1928, *Coming of Age in Samoa: A Psychological Study of Primitive Youth for Western Civilization*, New York: William Morrow and Company.
Micklethwait, John, and Adrian Wooldridge, 2009, *God is Back: How the Global Rise of Faith is Changing the World*, London: Allen Lane.
Milbank, John, 2006, *Theology & Social Theory: Beyond Secular Reason* (2nd edn), Oxford: Blackwell Publishing.
Mladin, Nathan, 2021, *Breaking Ground: The Church and Cultural Renewal*, London: Theos. Available at https://licc.org.uk/app/uploads/2022/01/Breaking-ground-full-report-compressed-FINAL.pdf (accessed 10.02.2023).
Montefiore, Hugh (ed.), 1992, *The Gospel and Contemporary Culture*, London: Mowbray.
Moreau, A. Scott, 2018, *Contextualizing the Faith: a holistic approach*, Grand Rapids, MI: Baker Academic.
Morgan, David, 2008, *Key Words in Religion, Media and Culture*, New York, NY: Routledge.
Mouw, Richard J., 2012, *The Challenges of Cultural Disipleship: Essays in the Line of Abraham Kuyper*, Grand Rapids, MI: William B. Eerdmans Publishing Company.
Moynagh, Michael, 2018, *Church in Life*, Eugene, OR: Cascade Books.
Muhanga, Margaret, 2009, 'Neo-colonialism Fuels Homosexuality in Africa', in *New Vision*, October 26, available at https://www.newvision.co.ug/new_vision/news/1233779/neo-colonialism-fuels-homosexuality-africa (accessed 23.09.2022).
Myers, Ken, 1989, *All God's Children and Blue Suede Shoes*, Wheaton, IL: Crossway.
Newbigin, Lesslie, 1986, *Foolishness to the Greeks: the Gospel and Western Culture*, London: SPCK.
—— 1989, *The Gospel in a Pluralist Society*, Grand Rapids, MI: William B. Eerdmans Publishing Company and Geneva: WCC Publications.
New York Times, 1926, 'Marital Tragedy', in *New York Times* (31 October) available at https://archive.nytimes.com/www.nytimes.com/books/99/07/04/specials/hemingway-rises.html?scp=1andsq=the%2520sun%2520also%2520rises%2520and%25201926andst=cse (accessed 24.12.2022).

BIBLIOGRAPHY

Nicholls, Bruce J., 2003, *Contextualization: A Theology of Gospel and Culture*, Vancouver, BC: Regent College Publishing.

Niebuhr, H. Richard, 1941, *The Meaning of Revelation*, New York, NY: Macmillan.

—— 1951, *Christ and Culture*, New York, NY: Harper and Row.

Nolan, Steve, 2005, 'Understanding Films: Reading the Gaps', in Anthony J. Clarke and Paul S. Fiddes (eds), *Flickering Images: Theology and Film in Dialogue*, Oxford: Regents Park College.

Nuovo, Victor, 1987, *Visionary Science: A Translation of Tillich's "On the Idea of a Theology of Culture" with an Interpretive Essay*, Detroit, MI: Wayne State University Press.

Pagola, José, 2012, *Jesus: An Historical Approximation*, Miami, FL: Convivium Press.

Parker, Andrew, Nick J. Watson and John B. White (eds), 2016, *Sports Chaplaincy: Trends, Issues and Debates*, London: Routledge.

Pescosolido, Bernice A., and Sigrun Olafsdottir, 2010, 'The Cultural Turn In Sociology: Can it Help Us Resolve an Age-Old Problem in Understanding Decision Making for Healthcare?', in *Sociological Forum*, 25.4.

Polanyi, Michael, 1964, *Personal Knowledge: Towards a Post-Critical Philosophy*, New York, NY: Harper and Row.

Portier, Philippe, 2011, 'Religion and democracy in the thought of Jurgen Habermas', in *Society*, 48.5.

Quality Assurance Agency, 2019, *Subject Benchmark Statement: Theology and Religious Studies*.

Re Manning, Russell (ed.), 2015, *Retrieving the Radical Tillich: his legacy and contemporary importance*, New York, NY: Palgrave Macmillan.

Ricoeur, Paul, 2016, *Hermeneutics and the Human Sciences: Essays on Language, Action and Interpretation*, Cambridge: Cambridge University Press.

Ritzer, George, 2011, *Sociological Theory*, New York, NY: McGraw Hill.

Romanowski, William D., 2007, *Eyes Wide Shut: Looking For God in Popular Culture*, Grand Rapids, MI: Brazos Press.

Rorty, Richard, 1979, *Philosophy and the Mirror of Nature*, Princeton, NJ: Princeton University Press.

—— 1989, *Contingency, Irony, and Solidarity*, Cambridge: Cambridge University Press.

—— 1991, *Objectivity, Relativism, and Truth: Philosophical Papers, Volume 1*, Cambridge: Cambridge University Press.

—— 1998, *Truth and Progress: Philosophical Papers, Volume 3*, Cambridge: Cambridge University Press.

—— 1999, *Philosophy and Social Hope*, Harmondsworth: Penguin Books.

Ryle, J. C., 1956, *Holiness*, Cambridge: James Clarke and Co.
Sanneh, Lamin, 1993, *Encountering the West: Christianity and the Global Cultural Process: the African Dimension*, London: Marshall Pickering.
—— 2003, *Whose Religion is Christianity? The Gospel Beyond the West*, Grand Rapids, MI: William B. Eerdmans Publishing Company.
—— 2009, *Translating the Message: the Missionary Impact on Culture* (2nd edn), Maryknoll, NY: Orbis.
Scharen, Christian, 2011, *Broken Hallelujahs: Why Popular Music Matters to Those Seeking God*, Grand Rapids, MI: Brazos Press.
Shorter, Aylward, 2006, *Toward a Theology of Inculturation*, Eugene, OR: Wipf and Stock.
Smith, Graeme, 2020, 'No longer "speaking truth to power"', in *Practical Theology* 13:1–2, pp. 75–86.
Smith, James K. A., 2006, *Who's Afraid of Postmodernism? Taking Derrida, Lyotard, and Foucault to Church*, Grand Rapids, MI: Baker Academic.
—— 2017, *Awaiting the King: Reforming Public Theology*, Grand Rapids, MI: Baker Academic.
Spillman, Lyn, 2007, 'Culture', in George Ritzer (ed.), *The Blackwell Encyclopedia of Sociology*,
Stackhouse, John G. Jr., 2008, *Making the Best Of It: Following Christ in the Real World*, Oxford: Oxford University Press.
Standing, Roger, 2004, *Finding the Plot: Preaching in a Narrative Style*, Milton Keynes: Paternoster.
—— 2013, *As a Fire by Burning: Mission as the Life of the Local Congregation*, London: SCM Press.
—— 2016, 'Before the Throne of God: Multicultural Church as Eschatological Anticipation', in *Missio Africanus*, 1.2 (January), available at https://missioafricanus.com/wp-content/uploads/2019/05/Standing_Before-the-Throne.pdf (accessed 13.02.2023).
Stanley, Brian, 1992, *The History of the Baptist Missionary Society, 1792–1992*, Edinburgh: T&T Clark.
Stassen, Glen H., D. M. Yeager and John Howard Yoder, 1996, *Authentic Transformation: A New Vision of Christ and Culture*, Nashville, TN: Abingdon Press.
Stott, John, 1990a, *Issues Facing Christians Today: New perspectives on social and moral dilemmas*, London: Marshall Pickering.
—— 1990b, *The Message of Acts (The Bible Speaks Today)*, Leicester: Inter-Varsity Press.
—— 1992, *The Contemporary Christian*, Leicester: Inter-Varsity Press.
Stott, John R. W., and Robert Coote, 1981, *Down To Earth: Studies in Christianity and Culture, the papers of the Lausanne Consultation on Gospel and Culture*, London: Hodder and Stoughton.
Strand, Michael, and Lyn Spillman, 2020, 'Cultural Sociology', in Peter

BIBLIOGRAPHY

Kivisto (ed.), *The Cambridge Handbook of Social Theory, Volume II: Contemporary Theories and Issues*, Cambridge: Cambridge University Press.

Strange, Daniel, 2015, 'Faithful Presence: A Theology for the Trenches?', in Collin Hanson (ed.), *Revisiting 'Faithful Presence: To Change the World' Five Years Later*, Deerfield IL: The Gospel Coalition, available at https://www.thegospelcoalition.org/article/revisiting-faithful-presence-to-change-the-world-five-years-later/ (accessed 08.11.2022).

Tanner, Kathryn, 1997, *Theories of Culture: A New Agenda for Theology*, Minneapolis, MN: Fortress Press.

Tasker, R. V. G., 1997, *John (Tyndale New Testament Commentaries)*, Leicester: Inter-Varsity Press.

Taylor, Charles, 2007, *A Secular Age*, Cambridge, MA: Harvard University Press.

Tenney, Merrill C., 1995, *John (Expositor's Bible Commentary)*, Grand Rapids, MI: Zondervan.

Theological Education Fund, 1972, *Ministry in Context: The Third Mandate Programme of the Theological Education Fund (1970–77)*, Bromley: TEF.

Thompson, E. P., 1963, *The Making of the English Working Class*, London: Victor Gollancz.

Till, Rupert, 2010, *Pop Cult: Religion and Popular Music*, London: Continuum.

Tillich, Paul, 1959, *Theology of Culture*, New York, NY: Oxford University Press.

—— 2014, *The Courage to Be* (3rd edn), New Haven, CN: Yale University Press.

Time Magazine, 1963, 'Barth in Retirement', May 31, available at https://content.time.com/time/subscriber/article/0,33009,896838,00.html (accessed 12.01.2023).

Tomley, Sarah, Mitchell Hobbs, Megan Todd, Marcus Weeks et al., 2015, *The Sociology Book: Big Ideas Simply Explained*, London: DK.

Turnau, Ted, 2012, *Popologetics: Popular Culture in Christian Perspective*, Phillipsburg, NJ: PandR Publishing.

Turner, Steve, 2013, *Popcultured: Thinking Christianly About Style, Media and Entertainment*, Downers Grove, IL: IVP Books.

Uberoi, Elise, 2016, *European Union Referendum 2016: House of Commons Briefing Paper Number CBP 7639*, 29 June 2016, available at http://researchbriefings.files.parliament.uk/documents/CBP-7639/CBP-7639.pdf (accessed 18.12.2022).

Van Til, Henry R., 2001, *The Calvinistic Concept of Culture*, Grand Rapids, MI: Baker Academic.

Vanhoozer, Kevin J. (ed.), 2003, *The Cambridge Companion to Postmodern Theology*, Cambridge: Cambridge University Press.

Vanhoozer, Kevin J., Charles A. Anderson and Michael J. Sleasman (eds), 2007. *Everyday Theology: How to Read Cultural Texts and Interpret Trends*, Grand Rapids, MI: Baker Academic.

Vernon, Mark, 2004, 'Reimagining the Divine', in *Third Way*, 27.4 (May).

Volf, Miroslav, 1996, *Exclusion and Embrace: A Theological Exploration of Identity, Otherness, and Reconciliation*, Nashville, TN: Abingdon Press.

—— 2011, *A Public Faith: How Followers of Christ Should Serve the Common Good*, Grand Rapids, MI: Brazos Press.

Wade, Dakota, 2020, *Paul Tillich's Theology of Culture (1959): A Summary and Analysis*, available at https://semperdiscentes.life/2020/01/11/paul-tillichs-theology-of-culture-a-summary-and-analysis/ (accessed 10.02.2022).

Walker, Andrew, 1996, *Telling the Story: Gospel, Mission and Culture*, London: SPCK.

Walls, Andrew F., 2009, *The Missionary Movement in Christian History: Studies in the Transmission of Faith*, Maryknoll, NY: Orbis.

Ward, Graham, 2005, *The Blackwell Companion to Postmodern Theology*, Oxford: Blackwell Publishing.

Ward, Pete, 2008, *Participation and Mediation: A Practical Theology for the Liquid Church*, London: SCM Press.

Warren, Max, 1971, *To Apply the Gospel: Selections From the Writings of Henry Venn*, Grand Rapids, MI: William B. Eerdmans.

Watkin, Christopher, 2022, *Biblical Critical Theory: How the Bible's Unfolding Story Makes Sense of Modern Life and Culture*, Grand Rapids, MI: Zondervan Academic.

Weinstein, Deena, 2005, 'Rock Protest Songs: so many and so few', in Ian Peddie (ed.), *The Resisting Muse: Popular Music and Social Protest*, Abingdon: Routledge.

Wenham, David, 1995, *Paul: Follower of Jesus or Founder of Christianity?* Grand Rapids, MI: William B. Eerdmans.

Wesley, Charles, 1745, *Hymns for the Nativity of Our Lord*, London: William Strahan.

Wesley, John, 1976, *A Plain Account of Christian Perfection*, London: The Epworth Press.

Wheeler, Ray, 2002, 'The Legacy of Shoki Coe', in *The International Bulletin of Missionary Research* 26.2 (April).

White, Hayden, 1973, *Metahistory: The Historical Imagination in Nineteenth-Century Europe*, Baltimore, MD: Johns Hopkins University Press.

—— 1999, 'Afterword', in Victoria E. Bonnell and Lynn Hunt (eds), *Beyond the Cultural Turn: New Directions in the Study of Society and Culture*, Berkeley, CA: University of California Press.

Wicker, Brian, 1975, *The Story-Shaped World: Fiction and Metaphysics:*

Some Variations on a Theme, Notre Dame, IN: University of Notre Dame Press.

Williams, Raymond, 1958, *Culture and Society 1780–1950*, London: Chatto and Windus.

Wright, Christopher J. H., 2020, *Here Are Your Gods: faithful discipleship in idolatrous times*, London: Inter-Varsity Press.

Wrogemann, Henning, 2016, *Intercultural Hermeneutics*, Downers Grove, IL: IVP Academic.

——2018, *Theologies of Mission*, Downers Grove, IL: IVP Academic.

——2019, *A Theology of Interreligious Relations*, Downers Grove, IL: IVP Academic.

Wuthnow, Robert, James Davison Hunter, Albert Bergesen and Edith Kurzweil, 1984, *Cultural Analysis: the work of Peter L. Berger, Mary Douglas, Michel Foucault and Jurgen Habermas*, Boston, MA: Routledge and Kegan Paul.

Yakimova, Milena, 2002, 'A Postmodern Grid of the Worldmap? An Interview with Zygmunt Bauman', in *Eurozine*, 8 November 2002, available at https://www.eurozine.com/a-postmodern-grid-of-the-worldmap/ (accessed 23.12.2021).

Young, Michael W. (ed.), 1979, *The Ethnography of Malinowski: the Trobriand Islands, 1915–18)*, London: Routledge and Kegan Paul.

Index of Biblical References

OLD TESTAMENT

Genesis	
1.1	66
1.31	60
1.26–28	60
10—11	75–6
11.9	75
12.3	70, 76
18.18	70
22.18	70

Exodus	
20.11	83

1 Chronicles	
12.32	126

Isaiah	
42.5	83

NEW TESTAMENT

Matthew	
1.1	70
4.13	65
5—7	178
5.14–16	179
18.19–20	124
22.34–40	71
22.37–40	178
22.39	131
28.18–20	70
28.20	121

Luke	
3.16	169
3.33	169
4.14	169
4.16–30	178
4.18–21	169–70
6.27–38	177
13.20–21	179
14.34	179
24.46–49	74
24.48–49	170

Mark	
7.31	64
8.35	179

John	
1.1	65
1.1–3	62

1.14	65, 66–7	17.26	133
1.32–34	72	17.26–27	83
3.1–8	73	17.28	xii, 83
10.10	130	17.30–31	84
14.14–16	73	17.34	84
14.26	73	21.23–26	81
14.26–27	73		
15.19–20	123	**Romans**	
15.26	73	8.4	79
16.7	73	8.9	79
16.8–11	73–4	8.9–10	85
16.8–13	166	8.14	171
16.13	159	8.26–27	164
16.13–14	73	10.11–13	85
16.14	160	12.1–2	139
17.4–5	69	12.2	138
17.14–15	123	12.4–8	79
17.20–23	69	13.9	168
20.19–21	72		
24.26	164	**1 Corinthians**	
		1.7—2.5	84
Acts		1.17	84
1.8	74, 169, 170	2.13	79
		9.19–23	80–1
2.1	88	9.20	81
2.2	162	9.21	82
2.2–15	164	9.22–23	xi, 81–2
2.4	74, 161	12.27–30	79
2.5–12	75–6, 83	14.29–33	169
2.6	88	16.15	84
2.15	167		
2.38–40	166	**2 Corinthians**	
2.41	88	1.17ff.	82
7.47	88	3	80
13.1	77		
15	x, 78	**Galatians**	
15.28	78	2.11–12	80
17.16–34	82	3.28	23, 80, 85

5.1	80	**2 Timothy**	
5.13	80	2.3–4	55
5.16	80		
5.18	171	**Hebrews**	
5.22	80	5.14	166
5.22–23	79		
5.25	79	**1 Peter**	
		1.1	192
Ephesians		2.11	192
4.11–13	79	2.13	192
6.10–17	55	4.17	193
Philippians		**1 John**	
2.6–8	68	4.10	130
2.7	130		
3.12	159	**Revelation**	
4.8	124	5.9	87
		7.9	87
Colossians		10.11	87
1.16–18	62	11.9	87
2.6–9	xv	13.7	87
3.10	85	14.6	87
		17.15	87
		21.23–26	87

Index of Names and Subjects

Action Research Church and Society (ARCS) 133–4
advertising 147–8
agency 175
Alexander, Jeffrey 98–100
anthropology 89–90, 92–7, 182–5
apologetics of presence 136
Argent (music group) ix
Athens 82–5
Augustine (saint) 164
Austin, John 143
Avatar (film) 151

Bailey, John Ariel 154–6, 164, 170–1, 197–200
Barthes, Roland 107
Bauman, Zygmunt 5–6
Benson, Dave 32, 200
Berger, Peter 5, 7–8, 10–20, 122, 185–6
Bevans, Stephen 32, 50, 51
Blakely, Jason 118
Bonhoeffer, Dietrich 159
Brown, Raymond 42
Bruce, F. F. 82
Brunner, Emil 133

Calder, Gideon 116

Calvin, John 165
Calvinism 53–4, 57
Carey, William xii
Carter, Craig 31–2
Certeau, Michel de 104
Childs, Peter 145
Christ, and culture 25–8, 55, 127
Christianity
  and Jewish culture x–xi, 42, 77–82
  and other historical cultures 152
church and state 137, 193
circumcision x, 42, 77–8
civilization 12–13
Clayton, John 41
Cobb, Kelton 191
Coe, Shoki 44–5
Collini, Stefan 109–10
colonialism 13, 23
consumerism 6, 122–3, 125
contextual theology 50, 51
contextualization xiii, 44–9
Corrie, John 48
Coupland, Douglas 5
Cox, Harvey 40
Cray, Graham 127
creation 59–63, 86

INDEX OF NAMES AND SUBJECTS

cross-cultural issues
  and modern missionaries
    xii, 47, 85
  in Roman Empire xii
Crouch, Andy 196
cultural analysis 144–51,
  155–8
cultural studies 90–1, 101–9,
  185–7
culture
  anthropological approach to
    18
  and the arts 14
  common heritage 1–7
  context of discipleship
    124–6
  definitions 17–20, 188–90
  differences 11, 87
  etymology 12–14
  evangelizing 177–80
  evolving 3, 5–6, 10–13, 15,
    55–7, 60, 89, 95, 124, 178
  five dimensions 156
  and history 14–15, 115,
    124
  popular 9, 14
  and power 16–17, 115
  reveals God's goodness
    59–61
  shared 14
  and social institutions 10
  and theology 22–51, 54,
    133–40, 154
  transmission 7–9
custom 3

Dannhauer, J. C. 138
de Graft, Joe 23

description
  'thick' 96, 99
  of the world 113–14
discernment 139, 166–7
discipleship xi, xv, 26, 58,
  71, 76–87, 120–32
  and host culture 152–3
  living from and for culture
    170–1
  starting point of
    hermeneutics 159–60
During, Simon 7, 103, 110
Durkheim, Emile 98

Eagleton, Terry 12, 13,
  15–16, 20
Edgar, William 127
Eliot, T. S. 24
ethics 68, 198

faith 57–8
faithfulness 129–32
fall, the 60–1, 193
film criticism 150–1, 194–5
film studies 31, 148–9
Fitch, David 130–1, 171–2
Foucault, Michel 4
Frankfurt School 103–4
Freud, Sigmund 89

Gallagher, Michael Paul 31
Geertz, Clifford 18–19,
  95–7, 182–3
Gentiles, converts to
  Christianity x–xi, 78
Godfather, The 123–4
Gorringe, Tim 30, 32
grace 61

Graham, Elaine 30, 136
Gruber, Judith 52
Gunton, Colin 56

Habermas, Jürgen 104, 137
Hall, Stuart 102–3, 106, 186
Hauerwas, Stanley 30
Hayakawa, Samuel 140–1
hegemony 105
Hemingway, Ernest 149–50
Herder, Johann Gottfried 13
hermeneutics
  historical development 138–40
  of suspicion 144–5
Herodotus 4
Highmore, Ben 12, 18, 20, 21, 120–1, 140, 158
Hoggart, Richard 101–2
Holmes, Stephen 55, 170
Holocaust 100
Holy Spirit 72–80, 85, 87, 159–71
humility 118, 158
Hunter, James Davison 10, 69, 128–32, 178–9, 192–3

identity
  Christian 52, 71, 78
  cultural 2–3, 8, 16, 67, 105
  human 62
  personal 109, 126
  social 101
incarnation 65–7, 86, 120–1, 130
inculturation 42–4, 67, 72, 121, 132

intercultural theology 50, 51–2
intuition xiv, 11, 15–16, 21, 142, 154, 163–4

Jenson, Robert 30
Jerusalem, Council of 77–8
Jesus
  commissions disciples 70–2, 74, 85, 87, 121, 160
  his use of power 129
  historical context 64–7
  kenosis 68–9
  metaphors for the Kingdom 179
  see also incarnation
John Cassian 138
Johnson, Richard 108
Johnston, Robert 31

Kant, Immanuel 38
Keener, Craig 161–3, 171, 172–3
Keller, Tim 31
kenosis 68–9
Kingdom of God 179
Krass, Al 45
Kuyper, Abraham 60, 62, 72

ladder of abstraction 140–1
language 2, 55–6, 63–7, 74–6, 104, 112
Lash, Nicholas 57
Lausanne Movement xiii, 46–7
logos 65–7
London Interdisciplinary School 165

INDEX OF NAMES AND SUBJECTS

Loughlin, Gerard 57, 63, 64, 121, 174–5, 195
Lynch, Gordon 197

McGrath, Alister 33
Malinowski, Bronislaw 94
Marsh, Clive 31, 41, 162, 193–4
Marshall, I. Howard 77–8
Milbank, John 50
Ministry in Context report 44–6
mission 169–71
mission studies 48
Mission-Shaped Church 44
missionaries 23
Mouw, Richard 60–1
multiculturalism 103

narrative 63–4, 195
nationalism 124–5
Newbigin, Lesslie 41, 47–8, 76, 122
Niebuhr, H. Richard 193–4
  on Christianity and culture xiii, 19, 24–32, 85
  on history 9
  sociological approach 49, 53
Nolan, Steve 194–5

Orwell, George 115

Pastoral Cycle 139–40
Paul (apostle)
  in Athens 82–3
  his understanding of discipleship 80–3

on the Holy Spirit 79–80
on the incarnation 68
language 55
mission to Gentiles x–xii, 42, 77
Pentecost 72–6, 88, 160
personal knowledge 142
Polanyi, Michael 141–2
popular culture 9, 14
postmodern theology 52
postmodernism 118–19, 142–3
poststructuralism 143
power 118, 198
Pragmatism 111, 113
prophecy 167–9
psychology 89
purity 129–30

Re Manning, Russell 33, 35, 37, 40
reading 146–7
reason 26
redescription 111–16, 164–5
religion, in Tillich's thought 35–6
religious symbols 39
Ricoeur, Paul 144–5, 147
Roman Empire, and Christianity xii
Romanowski, William 54
Rorty, Richard 110–16
Ryle, Gilbert 96

Saboteur (film) 174–5
Sanneh, Lamin xii–xiii, 84–5
Saussure, Ferdinand de 106–7

Schleiermacher, Friedrich 38
Schütz, Alfred 122
semiology (=semiotics) 96, 106–7
sin 26, 27, 61, 193
Smith, Graeme 116
Smith, James K. A. 123–4
social evolutionism 22–3
social imaginary 11
social sciences 118
socialization 8
sociology 97–101, 185–7
Stackhouse, John 30
storytelling 63–4
Stott, John 59–60, 84, 155
Strange, Daniel 172
Stuart, Douglas 150
subjectivity 109–10, 117
symbols 39

tacit knowledge 141–2
Tanner, Kathyrn 136, 165
theological education xiii–xiv, 45, 48
theology 187–90
  and culture 133–40, 154, 195
  freestyle 162–3
'thick description' 96, 99, 118, 164–5
Thomas, John Heywood 38–9

Tillich, Paul 24, 33–41, 49, 53, 85
Trinity 127
truth 113, 164–5, 166
Turner, Steve 127
typologies of Christ and culture 25–32

Ultimate Concern 36–8

vaccination 3
Van Til, Henry 53–4
Vanhoozer, Kevin 19, 52, 143, 147, 153, 155
Venn, Henry xii, 23
Vincent of Lérins 125
Volf, Miroslav 32, 121, 192

Walls, Andrew 71
Ward, Pete 32
Weber, Max 98
Wesley, Charles 22
Wesley, John 159
'*West Side Story*' 151
Westerns 102–3
White, Hayden 92
Willimon, William H. 30
worldviews 10–11, 129
Wuthnow, Robert 116

www.ingramcontent.com/pod-product-compliance
Lightning Source LLC
Chambersburg PA
CBHW022050290426
44109CB00014B/1051